The Misunderstood Child

A Guide for Parents of Children with Learning Disabilities

2nd Edition

The Misunderstood Child

A Guide for Parents of Children with Learning Disabilities

2nd Edition

Larry B. Silver, M.D.
Clinical Professor of Psychiatry,
Georgetown University
School of Medicine

TAB Books

Division of McGraw-Hill, Inc.

New York   San Francisco   Washington, D.C.   Auckland   Bogotá
Caracas   Lisbon   London   Madrid   Mexico City   Milan
Montreal   New Delhi   San Juan   Singapore
Sydney   Tokyo   Toronto

pbk   8 9 10 11 12 13 14 15 16 FGR/FGR 9 9 8 7 6 5
hc   1 2 3   4   5   6   7   8   9 10 FGR/FGR 9 9 8 7 6 5 4 3 2 1

Library of Congress Cataloging-in-Publication Data

Silver, Larry B.
     The misunderstood child : a guide for parents of learning disabled
  children/ Larry B. Silver. — 2nd ed.
       p.   cm.
     Includes bibliographical references and index.
       ISBN 0-8306-2954-8   ISBN 0-8306-2837-1 (pbk.)
     1. Learning disabled children.   2. Parent and child.   I. Title.
  RJ506.L4S55   1991
  618.92′85889—dc20   91-28978
                                                        CIP

Acquisitions Editor: Kimberly Tabor
Managing Editor: Joanne M. Slike
Book Editor: Annette M. Testa
Director of Production: Katherine G. Brown

The First Edition of this book was dedicated to:

THE CENTER SCHOOL, Warren, New Jersey
To its former director, Helen Goldberg, and the
dedicated professional staff for teaching me
about these children;
To the children, who shared with me their feelings,
thoughts, fears, and hopes;
And, to the former social worker, R. Joan Guilmartin,
who taught me the importance of the family.

This Second Edition is dedicated to:

The many children, adolescents, and their families
who continue to teach me about these invisible
disabilities and of the impact they have on
every aspect of their lives.

Thank you.

The joy of learning is often a nightmare for more than 10 million normal, bright, intelligent children—just because no one has recognized their learning difference. Understand their frustration—and begin to understand the problem.

Let no child be demeaned, nor have his or her wonder diminished, because of our ignorance or inactivity. Let no child be deprived of discovery because we lack the resources to discover his or her problem. Let no child— ever—doubt self or mind because we are unsure of our commitment.

The Foundation for Children
with Learning Disabilities
(now called the National Center
for Learning Disabilities)

Contents

Preface to the Second Edition

I WROTE THE FIRST EDITION of *The Misunderstood Child*, published in 1984, because I experienced the confusion, lack of information, and want for direction that so many families of children and adolescents with learning disabilities felt. I realized that knowledge was the key to helping the parents, children and adolescents, and their families overcome their problems. If they could be informed of learning disabilities and given an understanding of their critical role in helping their son or daughter, they would feel less helpless and would be able to do for their child or adolescent what they so dearly wanted to do—to help them reach above their disability and be happy, successful people.

As with every author, I feared that the information in the book would not be seen as helpful and that my book, like most books of this kind, would be published, exist until the first printing was gone, and then disappear. It did not. Parents found it helpful and told other parents of the book. Now, more than seven years later and after many printings, *The Misunderstood Child* remains popular and is recommended by one generation of parents to the new generation of parents who have just learned of their son's or daughter's learning disabilities.

For me, the greatest review of the book has come from the parents. No matter how often it has happened throughout these years, I am still brought to tears when a parent stops me at a meeting or takes the time to write to me to tell me how much the book has meant to him or her and how much it has helped him or her to assist his or her child or adolescent. There can be no greater satisfaction in life than learning that you have been of help to others.

In writing this second edition, I have changed none of the original information, but have updated several sections based on the new information of the past seven years and expanded the information on adults. Because Attention-Deficit Hyperactivity Disorder is a related disorder and many parents want more information on it, I have added extensive material on this topic.

Your child or adolescent with a learning disability, plus possibly Attention-Deficit Hyperactivity Disorder (ADHD) needs special understanding, support, and help from you and from your family. As with the first edition, I hope this book helps you to be that special parent and for you to have that special family.

Preface to the First Edition

WHEN A CHILD OR ADOLESCENT has learning disabilities, they interfere not only with academic work, but with all aspects of life—at home, in the community, in clubs, and in activities.

You, as parents, play a crucial role in helping your child or adolescent deal with these disabilities. You must be an *informed consumer*, knowing all that is known about these problems. You must be an *assertive advocate*, constantly trying to find the programs your child needs in school, at home, and out of school. This book will help you to become both.

I have also tried to help you help the other members of your family. As you know all too well, when your son or daughter with learning disabilities feels pain, everyone feels it. I discuss your feelings, problems, and needs, as well as the impact that the learning disabled child or adolescent has on his or her brothers and sisters.

A child or adolescent with learning disabilities needs special understanding, support, and help from the family. This book should help you to be that special parent, and your family to be that special family.

Notices

Ritalin	CIBA-Geigy Pharmaceuticals 556 Morris Avenue Summit, New Jersey 07901
Dexedrine	Smith, Kline, and French Pharmaceuticals 1500 Spring Garden Drive P.O. Box 7929 Philadelphia, Pennsylvania 19101
Cylert	Abbott Laboratories 14th and Sheridan Road North Chicago, Illinois 60064Pharmaceuticals, 556 Morris Avenue Summit, New Jersey 07901
Norpramine	Marion-Merrell Dow Pharmaceuticals 9300 Ward Parkway P.O. Box 8480 Kansas City, Missouri 64114
Catapres	Boehringer Ingelheim Pharmaceuticals 90 East Ridge P.O. Box 368 Ridgefield, Connecticut 06877
Wellbutrin	Burroughs Wellcome Company 3030 Cornwallis Road Research Triangle Park, North Carolina 27709
Mellaril	Sandoz Pharmaceuticals Rt. 10 East Hanover, New Jersey 07936
Tegretol	Geigy Division of CIBA-Geigy (see Tofranil)
Benadryl	Parke-Davis Division of Warner-Lambert Company 201 Tabor Road Morris Plains, New Jersey 07950

PART ONE

Introduction to Learning Disabilities & Possible ADHD

1

Your Task
as a Parent

VICTOR WAS A DISASTER in elementary school. He never sat still or paid attention in class, yet his teachers passed him along from grade to grade. By the fourth grade, when he was 10 years old, he still read at a first-grade level, and his math skills were no better. The school evaluated him and concluded that he had learning disabilities. The report also described Victor as "hyperactive" and "distractible." Despite this evaluation, Victor went into a regular fifth-grade program. There, his classroom and academic performance became even worse, and he also grew much more unpleasant and provocative at home.

By the time he finished the sixth grade, Victor could only be described as impossible. At school he did everything he knew of to get kicked out of class: he hid under desks, threw objects, and crawled around the floor barking like a dog. All of his disruptive tactics succeeded. His classmates thought he was funny, and he spent more time banished from the classroom than he spent in it.

The more trouble he got into at school, the more his parents tried to punish him at home. Soon the family was in chaos. When Victor rebelled against the limits his parents set as punishment, the parents fought with each other about how firm to be in enforcing them. His brother, already humiliated by Victor's behavior, spent more and more time at a friend's house to avoid the fighting at home. When the parents went to the school to try to get to the problem's cause, the principal told them that Victor's emotional disturbance probably stemmed from their own marital distress. She told them that the school could not be responsible for family problems and suggested that they go for psychiatric help. No one mentioned the fourth-grade evaluation.

By the time the parents did seek a private psychiatric evaluation, Victor was almost 13 years old. During the interviews, Victor's behavior shifted between quiet depression and open hostility. When quiet, he spoke of "being stupid." He made such statements as, "I can't read good, I can't do anything good, Maybe I'm just dumb." He saw himself as "bad." He was "ruining the family." He would add, "Maybe they should just send me away to school so I won't cause so much trouble." When he became hostile, Victor joked around, tried to break items in the office, and threatened to leave the room.

A new educational evaluation, updating the one done in the fourth grade, revealed multiple learning and language disabilities. Victor was three years behind in most academic skill areas. Psychological testing revealed a superior intellectual potential with a verbal IQ of 132, but a below average performance IQ of 98. Everyone who took part in the evaluation saw him as hyperactive and distractible. The recommendations included: (1) placement in a full-time special education program, (2) individual and family therapy, and (3) a trial period on a psychostimulant medication.

I met with Victor to review the findings. He paraded in, joking about what "some dumb teacher" had done. I put my arm around his shoulder and said, "I want to let you know what *all* of the tests show. You know, now that I understand your problems, I really admire you. I'd probably have thrown in the towel years before you did." Victor sat down looking sad. But he followed me with interest as I reviewed his strong and weak areas, interrupting to make comments such as, "You mean like when I read a page but forget what I read or I start to talk to someone and halfway through I forget where I started?" I then discussed the IQ test, subtest by subtest, showing him how particular learning problems interfered with his ability to successfully answer questions. I emphasized how bright he was, despite his experiences in school.

Later in our interview, I told Victor that I thought he had become the class clown to cover up for his feeling like a "retard." I told him that I didn't blame him, but that he could expect better of himself. Then I explained the proposed plan for special help. He understood what I described, but refused to go along with it because he didn't want to go to a different school than his friends. I also explained why I wanted him to try medication and described what it could do. He didn't like that idea either, but he agreed to try it "for a few days." As he left my office, I reassured him that I understood the pain and frustration he had gone through and that I really wanted to help him. He smiled and held out his hand. We shook hands and Victor left.

I reviewed the full evaluation and the series of recommendations once again in my meeting with Victor's parents. They seemed relieved to gain a better understanding of their son's difficulties, but were angry with the school and with themselves for not doing something sooner. They agreed with all of the recommendations.

The next meeting was a family session with Victor, his brother, his parents, and his maternal grandmother who lived with the family. We reviewed the whole evaluation again. During this session Victor behaved very provocatively, eventually forcing everyone to get angry with him. I pointed out to him what he was doing and the effect it was having, but he continued with his irritating, disruptive behavior.

After a series of meetings with the personnel at Victor's school, during which all of the data were again presented and discussed, it was agreed that he would go into a self-contained special education program, one in which he was to remain for the next three years, although we did not know that then.

Victor's problems were serious, but not as severe as those of many such children, and certainly not hopeless. If you have a child with learning disabilities plus possible Attention-Deficit Hyperactivity Disorder (ADHD) in your family, no doubt you recognize some of the elements in Victor's story. You can probably tell a more vivid, dramatic, and agonizing story yourself. If the child with a learning disability is *your* child, no doubt you also know just how Victor's parents felt—their denial, frustration, anxiety, depression, guilt, and despair. And you probably recognize best of all their anger—anger at the circumstance, and, perhaps above all, anger at their own bad luck. The parent's anger is as easy to understand as the child's, however differing. Unfortunately, understanding falls short even of a first step toward a remedy. All of the energy that goes into this anger must be rerouted toward educated action—patient, unremitting, effective action.

Victor's case is not typical—there is no "typical" child with learning disabilities—but, it is not unusual either. Although caught late, Victor's problems were caught in the nick of time. Let us now return to Victor's story.

Victor resented being placed in the special education program. Initially, he fell back on his old clowning act. But in the new program, each time he had to be removed from class someone sat down and discussed his behavior with him. The theme was, "You don't like it here, but how are you ever going to get back to regular school if you don't stay in class long enough to get the help you need? You're bright, and you can overcome your problems, but you can't do that until you are willing to work with us rather than against us." Victor's teacher also tried to point out the probable causes for his misbehavior. When he knocked over his desk, the teacher would say, "I guess it's easier to get mad at the desk than to get mad at yourself because you can't do the math. How about picking up the desk so we can sit down and I can help you."

I started Victor on a stimulant medication (discussed in a later chapter). His overactive behavior lessened significantly, as did his distractibility. Both his teacher and his family noted a calming effect. His father commented, "Victor went fishing with me and for the first time in his life, he quietly sat and enjoyed himself." His mother marveled over a family dinner during which Victor did not jump up and down once. More important, Victor noted a change. He enjoyed the relaxed feeling. He tried to explain the decreased distractibility. "You know what it's like when you are in a room and the refrigerator goes off. Suddenly you realize how much noise it makes. Well, the medication makes my head quiet. I never realized how much noise was going on up there." He remained on medication from that point on with no objections.

Victor's general stormy behavior, however, lasted throughout most of the first year. During this time Victor was in both individual and family therapy. The therapist saw Victor once a week and the family every other week. Although Victor had plenty of work to do on his own, most of the effort during the first year went into working with the family. The parents had to regain control of both Victor and their family life, and, with the therapist's guidance, they established a behavior modification program, including a point system of rewards for Victor and a "time-out" room where he went when events got out of hand. They also had to find ways to recognize and fill their own needs. Obviously, they had to learn to support each other through the crises with Victor, but they also had to occasionally get away for a weekend, even if they only went to stay with friends in town. As therapy progressed, they learned how to candidly and clearly speak to Victor, reflecting back to him just how he seemed to them and just how they reacted to his behavior, much as the teacher did. In the therapy, Victor's brother also received the support he needed. Encouraged in the belief that Victor had no right to abuse him or to embarrass him in front of his friends, he too learned how to protect his own interests and to deal more honestly with Victor. Unlike the past, his parents supported him in these efforts.

The first year was hard work. Victor made little obvious progress, but everybody felt good about the direction in which they were headed. During the summer, Victor continued to attend psychotherapy sessions and to take the prescribed medication.

The first week of the second year in the special school went especially bad. Victor was very angry. He wanted to be back in public school. He could see that it would be difficult for him to attend his old school, but he still wanted to be there. Then, slowly, he accepted reality. Increasingly he would answer his teacher's reflective comments with "I know! I know!" In therapy, the sad, frightened Victor was most often present. As he struggled with his anger, frustration, and helplessness, he also began to accept the idea that his future was up to him. If he was willing to work, his family and special education teachers would work very hard to help him. If he resisted, fought, or played games, his family and teachers would stick by him, but he would not make progress. Frequently, now, he asked to review past test results, especially the IQ test. He wondered at times if more medication would make him better sooner.

Victor began to work at school. He stopped a lot of the clowning behavior, and he learned that he could talk about his feelings rather than act them out. For example, one afternoon after a very frustrating hour of work on reading, he waited until the rest of the class went to gym, then sat down on the floor near the teacher's desk and cried. His teacher sat still and did nothing.

Finally Victor volunteered: "I'm just a retard. I'll never learn this stuff. You're wasting your time. My brain is just too dumb to learn." His teacher put his arm on Victor and just listened. Then he told him how glad he was that Victor felt safe enough to share such personal thoughts with him and that he could talk about his feelings rather than acting them out. He also told Victor that the work was indeed hard, but he reassured him that he was bright and would make it.

Victor made up two years of academic work during his second year in the special program. His attitude at home improved, and he formed a good relationship with his father. He returned willingly to the program for the third year and continued to make progress. At his request, the individual therapy and medication continued.

The next year, Victor returned to his local high school, taking only an hour a day of extra help in the resource room. He continued to need the medication. He completed high school and was accepted in a college that had a special program for students with learning disabilities. He decided to become a special education teacher. Whatever he does, I have no concerns about Victor's future.

We can never know how much better off Victor might have been had he received earlier help. Perhaps help came at just the moment when he was ready to make use of it. We will also never know what else Victor's parents could have done at an earlier stage, or if what they did do could have been better. Putting ourselves in their place, however, we can certainly suppose that knowing more sooner would have helped them to manage their distressing situation more effectively. The energy they spent doing their best might have gone into more productive activities than punishing Victor, the family, and themselves.

If you need not imagine yourself in the shoes of Victor's parents because you are already in them, I shall do the best I can to help you. I wish I could promise to give you a total understanding of the learning disabilities, ADHD, and the other problems associated with them, but I can't. The human services field is full of highly trained, concerned, responsible professionals, but many of the phenomena that are seen every day cannot be explained. I can promise you this, however, if partial knowledge is not quite power, it is at least the equipment you must have to fight for the best attention and treatment you can get for your child or adolescent.

What you must do is fight for the right attention. In a very unusual way, you are a consumer of services. These services may not be easily found and they will rarely be thrust at you. They are there, however. Your daughter or son will be their most important beneficiary, but you are the child's only agent in this matter. As your child begins to benefit from the right kind of attention, so will you and your family.

The point is that as soon as you recognize your situation, you must do everything in your power to become an *informed consumer* and an *assertive advocate* for your child or adolescent. No one and no single agency—not your family physician, your child's teacher, the schools, or anyone else—is as vitally concerned as you are, or as informed as you can and must be.

A child or adolescent with learning disabilities and/or ADHD confronts a series of Herculean tasks laid out over a long, long course. But the rewards are virtually certain: your daughter or son can improve, can learn to learn, and can grow toward becoming a normal, happy adult. That success depends on you—on your action, assertion, perseverance, and advocacy. The task of getting help for your child or adolescent may be smaller than the task that is facing your daughter or son, but it is compelling and immediate. It will take all of the strength and determination you have and more. It will baffle and frustrate you, but it will eventually bring reward. The task, however, is inescapable, imminent, and, above all, *ultimately yours alone.*

2

Basic Questions and Concepts

IN ORDER TO HELP your daughter or son most effectively, you must first have a fair understanding of her or his problems. It may help you, initially, to realize that 10 to 20 percent of the average school-age population have trouble with academic work. These youngsters fall into several broad categories: (1) some have mental retardation—that is, they have subnormal intellectual capacities, and therefore they will always function below normal levels; (2) some have emotional problems that stand in the way of learning and cause academic difficulties; and (3) some have average or above-average intelligence, but still have academic difficulties because of the way their brain or nervous system functions. Although such children may have problems with vision, hearing, or both, their learning problems are not caused by these impairments. The person whom we call "learning disabled" falls into this third group, often called the "neurological group." They represent between 3 and 10 percent of most of the school-age population.

Children and adolescents with learning disabilities may have one or more of a group of associated disorders. About 20 to 25 percent will have Attention-Deficit Hyperactivity Disorder (ADHD). In addition, some may have a tic disorder called Tourette's Disorder; some may have an Obsessive-Compulsive Disorder; and, some may have a seizure disorder. Most develop emotional, social, and family problems because of the frustrations and failures they experience. These emotional, social, and family problems are referred to as "secondary" to emphasize that they are the consequence of the academic disability and not the cause of the disability. Each of these problems will be discussed in detail in Part Two of this book.

These problems often occur in the same person. The most frequent pattern is to find:

1. Learning Disabilities
2. ADHD
3. Secondary emotional, social, and family problems

The discussion of these patterns begins by answering two preliminary questions that often plague parents who are confronting for the first time the diagnosis and treatment of their child with a learning disability plus possibly ADHD: "What do all of the terms mean that I hear used to describe my child?" And, "What causes these problems? Who, or what, is to blame?"

What Do the Terms Applied to My Child Mean?

What shall we call this child or adolescent? Everyone seems to have a different name for someone with this group of behaviors and problems. Let us take a quick look at the history of our understanding of this problem and review some of the different labels that have evolved throughout the years to describe it.

Prior to the 1940s in the United States, if a child had difficulty learning, he or she was considered to have mental retardation, exhibit emotional disturbances, or be socially and culturally disadvantaged. In the early 1940s a fourth group was identified, children who had difficulty learning because of a presumed problem with their nervous system. The initial researchers noted that these students had the same learning problems as individuals who were known to have brain damage (e.g., after trauma or surgery to the brain). Yet, these students looked normal; thus, it was considered that they also had brain damage, but that the damage was minimal. The term *Minimal Brain Damage* was introduced. Gradually, however, observations and testing revealed that no evidence of damage to the brain could be found in most of these children. In fact, research information began to point to the idea that the cause of the problem lay in how the brain functions—that is, the problem was physiologic and not structural. All of the brain mechanisms are present and operable, but some of the "wiring" is hooked up differently and, thus, does not work in the normal way. Scientists created a term to suggest this faulty functioning. The prefix *dys*, which means "difficulty with," was incorporated, and the term *Minimal Brain Dysfunction* (MBD) came into use. The literature on MBD described such children as having: (1) learning difficulties, presumed to be due to a dysfunctional nervous system; (2) problems with hyperactivity and distractibility; and (3) emotional and family problems that were considered to be a consequence of the first two sets of problems.

From the 1950s through the present, professionals from a number of different disciplines intensively studied the problem of MBD. Because each discipline trains its specialists and subspecialists differently and uses a different vocabulary, each investigator describes what he or she found somewhat differently, much as the blind men did when they studied the elephant. Only now are we able to see what the whole elephant may look like.

Educators specializing in children with academic problems—the "special education" professionals—studied the learning problems. Initially, they used labels that had been established for many years in schools of education to describe the primary presenting problem. Thus, children who had trouble with reading had *dyslexia* and were called dyslexic. Children with writing problems had *dysgraphia* and were called dysgraphic. Trouble with arithmetic was called *dyscalculia*. Other special educators found these terms too general and not helpful. They decided that they had to look for the specific reasons for the trouble with reading, writing, and mathematics. These professionals had to look for the underlying learning difficulties or learning disabilities. The term, *learning disability* was selected and has become the primary term used today.

If the learning disabilities are primarily in the areas of language use, some professionals might use the term, *language disability*. This disability is but a type of a learning disability. Some professionals might use such terms as receptive language disability, central language disability, or expressive language disability. Most professionals prefer the term learning disability or language disability.

Other professionals studied those children who were described as hyperactive and distractible. The first official term established in 1968 in the medical classification system for these children was *Hyperkinetic Reaction of Childhood* and with it came the concept of the "Hyperactive Child." The description noted overactivity, restlessness, distractibility, and a short attention span. In 1980 the term was changed to *Attention-Deficit Disorder* (ADD) to emphasize that distractibility with a short attention span was the primary clinical issue and that hyperactivity or impulsivity also might be present. Two subtypes were used: ADD with Hyperactivity and ADD without Hyperactivity. A child need only have one of the three behaviors (e.g., hyperactivity, distractibility, or impulsivity) to be diagnosed.

In 1987, the official classification for these children changed to ADHD to reflect that, although distractibility is the primary issue, hyperactivity is also an important factor of the disorder. These changes in names do not reflect ambivalence on the part of the professionals, but modifications that take into account increasing research information.

Many mental health professionals studied the emotional, social, and family problems. They clarified a very important issue. For the child or adolescent with a learning disability, the emotional, social, and family problems were not the cause of the academic difficulties. They were the consequence of these academic difficulties and the resulting frustrations and failures experienced.

Today, therefore, the term MBD is no longer used. In its place, the different components are identified and labeled, using current terms. Thus, today, MBD would include:

1. Learning disabilities

2. ADHD

3. Secondary emotional, social, and family problems

Each child or adolescent will have one or more of these problems.

Now to return to our question, what shall we call these children and what do the labels mean? If the child or adolescent has informational processing problems that are presumed to be neurologically based and that result in difficulties mastering academic skills and strategies, he or she will be identified as having a learning disability. If this individual is hyperactive, distractible, and/or impulsive, he or she will be identified as having ADHD. As will become more clear later in this book, learning disabilities and ADHD are two separate but related disorders (see Chapters 3 and 5). Further, if emotional, social, and/or family problems exist, it is critical to determine if they are the cause of the academic difficulties (this is not the type child or adolescent discussed in this book) or if they are the consequence of the learning disabilities plus possible ADHD.

Do not let different professionals who use different terms confuse you. Nor should you be confused by books you read that use different terms. Often, these terms suggest that the professional using them had trained at an earlier time and has not kept up with the progressive changing of concepts. If you are at a meeting for your child or adolescent and the professionals present are debating whether he or she has dyslexia or a learning disability, relax and understand that they come from "different schools of thinking" or they have not kept up with the literature. Both terms are the same and refer to the same child.

The important thing for you to know and remember is that all of these terms refer to the same basic problems in the same basic child or adolescent. Don't let the labels that are used here or those used by your physician, your child's teacher, or an evaluator confuse you. Everyone you consult will want to talk about that aspect of the problem in which he or she specializes. Don't think that the terms they use all refer to different disorders. All of these terms are simply names for different parts of the same problem—a problem that is big enough as it is without compounding it.

Do More Boys Have These Problems Than Girls?

Most of the literature on learning disabilities suggest that the ratio of boys to girls with this disorder is between 5:1 and 9:1. Many theories have been proposed to explain why more boys have learning disabilities than girls and none of these theories fully explained the statistics. Recent studies suggest that the number of boys and girls with learning disabilities is about equal.

These studies suggest two reasons why previous statistics showed such a high incidence for boys. First, there is referral bias. Boys who are frustrated are more likely to act out than girls. Girls are more likely to withdraw and be quiet. Thus, more boys are referred for evaluation and, thus, identified. The other reason relates to possible test bias. Many of the tests used to diagnose learning disabilities were standardized on boys. It is possible that there are subtle differences that identify problems more frequently found with boys and less frequently found with girls. Efforts are underway to minimize these biases. It is probably true that many more girls with learning disabilities are not diagnosed.

The statistics on ADHD have shown also a higher frequency of the disorder with boys than girls, up to a 5:1 ratio or higher. Recent studies show two patterns of importance. First, the same referral bias exists as with learning disabilities. Boys with ADHD are more likely to act out and, thus, be referred for evaluation. Girls, especially those with only distractibility, are more likely to withdraw and be quiet. They are seen as "out of it" or "space cadets." The ratio may be closer to equal.

Another pattern has been observed. There might be two types of ADHD. One consists of hyperactivity, distractibility, impulsivity, and disruptive behavioral problems. This pattern may be more frequent with boys. The other type consists primarily of distractibility. Academic difficulties rather than behavioral problems are noticed first. This pattern may be more frequent with girls.

What Are the Causes of Learning Disabilities and Associated Problems?

Once parents become aware that they have a child or adolescent with a learning disability and have accepted this reality, they immediately ask, "How could this happen? Why did it happen?" as if knowing the cause of something implies knowing its cure. Or, for some, knowing the cause offers something to blame for the problems.

The answers to the question of the cause for learning disabilities or for ADHD has not yet been determined. Most research suggests that for most such children, something affected the brain during pregnancy. There is probably no one cause. Any number of things, in any number of combinations, could have affected the nervous system. In most cases, there is no way to reconstruct what actually did happen to each child. I have evaluated children whose histories included major problems during delivery, suggesting stress to the brain, yet showed no evidence of learning disability. Children with similar complications do not have learning disabilities; whereas, children with completely normal deliveries have identical learning disabilities to children with stressful deliveries.

I would like to share with you what professionals do know and what the current state of knowledge suggests about these causes of learning disabilities and ADHD. The current view is that there is a biological-neurological etiology for learning disabilities and ADHD. How the disorder is manifested is influenced by psychological and social factors. That is, it is the interaction of both sets of influences that explain the picture seen at any time.

For example, some forms of learning disabilities may not cause difficulty in mastering academic materials until the third or the sixth grade. Thus, the child could be seen as normal until these grades. Similarly, how a child or adolescent expresses the frustrations that are caused by the learning disabilities and/or ADHD can be influenced by that child's culture and sex. For instance, a girl doing poorly in school and frustrated might withdraw and appear to be disinterested or depressed. She might never be referred for an evaluation. A boy, on the other hand, with the same problems might begin to misbehave and get into trouble. He is more likely to be recognized as having a problem and referred for an evaluation.

Brain Damage

It is possible that some children and adolescents with learning disabilities plus possible ADHD have subtle brain damage. Problems with blood circulation or with chemicals that do not normally occur in the body, called "toxins," or with chemicals normally in the body but existing at higher or lower levels than normal, called "metabolites," all may affect the developing nervous system of the fetus during pregnancy or at delivery. In addition, certain viral infections may affect the developing brain.

Surgery or accidents during infancy or childhood can affect the nervous system. Other possible factors during the early years of life include certain brain infections (e.g., encephalitis), high fevers, or lead poisoning. Sometimes the treatment for one illness can cause secondary damage to the brain. For example, the treatment for some forms of leukemia include total body radiation. Before it became apparent that the brain needed to be shielded, children undergoing such therapy often developed learning disabilities due to the small areas of bleeding in the brain that were caused by the radiation therapy.

One view is that if something is going to affect the brain, the resulting picture may depend on the intensity of the problem, the areas that were affected, and the amount of developmental growth occurring in these areas at the time of the incident. At one end of the spectrum of consequences is fetal or infant death. In the middle may be cerebral palsy, epilepsy, or mental retardation. The least severe consequence at the other end of the spectrum might be such disorders as learning disabilities or ADHD.

Maturational Delay

In some children, the brain matures more slowly than normal. Your child may have experienced a delay in muscle control such as in sitting, standing, or walking and accomplished these tasks at an age later than normal. Speech may also have been delayed, not starting, perhaps, until age four or five. Less apparent than muscle control or speech delays are lags in development of auditory perception, visual perception, abstraction ability, memory, and other functions.

The brain is continuously maturing with the laying down of new nerve pathways and the connections of these new pathways to older pathways. There are several major growth spurts during childhood: between the ages of 3 and 10 months; between 2 and 4 years; between 6 and 8 years; between 10 and 12 years; and between 14 and 16 years. The brain's final maturation process is not completed until a person reaches his or her early thirties. In general, girls' brains grow and mature more quickly than boys' brains.

Maturational delay can cause learning disabilities with some children. The problem is that the diagnosis is made in retrospect. At this time, it cannot be said that a delay occurred until after it has remedied itself. While the delay exists, the learning disabilities and other behaviors exist and treatment is essential. It is nice, however, to be the person working with the child when this maturation process suddenly takes place. Not only does this person get the pleasure of seeing the improvement, he or she also gets the credit for the child's progress.

Genetics

Most studies suggest that between 25 and 40 percent of children and adolescents with learning disabilities have inherited this type of nervous system. The disability runs in families: brothers and sisters may have similar difficulties; a mother or father may recall such a problem or still have the problem; or an uncle, aunt, or cousin may have such a problem. The same statistics appear to be true for ADHD.

Family studies, twin studies, and adoptee-foster home studies suggest an important genetic factor. For example, there is an increased risk for these disabilities in parents or children who have relatives who have these disabilities. If one of a pair of identical twins has a learning disability or ADHD, the other twin is much more likely to have these problems; whereas, a fraternal twin would be less likely to have these similar disabilities. The familial pattern appears to be clear. The genetic pathway or process is not yet clear.

Another interesting observation is that the incidence of adoption with children and adolescents who have a learning disability is five times higher than would be expected from the national norms for adoption. The same incidence is found with ADHD. One could speculate about the parents of children placed for adoption or about the possible risk factors that were experienced by these youths during pregnancy and delivery. The incidence may be higher with children who were adopted from Third World countries and from poverty areas within these countries. Often mothers received minimal or no care and may have been malnourished. The baby is often malnourished during the weeks or months before adoption. Proper intake of the appropriate foods is critical during fetal life and the early months of life if the brain is to develop properly.

At this time, the reasons for such a high incidence of these disabilities with children who were adopted remain unknown. Parents should not be discouraged from adopting children. However, they might try to learn as much as possible about the biological parents, the pregnancy, and the life of the baby between delivery and placement.

Biochemical Factors

The brain is made up of millions of nerve cells, each of which has to communicate with other specific cells. This communication has to take place in such a way that only one other cell, the right cell, is stimulated. Each cell produces minute amounts of specific chemicals that pass across a microscopic space (called a *synapse*) and stimulate the next, correct cell. The chemicals that transmit messages from one nerve cell to another are called "neurotransmitters." Once this neurotransmitter crosses the space and stimulates another cell, another chemical process occurs that breaks down or neutralizes the neurotransmitter.

The brain produces many different types of neurotransmitters. About 50 are presently known, with an estimated total being as many as 200. Current research supports the possibility that ADHD is due to a deficiency of a specific neurotransmitter in a specific area of the brain. Information on neurotransmitter related to ADHD is provided in more detail in Chapter 5. No data yet suggests a neurotransmitter factor as the cause of learning disabilities.

There are other chemical activities related to the developing brain and an expanding body of knowledge on these activities. These chemicals control brain and behavioral interactions. New research at the molecular level on the genetic process of transmitting messages from the hereditary-carrying gene to the developing brain offers much promise. Specific chemical messengers, called "neuroendocrines," travel to the brain throughout fetal development. Each binds with a particular cell or cell group that has the correct receptor site for this chemical. This binding results in growth of these cells. Each day different sites are stimulated to grow in a very exact and complex process, slowly weaving together the networks of neurons that make up the human brain.

Could these genetic messengers be affected or influenced, resulting in a differently functioning brain? Could this explain the familial pattern of inheriting these disabilities? Could certain drugs or other chemicals interfere with the biochemical messenger process, resulting in the absence of brain growth for that particular day or time that the chemical is present? And, would such a block during a brief time affect other brain growth that should link with this area of nongrowth? Research in molecular genetics and cellular biology offers promise of such answers. With these answers, lay hope for prevention or possible treatment concepts.

One set of studies was of enough concern that the information resulted in prevention efforts. It was found that 80 percent of pregnant women in the United States took over-the-counter or prescription medications during pregnancy or at the time of delivery. It was not known which of these medications crossed through the placenta into the fetus nor what effect these chemicals might have had on the chemically driven genetic process that was previously described. Further, it was found that some of the medications used at the time of delivery could no longer pass back to the mother to be metabolized by her liver. Thus, they remained in the infant's blood for a longer period until the immature liver could metabolize it. Could these medications explain the more subtle changes found in the brain or other organ systems with children? The answer is not available. However, as a preventive effort, pregnant women are advised to take no medications during pregnancy and there is an increasing effort to use no medications at delivery, opting for women to use more natural childbirth methods.

One area of research supports the possibility of a chemical blockage as an explanation for the faulty "wiring" present in children with learning disabilities. First, I will explain the brain's developmental process, then review this research. As the brain develops, new cells multiply and then migrate out to new sites in the brain. These cells migrate out beyond where they will be in the ultimately developed brain. More cells are produced than will exist in the "finished" brain. Once these cells reach their temporary position in the developing brain, they send out nerve endings toward the area of the brain to which they are to connect. If the nerve ending establishes a connection, the cell survives. If the nerve ending does not establish proper connections, the cell does not survive. Once this process is finished and the proper number of cells are present, these cells migrate again back toward their place of origin. Once they reach their ultimate location, the migration stops. The proper number of cells, each connected to their other correct areas of the brain, are then in place.

A research team has studied six brains of individuals who had been diagnosed as having "dyslexia" and who died in such a way that the brain was not affected. In each case, areas of the brain were found where cells had migrated out to their first position but had not migrated back to their proper site in the brain. In addition, there were too many cells and some had nerve endings that did not connect with other cells. Thus, for the first time we have evidence to support the "faulty wiring" concept of brain dysfunction. The reason(s) for the process are not yet known.

Fetal Development

As discussed earlier, events or experiences that take place during pregnancy, at the time of delivery, or soon after delivery can affect the infant's developing brain. Socioenvironmental factors also can have a negative effect on this developing brain. Examples include poor nutrition, absence of prenatal care, metabolic or toxic factors, infections, or stress. Each can result in difficulties during pregnancy, premature delivery, and/or a child born with a low birth weight.

Studies have shown a relationship between low birth weight and prematurity and later academic difficulties or of hyperactivity and distractibility.

Two major national Collaborative Projects are in progress, one in the United States and one in England. Children have been followed since the mother first learned of her pregnancy and volunteered for the study. Multiple studies have been done during certain age periods and extensive observational information has been accumulated. Studies done on these children at age seven (second grade) and age 10 (fifth grade) identified those who were having academic difficulties or who showed evidence of hyperactivity, distractibility, and/or impulsivity. Through a study of the data on each child, efforts were made to statistically find patterns or correlations with specific factors.

It must be noted that such data are suggestive at best and that factors such as socioeconomic status were not factored into the results. The information at both age periods found a suggestive correlation with the following factors: maternal cigarette smoking during pregnancy, convulsions during pregnancy, low fetal heart rate during the second stage of labor, lower placental weight, more breech presentations, and more of a specific type of inflammation called chorionitis. Also noted was a history of the mother drinking alcohol during the pregnancy. In these cases, the amount used was two or three drinks a day, far less than that consumed with a more serious disorder called Fetal Alcohol Syndrome.

Although there is not a firm association between these factors and problems found with the children, preventive efforts are in effect. Pregnant women are told not to smoke or drink during the pregnancy. Proper nutrition throughout the pregnancy is stressed. For reasons discussed earlier, mothers are told not to use over-the-counter or prescription medications during pregnancy and at the time of delivery unless it is essential. Researchers may not have the final results, but preventive efforts based on such studies are in effect.

Recent studies of substance abuse during pregnancy are distressing. Many of these babies, such as the "Crack Babies," show problems with hyperactivity, distractibility, and irritability. As these children now reach school age, many are showing evidence of learning disabilities. The most recent studies show that the problem is not just with a mother who uses drugs during pregnancy. Evidence now shows that if the father uses drugs, the genetic activity of his sperm are affected and can result in difficulties with the fetus and future baby.

Other Medical Factors

It has long been known that there is a higher incidence of allergies with children and adolescents who have learning disabilities as well as with those who have ADHD. Although several theories have been proposed to explain this relationship, no clear answers are known at this time.

There is a higher incidence of learning disabilities, especially language-based disabilities with children who had multiple ear infections during the first three years of life. It has been proposed that as a result of the infections, there might have been fluid in the middle ear; thus, the child's hearing was affected. Possibly, the lack of correct sound input to the brain during critical periods resulted in a delay or halt to the development of those areas of the brain involved with auditory processing and language.

Other General Factors

Studies to date have not shown a consistent relationship between learning disabilities or ADHD and such variables as birth order, number of siblings, times the family moved, family income, mother's age, mother's educational level, or the father's educational level.

It is suggested that there may be cultural factors involved as well. The importance of academic achievement or of being able to sit still and attend may be experienced differently by various groups. Thus, the same behaviors that might be identified as a problem in some cultures and families are not seen as such in others.

In summary, now that you have an idea of what is known about the causes of learning disabilities and the associated disorder, ADHD, you can understand why professionals in the field cannot yet speak in terms of "prevention" or "cure," only of "hope for preventive efforts" and "treatment." Treatment, however, does offer a very favorable outcome.

Basic Concepts

As you go about seeking treatment for your child or adolescent, keep these four ideas firmly in mind. You will need them to understand everything that happens to you from now on:

1. Your child or adolescent does not have mental retardation, nor is he or she primarily displaying emotional disturbances.

2. Your child or adolescent probably has a group of difficulties often found together. The most common are learning disabilities, ADHD, and secondary emotional, social, and family problems. Know which of these problems are affecting your son or daughter.

3. Learning Disabilities are Life Disabilities. These disabilities do not just interfere with school, they interfere with every aspect of your child's or adolescent's life—at home, with friends, in sports, in activities. You must learn to understand every aspect of your youngster's disabilities and how they affect him or her in all these areas, as well as how they affect you and the other members of your family.

4. You must learn to build on strengths while understanding and compensating for weaknesses. If possible, never magnify the weaknesses.

Your child's or adolescent's problems may seem overwhelming. But you must keep in mind that although this condition is unfortunate, it is not the worst thing in the world. Many people can help you understand more, not only about your situation and that of your child, but about what remedies will work. You must know as much as possible about what to ask, who to ask, and what to demand. The people you meet will help you learn more about what they can do and about what your child can do. Only you are motivated enough to push for appropriate testing and constructive remedies. Only you know your child well enough to see that he or she gets the best help you can find.

I will try to provide you with the understanding, knowledge, and other information you will need to help your child. You must be your son's or daughter's informed consumer and assertive advocate. No one can be more concerned about or involved with your child or adolescent than you. Ready or not, the job is yours. This book will help you accomplish your goals.

3

Specific Learning Disabilities

ALL OF US HAVE AREAS in which we readily learn. A few of us even seem to excel in limited areas with very little apparent learning—thus, the "natural" athlete, the musical "genius," the "gifted" artist. All of us also have areas in which our abilities will never be more than average and a few areas in which we cannot seem to learn anything. Children or adolescents with learning disabilities have areas of strengths and average ability too. These youngsters, however, have larger areas, or different areas, of learning weaknesses than most people. Each person with a learning disability displays a different pattern of strengths and weaknesses. You must learn as much as you *can* about the whole pattern that your child displays—the disabilities, of course, but also the abilities. What your child can do, and may indeed do well, is just as important as what she or he cannot do because it is these strengths upon which you must build.

You may have suspected a learning disability before your child entered school. This concern became real when he or she failed to learn the skills being taught.

He or she may have read letters backwards or confused certain letters. Or, he or she may have misunderstood what you said or have been slow in developing speech or muscle coordination.

In order to talk a little more usefully about learning disabilities, let me quickly outline a simple scheme describing what the brain must do in order for learning to take place. The first step is *input*—getting information into the brain from the eyes and ears, primarily, but, as I will discuss later, from other senses as well. Once this information arrives, the brain needs to make sense out of it—a process called *integration*. Next, the information is stored and later retrieved—the *memory* process. Finally, the brain sends a message back to the nerves and muscles—its *output*.

The brain does a great deal more than this, of course. Any learning task involves more than one of these processes; however, this simplified scheme will do for this purpose. Once again, then, the learning processes are:

Input	Memory
Integration	Output

Input Disabilities

Information arrives at the brain as impulses, transmitted along neurons, primarily from our eyes—called *visual input*—and from our ears—called *auditory input*. This input process takes place in the brain. It does not pertain to visual problems, such as nearsightedness or farsightedness, or to any hearing problems. This central input process of seeing, or hearing, or in any other way taking in or perceiving one's environment is referred to as *perception*. Thus, children who have perception disabilities in the area of visual input are labeled as having *visual perception disabilities*, and those with disabilities in the area of auditory input as having *auditory perception disabilities*. Some children have problems with one area of input; some have both kinds of perception disability; and, some may have problems when both inputs are needed at the same time (e.g., seeing what the teacher writes on the blackboard while listening to the explanation of what is being written).

Visual Perception Disabilities

Your child may have difficulty in organizing the position and shape of what he or she sees. Input may be perceived with letters reversed or rotated (e.g., a "u" might look like an "n"; an "E" might look like a "W," or a "3," or an "M"). The child may confuse similar looking letters because of these rotations or reversals: d, b, p, g, and q may be confused with any one of the others. All children show this problem until about age five and a half. This confusion with position or input becomes apparent when the child begins to read, write, or copy letters or designs.

Another child might have a *figure-ground* problem—that is, difficulty in focusing on the significant figure instead of all of the other visual inputs in the background. This occurs in real-life situations as well as in looking at printed matter or electronic images. For example, the child is told to pass the salt shaker but has difficulty finding it among the many dishes and platters. Reading requires focusing on specific letters or groups of letters, then tracking from left to right, line after line. Children with this disability may have reading difficulties. They skip words, or miss lines, or read the same line twice.

Judging distance is another visual perception task that can go awry. Information is received from each eye and combined to create three-dimensional vision. Your child may misjudge depth, bumping into things, falling off a chair, or knocking over a drink because the hand reaches too far for it. What you take for habitual carelessness or poor eyesight may in fact be just this type of perception error.

There are other types of problems associated with visual perception disabilities. While playing in an open field or gym, your child may become confused and disoriented because of trouble organizing his or her position in space. Or perhaps the child may have difficulty in understanding left and right or up and down.

One very common type of visual perception disability relates to doing activities when the eyes have to tell the hands or legs what to do. This is called a *visual motor* task. When such information is unreliable, activates like catching a ball, jumping rope, doing puzzles, or using a hammer and nail become difficult or impossible. To catch a ball, the eyes must find and focus on the ball (i.e., visual figure-ground). The child must then keep his or her eyes on the ball so that the brain can use depth perception to perceive the correct position and path of the ball and tell the various parts of the body exactly where and when to move. A child who has difficulty with figure-ground or who misperceives distance or speed, may have difficulty catching or hitting balls; thus, he or she may not do well with such sports as baseball or basketball. For similar reasons, this child might have difficulty with jump rope, four-square, or hopscotch.

Auditory Perception Disabilities

As with visual perception, your child may have difficulty with one or several aspects of auditory perception. Some may have difficulty distinguishing subtle differences in sound. Ours is typically a visual society; so, when I mentioned subtle differences in shapes, you know I meant the 26 letters in the English alphabet and the 10 shapes in our numerical system. There are 43 units of sound in the English language, called *phonemes*. A child may have difficulty distinguishing subtle differences in these phonemes. He or she might confuse words that sound alike: (e.g., blue and blow, ball and bell, can and can't). I might ask a child, "How are you?" and he or she may answer, "I'm nine." The child may have thought he or she heard an "old" instead of an "are," or in addition to the "are."

A child may have difficulty with auditory figure-ground. For example, the child might be watching television in a room where others are playing or talking. When you call out to him or her from the kitchen, you might be into your third paragraph before the child realizes that your voice (i.e., figure) is important to distinguish from the other voices and sounds (i.e., background). With this disability, it appears that the child never listens or pays attention.

As another example, I recall observing Mary in her fourth grade classroom. She had been evaluated and found to have learning disabilities, one of which was an auditory figure-ground problem. She later helped me understand what I observed, but let me tell the story as it happened. She was at her desk reading a story. Other children were talking in the back of the room; there was noise of movement in the hall and noise from traffic heard through the open window. The teacher suddenly said, "Children, let's do math. Open up your book to page 38 and try problem five." Mary looked up to listen to her teacher as she heard "problem five." She looked over and saw her friend take out her math book. So, she did the same. She then looked over the shoulder of the boy in front of her to see on which page she could find problem five. At that moment the teacher shouted, "Mary, stop bothering John and get to work." The teacher then looked at me sitting in the back of the room and said, "See what I mean." Mary was confused and hurt because she did not know what she had done wrong. This was the only brain she had ever had and she did not know that it was different. She only knew that she was trying hard and suddenly the teacher was angry with her. The teacher was frustrated with Mary because she did not know of her disabilities.

Some children cannot process sound inputs as fast as normal people can. This problem is called an *auditory lag*. It is as if this child has to concentrate on what he or she heard for a second longer before it is understood. Thus, he or she is concentrating on what was just heard while trying to hold on to what is coming in so that it can be concentrated on next. Soon, he or she cannot keep up and parts of what is said are missed. For example, a teacher might explain something in class. This child misses parts of what was said, and thus, asks a question. The teacher becomes annoyed and says, "I just explained that. Why don't you pay attention."

Other Perception Disabilities

Sensory Integrative Disorder

Several other sensory inputs are critical to functioning. Difficulty in correctly receiving these sensory inputs interferes with awareness of the body and body movements. These sensory inputs involve nerve endings in the skin (i.e., tactile input); in the muscles (i.e., proprioception input); and in the inner ear (i.e., vestibular input). This group of sensory input difficulties is called Sensory Integrative Disorder.

Children with *tactile perception* difficulties confuse input from the nerve endings near the surface of the skin for light touch and from nerve endings deeper in the skin for deep touch or pressure. They may be tactilely defensive. From early childhood he or she will not like being touched or held. This child or adolescent is sensitive to touch and may perceive it as uncomfortable. Often parents notice that from birth this child did not like to be held or cuddled. He or she may complain of the tag on the back of a shirt, the belt being too tight, the clothes feeling uncomfortable. He or she might wear socks inside out, complaining that the seam bothers their feet. Parents learn that this child does like deep touch and can be calmed down by rubbing hard over his or her arms, legs, or back. Some children with tactile sensitivity feel defensive and try to avoid people getting too close. This child might be walking down the hall and another child lightly brushes against him or her. The child might respond as if the touch was a major blow and hit the other child. Another child may experience touch deprivation and the need for body contact. This child might walk around the classroom touching other children to the annoyance of the children and the teacher.

Proprioception perception informs the child of joint position, muscle tone, movement, and body position. These inputs help the child adapt so that he or she can hold his or her body upright or to hold, push, pull, and carry. A child and adolescent having difficulty with this sensory input may be confused with his or her body in space and may have difficulty with muscle tone and maintaining posture. The child will have difficulty changing his or her body in order to keep from losing balance. He or she may have difficulty with running, jumping, or climbing. This child may also have difficulty with muscle planning and the coordinated use of muscles in such activities as buttoning and tying. A child with this disability experiences a proprioception deprivation. This child might stomp his or her feet or appear to like to bump into walls.

Vestibular perception is necessary to tell where one's head is in space and to know how to handle gravity. These inputs are needed to interact with space and sense body movements in space, particularly in making adjustments with the body to adjust for changes in the position of the head. This information helps the child know where his or her body is in space (e.g., upside down, lying on stomach, lying on back) and how he or she is moving (e.g., fast, slow, around, forward, backward). A child may experience vestibular deprivation and enjoy spinning in chairs or on swings.

Depending on which sensory systems are involved in the Sensory Integrative Disorder, a child or adolescent may have problems with tactile sensitivity, body movements coordination, and adaptation to the position of the body in space. In addition, he or she may have difficulty with muscle planning; that is, having the ability to easily direct his or her body to perform activities in a smooth, coordinated manner and in the right sequence of activities.

Taste and smell

No research has been done to explore if the taste and smell sensory inputs might be received with difficulty with a child or adolescent who has learning disabilities. Since this individual has difficulty with other sensory perceptions, it is possible that these inputs can also be involved.

I have had parents report that their child's taste is supersensitive. For example, he or she does not like certain foods because they "taste funny" or "feel funny in my mouth." Other parents report that their child smells things that they do not. These children seem to be very sensitive to smells or appear to smell some things differently.

Integration Disabilities

Once the information coming into the brain is registered, it has to be understood. Let me illustrate this process by asking you to do something. I want you to print the following three symbols in your brain—a "d," an "o" and a "g." No problem with visual perception; so, it is correctly printed. There are at least three things you would have to do to make sense out of (i.e., integrate) these three symbols. First, you would have to place the symbols in the right order, or sequence the inputs. Is it "d-o-g," or "g-o-d," or "o-g-d," or what? Second, you have to infer meaning from the context in which the word is used. For example, "the dog" and "you dog" have very different meanings. In one case you are naming a pet and in the other case you are insulting someone. Thus, you have two abstract meanings in these words. Finally, you have to take this word now that it is recorded properly and you know what it means, as well as take in all of the other words that are pouring into your head plus the many memory tracks being stimulated by these words and pull them all together or organize them in a way that can be understood.

The process of integrating inputs, of understanding what your brain has recorded, thus requires *sequencing, abstraction,* and *organization.* Your child might have a disability in one area or in more than one area. Since inputs are processed through two pathways—visual and auditory—some children might have a *visual sequencing disability* or an *auditory sequencing disability.* So, too, the other integrative tasks might involve one input mode and not the other.

Sequencing Disabilities

A child with such a disability might hear or read a story; but, in recounting it, he or she may start in the middle, go to the beginning, then shift to the end. Eventually the whole story comes out, but the sequence of events is wrong. Or a child might see the math problem as $16 - 3 = ?$ on the blackboard, but write it on the paper as $61 - 3 = ?$ Or, a child might see $2 + 3 = ?$, and write $2 + 5 = 3$. The child knows the right answer but gets the sequence wrong. Spelling words with all of the right letters but in the wrong order can also reflect this disability.

A child might memorize a sequence—the days of the week or the months of the year—and then be unable to use the sequence. He or she can recite the months of the year; however, if asked what comes after August, the child pauses before answering, "September." The child had to go back to January and move forward to get the answer. Using the dictionary can be very frustrating. The child has to return to "a" each time to know if the next letter is above or below in the alphabet sequence.

A child with a sequence disability might hit the baseball then run to third base rather than to first or have difficulty with board games that require moving in a particular sequence. When setting the dinner table, he or she might have difficulty remembering where to properly place each item. The child may also have difficulty with the sequence of dressing. Parents might walk into the child's bedroom in the morning and not know whether to laugh, cry, or bite one's tongue. The child may have his or her pants on, but is holding his underpants, or he or she has the shirt on, but is holding an undershirt.

Abstraction Disabilities

Once information is recorded in the brain and placed in the right sequence, one must be able to infer meaning. Most children with learning disabilities, if they have abstraction difficulties, have only minor problems. Abstraction is such a basic intellectual task that if the disability were too great the child might be functioning at a level of mental retardation.

Some children do have problems with abstraction. For example, the teacher may be doing a language-arts exercise with the class. The teacher reads a story about a police officer, then begins a discussion of police officers in general, asking the students if they know any men or women who are police officers in their neighborhoods, and, if so, what do they do? A child with an abstraction disability may not be able to answer such a question. He or she can only talk about the particular officer in the story and not be able to generalize with all law officers.

I remember observing a group of approximately 10 children with learning disabilities as they sat at a table working with their teacher. One child was known to have difficulty with abstraction. Two other children were talking to each other throughout the lesson. When the teacher tired of the noise, she said, "Class, will you please be quiet." The child with the abstraction difficulty looked up and complained, "I was not talking." The teacher agreed and tried to explain that she knew he was not talking but that she was referring to the class in general. He was upset and took her statement literally. If the class was talking, then, she meant he must be talking. And, he was not talking. He would not stop as he continued his protest about being accused of doing something he did not do.

A child or adolescent with abstraction problems does not understand jokes, either. He or she does not know when to laugh. Furthermore, this child is often confused by puns or idioms. He or she seems to take things literally and to misunderstand what is said.

Organization Disabilities

If your child or adolescent has difficulties with organization, you will not need a formal test to know. Look at his or her notebook, locker, or bedroom. He or she is "disorganized" in all aspects of life. The notebook will be a mess with papers in the wrong place or falling out. The bedroom will be disorganized and a mess no matter how many times you yell to keep it clean. This child might have difficulty organizing time and never be able to plan ahead.

This child or adolescent never seems to bring home what he or she will need to do for homework. Somehow, homework never gets back to school, even when it is done. He or she is always losing things such as coats, books, and assignments.

Information, once recorded, sequenced, and understood, must be integrated with a constant flow of information and must be related to previously learned information. A child may have difficulty pulling together multiple parts of information into a full or complete concept. He or she might learn a series of facts but not be able to answer general questions that require using these facts. This student answers the questions at the end of the chapter (putting parts of information from the chapter together with the correct question to get the answer). However, the same student cannot tell you what the chapter or book was about. The child or adolescent might tell you about what he or she wishes to write. Then, when it is put on paper, it is disorganized with the facts in the wrong order and disconnected.

Memory Disabilities

Once information is received, recorded in the brain, and integrated, it is stored so that it can be retrieved later. This storage and retrieval process is called *memory*. For this purpose, we can consider that there are two types of memory: short-term memory and long-term memory.

Short-term memory is the process by which you store and hold information by method of concentration and repetition. For example, when you call the information operator for a long-distance telephone number, with the area code you get a 10 digit number. Like most people, you can probably retain these numbers long enough to dial the number if you do it right away and nothing interrupts your attention. However, if someone starts talking to you in the course of dialing, you may lose the number. Similarly, you might go to the store with five items in mind to buy, but by the time you get there so many different impressions have intervened that you've forgotten an item or two on your list.

Long-term memory refers to the process by which you store information that you have often repeated. You can retrieve this information quickly by thinking of it. For example, you can come up with your current home address and telephone number quite readily by thinking about it.

If your child or adolescent has a memory disability, it is most likely a short-term one. Like abstraction disabilities, long-term memory disabilities interfere so much with functioning that a child who has such disabilities is more likely to be classified as having mental retardation. It may take 10 to 15 repetitions throughout several days for a child with this problem to retain what the average child retains after three to five repetitions on one occasion. Yet, this same child usually has no problem with long-term memory. He or she will surprise you at times by coming up with events that happened years ago in great detail about which you may have forgotten.

A short-term memory disability can occur with information learned through what one sees, a *visual short-term memory disability*, or with information learned through what one hears, an *auditory short-term memory disability*. The two disabilities might exist in the same individual.

This child might read through a spelling list one evening and really seem to know it because he or she is concentrating on it. The next day he or she has lost most or all of the words. Similarly, a teacher might review a math concept in class until the child understands and remembers it (because he or she is concentrating on it). Yet, when it is time to do the math home-work that night, he or she has forgotten how to do the problems. Likewise, this child or adolescent might read a few paragraphs and remember each as he or she reads it, but by the time he or she gets to the end of the chapter, nothing is remembered.

If your son or daughter has this disability, you have learned the hard way that you cannot give him or her too many instruc-tions at the same time. "Run upstairs, wash up, get in your paja-mas, then come on down again for a snack." Forget it, he or she will not remember that many instructions.

Your son or daughter might drive you crazy by constantly stopping in the middle of what is being said and saying, "Oh for-get it" or "It's not important." If your child exhibits these behav-iors, it is possible that he or she has a short-term memory disability. This child or adolescent starts to speak knowing what he or she wants to say. However, part way through, the flow of ideas is forgotten. It is embarrassing to say, "I'm sorry. What was I saying." It is easier for the child to say, "Oh forget it."

Output Disabilities

Information comes out of the brain either by means of words, language output, or through muscle activity, such as writing, drawing, gesturing, or motor output. A child or adolescent hav-ing problems communicating may have a *language disability* or a *motor disability*.

Language Disability

Two forms of language are used in communication, spontaneous language and demand language. You use *spontaneous language* in situations where you initiate whatever is said. Here you have the luxury of picking the subject and taking some time to orga-nize your thoughts and to find the correct words before you say anything. In a *demand language* situation, someone else sets up a circumstance in which you must communicate. In other words, a question is put to you, not vice versa. Now you have no time to organize your thoughts or to find the right words. You have only a split second in which you must simultaneously organize, find words, and answer more or less appropriately.

Children with a *language disability* usually have no difficulty with spontaneous language. They do, however, often have problems with demand language. The inconsistency can be quite striking. A youngster may initiate all sorts of conversations, may never keep quiet, in fact, and may sound quite normal. But, put into a situation that demands a response, the same child might answer "Huh?," "What?," or "I don't know." Or, the child may ask you to repeat the question to gain time, or not answer at all. If the child is forced to answer, the response may be so confusing or circumstantial that it is difficult to follow. She or he may sound totally unlike the child who was so fluently speaking just a minute ago. This inconsistency or confusion in language behavior often puzzles parents and teachers. A teacher might put a child down as lazy or negative because he or she speaks all of the time in class. However, if the teacher calls on the child to answer a question, he or she often will say, "I don't know."

Motor Disabilities

If a child has difficulty coordinating the use of groups of large muscles such as those in the arms, legs, and trunk, this is called a *gross motor disability*. Difficulty in performing tasks that require coordinating groups of small muscles such as those in the hand is called a *fine motor disability*.

Gross motor disabilities may cause your child to be clumsy, stumble, fall, bump into things, or have trouble with generalized physical activities such as running, climbing, or riding a bike.

The most common form of a fine motor disability shows up when the child begins to write. The problem lies in an inability to get the many muscles in the dominant hand to work together as a team. His or her handwriting is poor. The child awkwardly holds a pen or pencil and writes slowly; thus, his or her hand gets tired. The child seems not to be able to get his or her hand to write as fast as the head is thinking. Watch your own dominant hand as you write something and notice the many detailed fine muscle activities that it takes to write legibly. Writing requires a constant flow of such activities. Now place your pen in your nondominant hand and try to write. If you go very slowly, it is tedious but your handwriting is legible. If you go at a regular pace, however, your hand aches and your handwriting immediately deteriorates. Shape, size, spacing, and positioning—everything about the handwriting looks awful no matter how hard you try. A child with a fine motor disability goes through this all of the time.

Some may only have this fine motor problem. Usually, however, the child has a broader problem called a *written language disability*. In addition to the problems with the mechanical aspects of writing, he or she has difficulty getting thoughts out of the brain through the motor pathways, creating spelling, grammar, and punctuation problems. The same child who gets 100 on spelling test misspells words when writing. The child knows all of the rules for grammar, yet, makes errors when writing. This son or daughter will explain what will be written on a report with excellent ideas and vocabulary. Later, you read what was written and find a few incomplete sentences with confused information.

A written language disability is very frustrating and can be very serious. Most schools do not grade you on what you know but on what you put down on a piece of paper. If you cannot copy off of the board fast enough, take notes, or write in class, you have a problem. Of necessity, homework requires writing. Think of copying off of the board. First you have to look at the word (i.e., visual perception). Then, you have to retain the word (i.e., visual short-term memory). Finally, you have to copy the word on the paper (i.e., fine motor activity). Children with visual perception, visual short-term memory, and fine motor disabilities may have to copy one word or letter at a time, never finishing the work.

Establishing Your Child's Profile

Obviously the learning process is much more complex, but this simple model for describing learning disabilities should be more than adequate. When you read reports or sit in on conferences, these are the terms used.

The important thing is that you must know your son's or daughter's specific profile. Each child or adolescent with a learning disability will have a different combination of disabilities and abilities. You must know your own son's or daughter's areas of learning disability and abilities.

Look at the checklist of learning disabilities below. Do you know where your child's disabilities lie? Where his or her strengths exist? Where the weaknesses are? You must know this information in order to learn how to build on strengths rather than magnify weaknesses when selecting chores, activities, sports, or camps. You must know this information and how to best help your child with his or her homework. If you do not know, ask the special education team at your school or the person who did the testing.

Learning Disabilities
Input
- ~ Visual Perception
- ~ Auditory Perception

Integration
- ~ Visual Sequencing
- ~ Auditory Sequencing
- ~ Visual Abstraction
- ~ Auditory Abstraction
- ~ Visual Organization
- ~ Auditory Organization

Memory
- ~ Visual Short-Term Memory
- ~ Auditory Short-Term Memory

Output
- ~ Demand Language
- ~ Gross Motor
- ~ Fine Motor

In the previous chapter, I noted that with about 40 percent of children and adolescents with learning disabilities, such disabilities appear to be a familial pattern—that is, the problems are inherited. This means that there is about a 40 percent possibility that one parent also will have learning disabilities. As you learn about your child, you might say, "That's me." This may be the first time in your life that you understand why you have had so much difficulty in school and in life. If so, learn about yourself. The new knowledge will be valuable. This knowledge may be needed when help for your son or daughter is discussed. As one mother once said, "You keep telling me that I have to help my son be more organized with his work. But, I have not been organized one day of my life. How can I help him when I have the same problem?"

Other Neurological Problems Associated with Learning Disabilities

The association of Attention-Deficit Hyperactivity Disorder (ADHD) with learning disabilities as well as the possible presence of a Sensory Integrative Disorder have already been noted. However, two other possible neurological problems should be mentioned: perseveration and persisting immature reflexes.

You might also note physical differences with your son or daughter: ears may be set slightly lower or higher on the head than normal, eyes may be placed wider apart or closer together than normal, teeth may be spaced further apart than normal, or certain fingers or toes may be longer or shorter than normal.

None of these difficulties is necessarily associated with learning disabilities. However, they do appear to reflect other areas of neurological difficulty or other evidence of stress on the fetus during pregnancy. Since they may occur in your son or daughter, they are briefly discussed.

Perseveration

At times your child may repeat a word or a phrase over, repeatedly ask the same question, or start an activity and persist in it beyond the bounds of good sense. Repetitive behavior like this may be another evidence of abnormal brain activity. It is as if his or her "circuits are jammed." The youngster lines up cars or soldiers, for example, then keeps on lining them up without apparent purpose, or starts talking about something or asks a question and cannot get off it and onto another topic. Someone usually has to intercede and help the child change to something else.

We do not understand this behavior, nor do we have a treatment for it. The best approach is a very practical one, although not always an easy one. Try to help the child break the pattern. With activities, you might put away the objects the child is using. With questions, you may have to say that you will not answer any more of them, then try to ignore the questions or walk away.

Persisting Immature Reflexes

During the first few months of life, certain automatic body responses, or *reflexes*, usually disappear. These reflexes are normal in a newborn infant, but as the brain matures, it suppresses or controls these behaviors. For some children who will turn out to have learning disabilities, these reflexes persist longer than normal. These characteristics may also persist in babies who will *not* develop learning disabilities, so don't take this as a sign, simply as a possible clue.

These reflexes may have interfered with your feeding and holding the baby, and if this happened it may have created ambivalent feelings in you and frustrations in your infant. Since what I am about to describe occurred when your child was young, it is too late to offer help. However, if you can look back and understand your feelings, you may be able to more realistically think about that time and feel less anxious or guilty.

One such reflex is called the *tonic-neck reflex*. When you turn your infant's head to one side, the arm on that side automatically extends and moves out, while the arm on the other side bends, going up over the head. This reflex is present at two weeks of age, peaks at about two months, then declines, often completely disappearing by 16 weeks. If it persisted in your child, you may have noticed that when you held your infant and turned his or her head toward the bottle or nipple, his or her arm moved out as if to push you away.

Another persistent reflex relates to a behavior that is characteristic of young infants. When muscles are stretched, they reflexively contract. This is called a *stretch reflex*. For example, as you held your infant to feed him or her, you may have noticed that when you put your finger into the infant's hand, his or her fingers closed around your finger. Another stretch reflex occurs when the pressure of your upper arm against the baby's back causes the back muscles to contract—that is, the baby arches his or her back. If both the *back-arching stretch reflex* and the *tonic-neck reflex* are present, when you pick up your infant, place him or her in your arm, and turn his or her face toward you, he or she will seem to "back off" and "push you away," almost as if it were rejecting you. Perhaps these behaviors were the earliest examples of your child's "invisible" disability that were not understood and resulted in a conflict in relating. The consequence may be poor interaction with the people who are most important and necessary to the baby—you, the parents.

A third suggestion of immature reflexes occurs when the *startle reaction* persists. Normally, if an infant's head is lowered or dropped quickly, he or she will startle—the back extends, the arms extend and move out, the hands and fingers are held wide open and the legs may do the same. This reflex usually disappears by three to four months. If it continues beyond this time, it may be another evidence of subtle neurological difficulties.

As I discussed earlier under Sensory Integrative Disorder, hypersensitivity to touch can be another possible evidence of an immature nervous system during early infancy. Some infants perceive touch as unpleasant or painful. They appear to be tactilely sensitive and develop tactile defensiveness. When a parent holds such a baby, it cries. The more you try to comfort the baby by holding him or her tighter or by cuddling, the more the child cries. Some parents report that they intuitively learned to place their baby on a pillow and then hold the pillow, or place the child on the bed and prop up the bottle beside him or her.

Such hypersensitivity may, for some infants, suppress by the fifth or sixth week of life. Some cases of proposed "milk allergies" may instead be cases of tactile sensitivity. It is not that last change in the type of milk or formula at six or seven weeks that finally worked; rather, the tactile sensitivity phases out at that age and the child can relax when eating. Any milk or formula given at this time might work.

Some infants seem more irritable and active from birth than normal. It is as if the child's nervous system is easily upset and he or she has difficulty calming him- or herself. Any activity, sound, or movement can make the child shake or cry. Nothing appears to comfort him or her.

Motor disabilities may be present early. Poor coordination of the muscles in the tongue, cheeks, lips, and throat can cause eating and swallowing problems. The baby uses the same muscles to eat as he or she does to swallow, and if the baby swallows poorly, saliva builds up, causing excessive drooling.

Note once again that none of these problems have any necessary correlation with learning disabilities. To the degree that they may coexist, and because they constitute problems in and of themselves as well as occasionally indicating other conditions, you should be aware of them and of what they may possibly mean.

4

Learning Disabilities Are Life Disabilities

AS YOU READ CHAPTER 3, the impact of learning disabilities on class participation, mastering academic skills, and learning successful study skills is apparent. Learning disabilities definitely are school disabilities. It is equally crucial for parents and for other adults who work with children and adolescents to understand that learning disabilities are life disabilities. The same disabilities that interfere with reading, writing, and arithmetic also will interfere with sports and other activities, family life, and getting along with friends.

The special education professional must know your son's or daughter's areas of learning ability and disability in order to develop the necessary educational program. You must also know your son's or daughter's areas of learning ability and disability to know in what sports or activities he or she is most likely to succeed, what chores to assign, what camps to select, and countless other crucial decisions. With these strengths and weaknesses known, you can use this understanding to maximize your child's growth and success, and to minimize frustration and failure in the family and outside world.

Input Disabilities

A child or adolescent with visual perception difficulties may have problems with sports that require eye-hand coordination such as catching, throwing, or hitting a ball. The ball could be a baseball, basketball, or football. The first task in order to achieve eye-hand coordination is to look in the correct direction and spot the ball. This activity requires visual figure-ground skills. If the child has a disability in this area, he or she may not spot the ball and will stand there as the ball hits him or her or the ground. The second task is to keep one's eye on the ball. By doing this, the brain can use depth perception to track the ball and to inform the body, legs, arms, and hands where to be at the right time to catch the ball. Individuals with visual perception problems might play sports poorly and, thus, avoid them. They might intuitively have learned that they do best in sports that do not need or require only minimal eye-hand coordination (e.g., swimming, soccer, certain track and field events, horseback riding).

What about jump rope? First, the child or adolescent must spot where the rope hits the ground (i.e., visual figure-ground). Then, he or she must focus on this spot while running toward the rope so that the brain can use depth perception to inform the body when and where to jump. Thus, you can also see the potential problems with four-square, hopscotch, and other activities if visual perception problems exist.

An individual with depth perception problems may fall off of his or her seat, bump into things, misjudge the distance to a drink and knock over the glass. He or she may be confused by large, open spaces such as gyms, parking lots, and shopping malls.

A child or adolescent with an auditory perception problem might misunderstand what adults or friends say and thus respond incorrectly. This child may have difficulty knowing what sounds to listen to when there are competing sounds. Such a child might miss what is being said to him or her by parents or friends because he or she was listening to one sound (e.g., television, stereo) and not realize that another sound started (e.g., a friend talking to him or her). A child may also have a delay in processing speech (i.e., auditory lag). He or she may appear to be not listening or to be staring into space. This individual is often called an "air head" or a "space cadet."

Integration Disabilities

Individuals with sequencing problems may confuse the steps involved in playing a game, might hit the baseball and run to third base rather than first, or might have difficulty dressing. For example, you may walk into your child's bedroom and not know whether to laugh, cry, or bite your tongue because he or she has his or her pants on but is holding underpants. Or, he or she has a shirt on but is holding an undershirt. This same child or adolescent might have difficulty following directions, making the bed, building models, or setting the dinner table properly.

Much of humor is based on subtle changes in the meaning of words or phrases. An individual who is having difficulty with abstraction may miss the meaning of jokes and be out of place with friends. In a crowd, he or she has no problem—when everyone else laughs, it is time to laugh. However, in a one-to-one situation, the friend might get angry because he or she did not laugh. The child might have similar difficulty with puns or slang expressions. Some children with this problem appear to be supersensitive or paranoid because they take everything said literally.

Organizational problems often create family conflicts. A child or adolescent with an organization disability has difficulty keeping his or her room organized. It is always disorganized. Necessary books and papers are not brought home from school; the right work never gets back to school. Coats and books and everything else imaginable are lost. Often, a child with organizational problems has difficulty with the concept of time. He or she cannot plan ahead and panics the night before a big project is due. He or she is also always late. Friends may complain that this individual can never get his or her act together. Furthermore, this child will forget what is planned or what he or she is supposed to do.

Parents often get angry with this child when it comes to homework, thinking that he or she is too dependent on them and will not work unless someone does it with him or her. In reality, he or she may not be able to start homework until someone sits and helps to organize what needs to be done.

Memory Disabilities

Children and adolescents with short-term memory disabilities can have problems communicating and in social interactions. If your child has a memory disability, he or she might meet someone that he or she has known for a long time, but not remember that person's name. You might ask your son to go into the garage and get the hammer, some nails, and a ruler, and he may return with only the hammer. Or, you may say, "Run upstairs and get into your pajamas. Then, wash up, brush your teeth, and come back downstairs," and he or she may do only one of the commands. He or she cannot handle this many verbal instructions. You find yourself yelling because he or she never does what you ask.

An individual might frustrate family and friends because he or she starts to talk and then stops in the middle, saying, "Oh, forget it" or "It's not important." In reality, the child's flow of thoughts were forgotten and he or she covered it up with these comments.

Output Disabilities

The inability to write quickly and legibly or to spell can be a problem with games, activities, taking telephone messages, or writing a note to a friend. Mistakes are laughed at or associated with not being smart.

Motor coordination difficulties can cause problems with buttoning, tying, zipping, playing games, cutting up food, getting food into the mouth rather than on the face, and so many other daily life tasks.

Success in sports is essential for peer acceptance as a child. Problems with motor coordination resulting in clumsiness and poor sports ability can be painful to the child and can lead to peer rejections.

Expressive language problems make communications difficult with family and friends. An individual may have problems with small talk or interacting in a conversation. Often he or she becomes shy and avoid talking or being with people for fear that he or she will say the wrong thing and appear to be foolish.

Learning disabilities are life disabilities. Unless parents and other important people in the child's or adolescent's life understand the disabilities, everyone experiences frustration. The child or adolescent cannot do certain things and gets rejected, yelled at, punished, or all of the above. For example, "If you just tried harder, you could play baseball as well as the other kids," or "How could you have forgotten to tell me that you were supposed to be at your friend's house a half an hour ago."

Parents become angry and feel frustrated, saying, "No matter how many times I tell him to do something, he does not listen." Or, for example, "Your room's a mess again. You cannot go out until you straighten it up"; "Why don't you look where you are going"; or "You are such a mess. Why don't you look at what you are doing so you don't knock everything down."

What does it feel like to be this child or adolescent. Let me have Jill explain. She wrote this essay (copied exactly as she wrote it) and sent it to me shortly after starting college in a special education program. We had worked together for many years and she understood her learning disabilities. It was this knowledge of herself that helped her describe her life.

> I think that when I was born I was put in a rocket ship and taken to another planet—earth. I never felt that I was like anyone else here. From the time I was five, I can recall feeling like an outsider. I first remember feeling like an alien when I tried to communicate. People would raise their eyebrows and make other facial expressions of confusion when I tried to express myself. I was aware of starting a sentence in my head but only the last half came out of my mouth. I know how E.T. must have felt. It was like I was speaking another language and thinking on another wavelength. Constant rejection created feelings of isolation and isolation created anger and anger created self-defeat. I could not judge time and was anxious about being late. I never got a joke (no matter how simple) because it was abstract, and I could never get myself or my work in order because of my sequencing problems. Printing was murder because of my perceptual problems and my spacing was the worst. I could never remember anything but the first part of a direction and the noise level of the then popular "open classroom" drove me crazy. I always wondered why everyone got everything the leader said but me. Definitely wrong planet!

> I found one accepting person to be friends with and stuck to her like glue. Most of my anger at my environment and my inability to control it or even make sense out of it was directed at my parents and brother because I knew they couldn't leave me like the others, no matter what I did. Once I kicked a hole in the wall because I couldn't find my shoes and that proved how dumb I really was. Only a moron could lose their shoes—I wanted to kick myself but was at least smart enough to choose the wall instead. It was so hard getting through everyday life; things that other people automatically did re-

quired constant thought and concern for me. To protect myself, I built a wall around myself.

I could only handle myself and my needs. No one else mattered, not my family or friends. My family was angry at my self-centered ways. I was the black sheep—the alien—the different one. I never understood why everyone was so angry at me. Why didn't they understand that I was just surviving? My daydreams were of me in a rough and choppy ocean where a storm was raging. I was all alone in the middle of a great black sea. It took all of my strength just to stay above the water. I had no energy left to call for help or even notice if anyone else was around. That's how my life was. I had to be self-centered to survive.

School was no haven. The teachers said I was unmotivated and not paying attention. Some even yelled at me and physically shook me. One teacher who really thought she understood learning disabilities would say, "Does everyone understand?" And then she turned to me, as the class followed her gaze, and said, "and do you, Jill?" I suddenly felt my antennae's sprouting from my head. Everyone knew I was different when I was taken from the room for tutoring and later I had to lie about Special teachers and the "resource room" (a place for the "slower kids"). In school, it's every teenagers nightmare to be different. By high school my conversations had improved to the point where I was accepted as an "airhead" but I still had to keep my special "help room" a secret. With careful planning I could sneak into the resource room just as the bell rang and everyone was out of the halls. Talk about being different—when someone asked who my English teacher was, no one knew her because only "SPEDS" (Special Education students) had her and normal kids didn't know she existed.

High school was a turning point. I started noticing things. Dr. Silver, a psychiatrist, who really understands how to explain learning disabilities, made me aware of ways to compensate for my shortcomings. I began to read people from their faces and body language. If their faces looked confused, I would say, "Did I say something wrong?" Or, I would make a joke. Sometimes I would just start over. Dr. Silver showed me how to use little tricks to get around my disabilities like leaning forward to concentrate on a professor's lecture and this trick also helped force out disturbing background noises. Dr. Silver explained that with my auditory discrimination problems, bars with large crowds would become very difficult social meeting places for me. I feel like I'm there, people are there, music is there but I'm in a plastic bubble separated from everything. All of the noises, the conversation, the band, the glasses clinking—are all amplified and blended together like a senseless drone. I can't hear anyone's conversation because I only hear parts of what they say and none of it makes sense. I try to fill in the missing parts but my answers must be off the wall from the reactions I got. I keep thinking in the middle of everyone having fun, "Scotty, beam me up. Get me out of here!!"

At college, there is a wonderful learning disability program, the term L.D. has come to mean learning desirable to me. I have found my planet! People like me do exist and they aren't crazy. We even joke about being L.D. Its like a private club and its not unpopular. At dinner, if someone forgets their silverware there is a chorus of "L.D., L.D., L.D." and a knowing smile of acceptance. Once, four of us got lost driving to a dance and my friend, the driver, said, "Oh, no! Four L.D.s and no one has a pencil." She quickly assigned one part of the directions to each of us. "You remember the first part, you the second, and you the third." We all laughed at ourselves. At this college I cannot use L.D. as an excuse. I found that in real life no one really cares if I'm L.D. They only care if I don't try. It's results that count, not excuses. I really wanted to be a radio d.j., but I knew that with my disabilities it would be impossible. How could I "cue" records, answer phone requests and check scripts all at the same time. But, guess what? The girl voted "Biggest Airhead—Class of 1984" just got her F.M. license. Everyone from professors to students had quizzed me whenever they saw me. No one let me quit.

Life is still not a breeze. My friends, who say they understand, still get mad when I say I can't listen to the radio, talk, and hear directions at the same time. They still can't believe it when I go left when they say right. Actually I have more trouble understanding why I do the exact opposite, but I know I'm not dumb or an airhead. That's how my brain works or doesn't work. That's me. I'm not different. I'm special! No one is more sensitive to others than I am. I am my own friend and

I have recently begun to feel better about myself and to like myself. I am having success. I will be an L.D. forever. It will never go away, but each day I learn to handle another thing or work something out and things get better for me. How many people can say that??

5

Attention-Deficit Hyperactivity Disorder

AS I MENTIONED EARLIER, about 20 percent of children and adolescents with learning disabilities also have Attention-Deficit Hyperactivity Disorder (ADHD). These disorders are related but not the same. It is important to clarify if your son or daughter has ADHD.

In this chapter I describe in detail what ADHD is and is not. In Chapter 12 I review some of the same material found in this chapter, but expand the information to discuss the evaluation process. You may find parts of the two chapters redundant; however, I believe this necessary in order to start a concept in this chapter and then build on it in Chapter 12.

What Are ADHD Behaviors?

The official classification system identifies the essential features of ADHD as having "developmentally inappropriate degrees of inattention, impulsiveness, and hyperactivity." Although many persons with ADHD show problems in each of these areas, some will have only one or two of these behaviors. It is not necessary to have all three behaviors to have ADHD. For example, a child can be relaxed, even hypoactive, and still have ADHD if he or she is distractible and/or impulsive.

Hyperactivity

The hyperactive child used to be described as one who ran around and could not stand or sit still. Although some children may be this way, the typical hyperactive child just displays fidgety behavior. If you look, you will see that some part of the child's body is always in motion, often purposeless motion. For example, this child's fingers are often tapping or playing with a pencil, his or her leg is swinging, or he or she is twisting or squirming in a chair. Teachers may report that this child sits with one knee on the floor. You may remember that this son or daughter has never sat still through a whole meal in his or her entire life. Some appear to be verbally hyperactive—talking constantly.

Distractibility

A child or adolescent who has difficulty knowing what to attend to in his or her environment can be described as distractible. With such a child, all stimuli come in and may be focused on, creating a distractible state, causing the child to have difficulty sustaining attention, have a short attention span, and have difficulty staying on a task. If the individual is auditorily distractible, he or she will hear and respond to sounds that most would hear and tune out. Teachers report that if someone in the back of the room is tapping a pencil or talking, others can ignore it but this child must turn and listen. If someone is talking in the hall or someone is dribbling a basketball outside on the playground, somehow this student looks up and says, "what's that?" You notice that when you are reading a story to this child or doing homework with him or her, he or she responds to every sound (e.g., a floorboard creaking in another room, the dog wagging his tail, a car horn a block away). If the person is visually distractible, he or she might be distracted by the design on a rug, a picture, or other objects in the room. If outside, he or she will notice birds flying, clouds going by, or the trees and not stay focused on the appropriate activity. You may notice that you send this child to get something; however, on the way he or she sees something and starts to play with it. Then, something else is seen and he or she goes to it. Somehow, the child never gets to the original point.

A child or adolescent who is distractible appears to be able to attend to certain tasks for long periods of time. You might wonder if your son or daughter could be distractible if he or she can spend hours watching television or playing a video game. These tasks are usually ones that are enjoyable with high motivation. It appears that to be able to attend like this, this child or adolescent has to apply extra "filters" to block out the sounds on which he or she does not want to focus. This child appears to be in a trance. You can often not get through to him or her by just talking. You have to shake him or her or stand between the child and the activity to get his or her attention. If your son or daughter is distractible, you might notice that he or she can have what is called *sensory overload*. For example, if he or she is at a birthday party that is noisy, in a busy shopping mall, or at the circus or a sports event, he or she gets irritable, upset, and complains of the noise. The child might have a headache and want to leave. It appears that if there is too much auditory stimulation, the child cannot block out the input and he or she feels overloaded.

Impulsivity

An individual with impulsivity appears to not be able to reflect before he or she talks or acts. Thus, this person does not learn from experience, since he or she cannot delay action long enough to recall past experiences and consequences. He or she says something and may be sorry it was said before the statement is complete. The child gets upset and acts by hitting or throwing something. He or she will also turn quickly and knock things over. The child might fail to wait his or her turn and speak out, or answer a question before the teacher finishes asking it. Because of the impulsive behavior, this child appears to have poor judgment and may be accident prone.

How Is the Diagnosis Made?

There are many reasons why children and adolescents might be hyperactive, distractible, and/or impulsive. It is important to understand that not all who show these behaviors have ADHD. All too often a teacher says that a child cannot sit still or pay attention, but this does not mean that the child has ADHD.

The most common cause of hyperactivity, distractibility, or impulsivity with children, adolescents, and adults is anxiety. This anxiety can be a reflection of emotional problems or of an immediate stress. If the behaviors are due to anxiety, it is not ADHD. When someone is anxious he or she can be restless and active. Children often show anxiety by an increased activity level. If a child has a learning disability, the hyperactivity might relate to anxiety about school work and only be noted in school or when he or she has to do specific tasks.

Depression is the next most common cause of these behaviors. Again, the depression might reflect an emotional problem or current stress. If the behaviors are due to depression, it is not ADHD. Depression can be expressed at all ages by withdrawal and difficulty interacting or by agitation and difficulty concentrating. Each state can result in distractible behaviors.

Many types of learning disabilities and other related disorders can cause behaviors of hyperactivity, distractibility, or impulsivity; however, they are not ADHD. For example, a child with an auditory perception problem will appear to be auditorily distractible. Other learning disabilities may make the work so difficult that the child appears to be not paying attention. Or, the anxiety caused by the learning disability can produce hyperactivity or distractibility. A Sensory Integrative Disorder can cause fidgety behaviors as the child tries to adjust his or her body in space or responds to tactile discomfort.

How then does the clinician make the diagnosis? The answer will be discussed in Chapter 12. As you will learn, the diagnosis is made primarily by the clinical history.

If your child or adolescent has a learning disability and/or Sensory Integrative Disorder, the impact that these disabilities might have on the observed behaviors must be considered before the diagnosis of ADHD can be clarified. Often the special education team can help with this question.

How Long Does ADHD Last?

The long-term studies show that previous beliefs (or wishes) that these children outgrew ADHD at puberty is not correct. About 50 percent of children with ADHD mature out of the behaviors during puberty; however, 50 percent will continue to be ADHD throughout adolescence. Of this 50 percent, about half (i.e., 25 percent of the initial group of children) will continue to be ADHD into adulthood. Some studies suggest that this figure might be higher than 25 percent. No clues can tell us which pattern each child will follow. Often, if there is a family history of ADHD, one can get a possible clue. If a parent had ADHD but improved in high school, the child might be one who improves at puberty. If the parent still has ADHD, the child might be one who will continue into adulthood.

What Causes ADHD?

The current understanding is that ADHD is a neurological disorder. How it is manifested is influenced by age, sex, and psychological makeup, as well as by social and cultural factors. It is the interaction of both influences that explains the clinical picture that is seen. As an example, a girl with distractibility who is doing poorly in school and frustrated might withdraw and appear to be disinterested or depressed. A boy with the same problems might begin to misbehave and get into trouble. Each has ADHD. The boy is more likely to be recognized and diagnosed than the girl.

One biological theme is the apparent genetic influence. Between 30 and 40 percent of children and adolescents with ADHD have inherited a familial pattern. A parent, sibling, or other biological relative also will have or had ADHD.

The current research strongly suggests that ADHD is due to a neurological dysfunction caused by a neurochemical deficiency in the brain. This concept and its implications for treatment will be discussed in detail in Chapter 14.

How Is ADHD Treated?

The treatment for ADHD, like the treatment for learning disabilities, must include several approaches. First, the child, adolescent, and family must be educated on ADHD, what it is, and what it is not. Second, individual and family counseling may be needed to learn more about the behaviors and to change established patterns of behaviors or parenting. It is equally important to work with the school system in developing appropriate interventions and accommodations. Third, use of appropriate medication is necessary. Each of these treatment approaches will be discussed in detail in Chapter 14.

It is crucial that the correct diagnosis be made. As I mentioned, all children and adolescents who are hyperactive, distractible, and/or impulsive are not ADHD. Furthermore, all related problems must be identified and treated as well. Treatment for a learning disability will not treat ADHD; treatment for ADHD will not treat a learning disability. Medication alone will not help all aspects of ADHD. To treat a learning disability and ADHD, the educational and counseling efforts are equally important.

PART TWO

Problems in Psychological, Emotional, & Social Development

6

Normal Psychosocial Development

A MOTHER CALLED ME about her child. Her son refused to leave her, and began clinging and crying if she tried to walk away. If she left him with someone else, he threw a tantrum. What should she do with him? I couldn't say anything until I found out her son's age. If he were one year old, this behavior could be quite normal. If he were two, I would be slightly worried. If he were four or eight, I would be very concerned. If he were 15, I would be alarmed. *Normal* behavior has a great deal to do with your son's or daughter's age and the stage of development that the child is in at the time.

All children go through stages of psychological and social development, and most do so with minimal difficulty. They may occasionally face a stressful situation—being in the hospital, getting used to a new baby brother or sister, or coping with their parents' divorce—and briefly retreat back to earlier behaviors. But ordinarily they soon rally and move ahead again. Growth means many steps forward with occasional steps backward.

Much of this psychological and social—psychosocial—growth interweaves with stages in physical growth. As the brain and body mature, the child develops new abilities with which to handle problems. This same growth, however, also introduces new problems.

Many children go through the various stages of development noticeably, but without serious problems, while some progress with few obvious difficulties. Some children and families find certain stages of growth more difficult than others. The child with a learning disability, however, may have trouble with some or all stages of psychosocial development. First I'll review what is understood to be normal development. Then you will see the ways in which learning disabilities inhibit or alter this development.

Normal Child Development

The newborn infant functions primarily as a physiological being—the brain receiving messages from the body and sending messages to the body to respond. During the early weeks and months, the baby begins to become conscious of certain significant people, recognizing, for example, mother's or father's voice, image, or smell. As the infant begins to relate to his or her world, he or she is unaware of any distinction between his or her body and objects in the environment—he or she has no sense of any boundaries. People, pets, food, furniture, favorite toys—all objects outside of the self appear to be merely extensions of the child. For now, the infant and his or her world are one. This stage of development is depicted in Fig. 6-1.

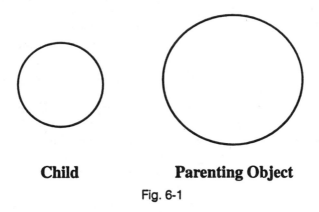

Child   Parenting Object

Fig. 6-1

Basic Trust

Gradually the infant begins to discover that objects have extensions and limits to them as well. The child discovers his or her fingers, and hands, toes and feet, and finds that these objects belong to the same body that he or she has begun to experience. By about three months, the infant can recognize certain pieces of the external world and relates to these "part objects" in special ways that acknowledge their importance. Now, for the first time, the "social smile" can be seen. The child looks at a part of a face and smiles. This social smile is an early psychological landmark of normal development.

By about nine months, an infant has completed the process of discovering where he or she leaves off and the world begins. The child discovers that there are many human objects in the world. Having learned to associate pleasurable experiences with certain human objects, the baby begins to comprehend that these specific human objects are very important—that they are absolutely necessary, in fact. Thus the baby learns to place a *basic trust* in these key people and becomes *totally dependent* on them.

With the establishment of basic trust, the infant masters the first major step in psychosocial development. But now the baby becomes upset if he or she is left alone. The child fears separation and strangers. Before this stage, anyone could pick up the baby and get a smile. Now if someone unknown or not very well known picks up the baby, he or she starts to cry. This fear, which normally appears at around nine months, is another psychosocial landmark. This stage of total dependency is depicted in Fig. 6-2.

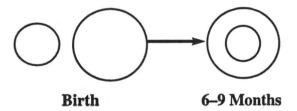

Birth   **6–9 Months**

Fig. 6-2

Separation

The next task in psychosocial development is *separation*. The infant must realize that he or she can separate from these significant people and still survive, and then learn how to do that. Mastery of this stage of development involves several steps that start at about 9 to 12 months and usually finish at around 3 to 3½ years. This accomplishment of separation, which leads to a sense of an autonomous self, is illustrated in Fig. 6-3.

Initially (see "a" in Fig. 6-3), the infant must have some form of sensory connection with the significant person. The baby cries, hears a parent's footsteps in the hall, and stops crying. This auditory linkage is enough. Or the infant crawls behind a chair, loses sight of a parent, and cries. When the parent moves into view, the child stops crying. This visual link, the sight of the parent, re-establishes the necessary contact. For example, the baby cries at night. When the mother or father picks him or her up in the dark and holds him or her, the child stops crying. The touch, smell, and voice of the parent reassures the infant that the intimate connection is not broken.

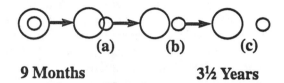

(a) (b) (c)

9 Months **3½ Years**

Fig. 6-3

Beginning at about 18 to 24 months, the child slowly learns to separate for longer and longer periods of time (see "b" in Fig. 6-3). However, the toddler still must frequently return to the parent to "refuel" or "tag up." A hug or a kiss or a cookie will do, and the child is off again. Some children find these early efforts at separating easier if they can take something that reminds them of a parent along with them. Children usually select these favorite items, which are commonly called "security blankets" but more properly called *transitional objects*, because they have a familiar smell, soft touch, or the cuddly feel that they have learned to associate with the parent.

By about three to three-and-a-half years, the child can finally separate from his or her parents with no discomfort (see "c" in Fig. 6-3). This full mastery of separation is yet another landmark in psychosocial development.

Two major psychological events take place during this stage, one is internally motivated, and the other, externally caused. Each aids in mastering separation and in establishing autonomy, and each has a major influence on personality development. The internal event is *negativism*, and this begins at about age two. During the "terrible twos," the child responds to most requests or comments with "No," or "No, I do myself." The child is beginning to separate and to show that he or she has a mind of his or her own. Although exasperating to parents, this healthy step toward separation and autonomy is a very necessary one.

The other event that occurs at about age two is *toilet training*. In learning to accede to this requirement of the outside world, the child confronts two new tasks that have to be mastered. First, the child must alter his or her concept of love and relationships. Until now the child has perceived the whole world as being there to take care of him or her. Love and caring were automatic and free. Suddenly the child faces a situation in which love is no longer free and available on demand. Now if the child wants love, he or she must do something to get it. Loving relationships no longer center totally around one's wishes and needs; now the child must learn to participate in a give-and-take process. Urinate in the potty and mommy loves you; urinate in your pants and mommy frowns. Getting love sometimes requires doing what is wanted; that is, what is lovable. To receive pleasure requires pleasing. This forces the child to make a revolutionary shift in her or his concept of the world, people, and relationships.

Toilet training introduces a second new concept that provides the child with a new way to handle angry feelings. For the first time the child has an active weapon in the battle to get what he or she wants. Prior to this, the child could cry or have a tantrum, but the parents could choose to ignore it. Prior to this, the child experienced anger and expressed it openly by crying, screaming, kicking, or hitting. Now the child begins to realize that there are different ways to express anger, and that the way one does express anger has a great deal to do with getting and keeping love. Direct expressions of anger don't work. The price one has to pay may be too great. A child now learns that more indirect expressions of anger work somewhat better than hitting and yelling. Now when angry with a parent the child can squat right in front of them, preferably when company is around, and, with a big smile, "make" in their pants. If they are pleased with mommy and daddy, they will "make" on the potty. The child begins to learn the importance of controlling anger, or more precisely, of learning subtler, more ambiguous, and therefore more acceptable ways to express anger.

These issues—the reciprocal nature of loving and being

loved and pleasing and being pleased, and handling angry feelings—are struggled with individually and together. The two themes often interrelate: at this age one can readily love and hate the same person at the same time or hurt and care for the same person at the same time.

Individuation

When the child has mastered the first major task of development, establishing basic trust, and the second major task, handling separation, he or she is ready for the third task, individuation. This task involves asking and trying to answer the question, "Who am I?" Now that the child knows that he or she is a separate person who can survive without being totally dependent on important people, what kind of person is that child? The struggle to answer these questions usually takes place between the ages of three and six years of age.

At this age, the brain is still immature, and not all thinking is based on reality. Fantasy, which seems as real as what is real, forms one basis for a lot of the child's thinking. If the child thinks something is so, it may as well be. A child at this age, then, can have opposite beliefs and feelings simultaneously, with no notion that a contradiction exists or that only one of two or more different possibilities can come true. For example, loving and hating, wanting and not wanting, going to a movie and at the same time going on a picnic—the child excludes nothing and sees no problem with believing in all possibilities coming true at the same time.

The child also tries out many roles. If he or she pretends to be Superman, she or he is Superman. What is it like to be big? Little? Aggressive? Submissive? A boy? A girl? Children play "house," "school," or "doctor," exploring various roles and different situations. One day your daughter may act like a boy, the next day a girl, or a mommy, a daddy, a teacher, a gangster, E.T., or Miss Piggy. Your daughter or son tries to learn about people and how to do activities, and attempts to master those concerns through repetition in play. For example, children must learn to listen to adults other than their parents. When they play school, they take turns being the teacher who gives instructions and orders, and then the pupil who must listen and obey. When they play doctor, they take turns being the doctor who explores and the patient who is explored.

Whenever a child tries to "be" someone else in the family—for instance, mother or father—he or she has to compete with that person for her or his identity and roles as well as with any sibling who may also want to be that parent. The child also has to try to attract the attention of the other parent. So another characteristic of this age period is the child's tendency to cause splitting and tension between parents as well as among siblings. Children learn with remarkable aptitude how to divide parents, getting one closer to them and pushing the other away. Thus, on one day a child may seem close and loving, yet on another day he or she is irritating and hostile.

For the first time, in Fig. 6-4, the diagram of the child's relationships must include both parents.

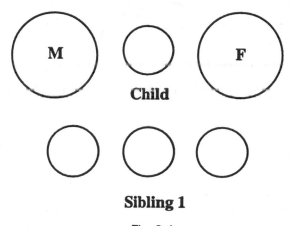

Child

Sibling 1

Fig. 6-4

If the boy or girl wants to play "being mother," then mother must be pushed away, along with any siblings who might compete for her role, as in Fig. 6-5.

If the child wants to play "being father," then father has to be pushed away, along with any siblings who might want that role, as in Fig. 6-6.

Because both splits occur from time to time, the diagram of the child's relationships has to look like that which is depicted in Fig. 6-7.

A child's thoughts at this age are magical—that is, they are not reality-based, and the child often has trouble distinguishing

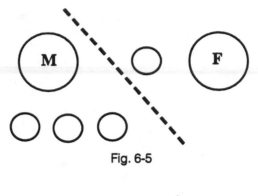

Fig. 6-5

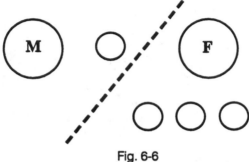

Fig. 6-6

among his or her actual feelings, thoughts, and actions. The child's thoughts, especially his or her angry thoughts, scare him or her. Nightmares are common. A child worries that others, like his or her parents, know what he or she is thinking and that they will retaliate. This magical fear of retaliation causes the child to worry excessively about body integrity and body damage. Any

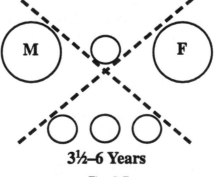

3½–6 Years

Fig. 6-7

cut or scratch is a disaster. This is why this age is often called the "bandaid" stage.

During these frustrating fours and fives, most children and their parents do have a lot of fun. The child is animated, uninhibited, and imaginative, and enjoys interacting and playing. However, the child can cause stress between parents and among siblings and have trouble sleeping, have nightmares, or want to sleep with parents. One minute you love and cuddle the child, the next you feel like giving him or her away to the nearest stranger. All of this is normal.

By about age six, most children begin to find preliminary answers to the question, "Who am I?" Little girls begin to learn that they are to become "just like mommy" and enjoy playing this role. They give up wanting daddy all to themselves and look forward to some day having someone just like their father. Little boys begin to learn that they are to become "just like daddy." They give up wanting mommy all to themselves and settle for the idea of having someone just like their mother some day (e.g., "I want a girl just like the girl that married dear old dad"). Although some of these self-assessments may later change, it is through this process of identification that children learn to become more or less like the parent of the same sex. (The child in a single-parent family may have more difficulty working through this stage of development. Most make it through, but if you think that consulting a mental health professional would help, don't hesitate to get advice yourself and, perhaps, help your child.)

During this time, between about age three and age six, most children are struggling to establish basic assumptions about their identities. Parents also now do their imprinting of stereotypical sex-role behaviors. If a boy reaches for a doll to play with, he is brusquely told that boys play with trucks or guns, not with dolls. Cultural clichés like this always amaze me—adult men must know how to relate lovingly to their children, among other people, not how to use guns; and, adult men know that. Adult women must know how to express themselves productively, not just how to use eye makeup; and, adult women know that. Still, many continue to teach little girls that they play with dolls and do tasks in the kitchen; they do not work with tools or excel in sports. Girls are taught that it is acceptable to express love and sadness, but not self-assertion or anger. Boys learn that it is acceptable to express anger, but "big boys don't cry."

Fortunately, the consciousness-raising efforts of the women's movement have helped to free more and more families from the need to pass along these stereotypes. Children must feel free to explore and to learn many roles to become fully developed males or females. They must learn that true maleness and femaleness has nothing to do with the things one does or how one expresses different emotions, but instead with the kinds of resources and experiences one has, the kinds of relationships he or she can sustain, and the respect developed toward oneself and others.

Toward the end of this stage, at about age six, two changes take place that help the child master the process of individuation. The central nervous system takes a large maturational leap forward, and this helps the child to move from nonreality-based thinking to reality-based thinking. Contradictory feelings and thoughts can no longer coexist with equal power. The child begins to understand that feeling or thinking one thing means that he or she cannot believe in its opposite at the same time with equal conviction. In other words, the realization dawns that one cannot do or be two (or more) things at the same time. The child can now distinguish between reality and fantasy. For example, the child might pretend to be Superman, but he or she now knows it is only pretend.

The other change during this stage involves the child's emerging awareness of the various accumulated values and value judgments that he or she has learned. At about this age, the child fuses into an established conscience called the *superego*. This "voice," or conscience, stays with one throughout one's life, and becomes increasingly significant. It "tells" the child which thoughts, feelings, and actions are acceptable and which are not. Initially, the parents teach these values, and the child usually adopts them fairly automatically. He or she may rebel, but that is more because the child wants his or her own way, not because any serious questions about moral or intellectual validity come up. In adolescence, as we shall see, these values are routinely reviewed and reconsidered.

Latency

Once the child has mastered the third task of development, individuation, he or she moves into a period of consolidation. Sometime around age six, the child becomes free to move out of the family and into the community. With the major psychological work of childhood done, the child's energy is freed to range more widely, in school and other learning activities, and in expanding relationships. This period, which lasts about six to eight years, is called the *latency* period, illustrated in Fig. 6-8.

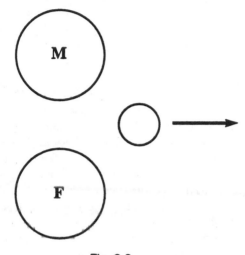

Fig. 6-8

During the latency period, a child learns to relate to adults other than his or her parents and to children other than his or her siblings. The child begins to focus on relationships with children of the same sex, and may ignore or move away from peer activities that include children of the opposite sex. Boys prefer boys and often don't like girls. Girls prefer girls and may avoid boys. Very intimate "chum" or "best friend" relationships develop, and the child's behavior that you got used to during the individuation stage changes completely. A boy will shrug and push mother away if she tries to hold or kiss him. Two boys or two girls may walk down the street arm in arm. During this period, children explore and learn the ability to relate to people of the same sex and form both intimate and casual friendships with them.

The latency period also covers grades one through six. Massive knowledge must be learned and mastered from reading, writing, and arithmetic to subject information and study skills. A child who did not resolve or master each stage of psychosocial development before entering these grades, can have difficulty functioning in school or mastering the required tasks.

By the age of 12 to 14, this period of consolidation ends. Adolescence arrives, and with it, new tasks to master. Everything is about to change—possibly for the worse, but eventually for the better. Each stage of psychosocial development for the child must be mastered, and he or she must feel comfortable entering adolescence. If any previous developmental stage was not resolved, the child might have more difficulty with adolescence.

Normal Adolescent Development

Adolescence is a difficult time for almost anyone, and for almost all parents. The period of adolescence prepares a person to move out of his or her childhood and into adulthood. This transition has to be unique for each generation. Parents often rely on their own models and experiences, responding to their teenage children as their parents did to them or as they think they should have been responded to. The difficulty is that these role-models and experiences more or less successfully prepared today's parents for the last third of the twentieth century. Today's adolescents have to learn to live in the first part of the twenty-first century. You will have to speculate right along with your teenage child on the strengths, attitudes, and skills needed for adulthood. Your own life experiences will be out-of-date and probably too restrictive.

As parents of an adolescent, you must teach your youth the values that you believe are important, but you must also take into account the unique issues that your teenager struggles with in the world as it is now and as it will be for him or her. You have to give your teenager roots and wings at the same time. The adolescent will need the roots—the security that comes with a solid foundation—in order to spread his or her wings and fly.

The adolescent must rework most of the psychosocial tasks of childhood. Physical growth still plays a major role in the stages of psychological growth. Some adolescents go through these stages with little or no difficulty; others have problems with a stage, then regroup and move forward.

Problems with Physical Change

It is useful to distinguish between puberty—the period of physical changes—and adolescence—the period of psychosocial changes. Ideally, the two occur hand-in-hand. However, with some teenagers, these processes get way out of sync. When one is out of phase with the other, the person has to cope with even more stress than usual.

Think of a girl who, at 10 or 11, is taller than all of the other girls, full-breasted, and already menstruating, or the 17-year-old boy who is 5 feet tall, with peach fuzz and a high voice. Both are physically normal, but each is at a different end of the normal growth curve. And, each has additional stresses with which to cope. The reverse can be equally stressful. For example, the boy in sixth grade who is already almost 6 feet tall and growing a beard; or the short, flat-chested young woman who still looks like "a little girl" as she graduates from high school. Each must cope with more than their share of the stress that adolescence normally brings.

Just as children do, adolescents have feelings and thoughts that cause conflicts and tension. However, their physical growth has also given them capacities for action and reaction that no child has. When a 6-year-old boy cuddles with his mother, he feels pleasant sensations; when a 14- or 15-year-old boy does so, he may be embarrassed when he has an erection. A little girl can thoroughly enjoy sitting on her father's lap, but a 13 year-old girl who does so may have physical sensations that worry her. Wrestling with or tickling a sibling of the opposite sex can become both sexually stimulating and distressing. These new reactions that come with physical maturation may be so upsetting that the adolescent feels forced to transfer the relationships that cause these feelings to "safer" people outside of the family.

The same is true for angry feelings. For example, it is one thing for a little boy to feel rage at his mother when his eyes are at the level of her kneecaps. However, it is another situation when the angry adolescent realizes that he is taller and bigger than his mother and that he could really hurt her.

The distress and loss of confidence caused by these physical and emotional changes encourages the early adolescent to become more dependent on home and parents. But, the same newly discovered emotional feelings and physical reactions make it more difficult to explore and work out relationships and problems with parents and siblings. Thus, there is conflict— within the adolescent, and eventually within the family. The adolescent pulls to become more dependent and childlike while at the same time, he or she pulls to become more independent and adultlike.

Initially, the early adolescent may attempt to cope with all this by using fantasy, choosing to relate to people who are unavailable and therefore safe. For example, boys and girls have "mad crushes" on movie stars, rock musicians, and sports heroes. The probability of a rock music star suddenly knocking on the door of an adolescent girl and asking her for a date is remote enough to allow her to safely fantasize a relationship with him. Gradually, however, the young adolescent will begin to explore relationships with real, potentially available people. At first, these interactions are likely to occur within groups, then within smaller groups, and finally with individual people. Very early dating is usually narcissistically motivated: the adolescent wants to date someone who makes him or her *look* good—the cheerleader, the football hero, someone whom everyone thinks is desirable. Often a boy behaves toward his date much as he would toward a boy friend, clowning around, showing off, or hitting. Later on, both adolescent girls and boys will date someone who makes them feel good. Looks are still important, but less important than personality.

Independence

The first task of adolescence is to move from being a *dependent* person to being an *independent* person. The initial struggle often revolves around the concepts of sex roles and identification. The old techniques that the child used to master separation may turn up again.

Negativism reappears—"No, I can do it myself," "Don't tell me how long my hair can be," "Don't tell me how short my skirt can be." This negativism is a renewed attempt to tell first you and then the world that this growing person has a mind of his or her own. And again, it becomes an active verbal way of expressing anger. An adolescent seizes almost any opportunity to exploit an issue that shows that he or she has a mind separate from his or her parents. Parents and an adolescent may argue about the choice of friends and peer groups, school plans and courses, points of philosophy and etiquette. Clothing and hair styles have always been favorite issues with which to prove one's independence. The casual or unisex theme of today resembles the "cause" of every other generation—the "flappers," the "zoot-suiters," the "rockers," the "hippies," and so on. Each generation recalls how they used clothes, hairstyles, and other external badges (e.g., earrings for boys; multiple earrings for girls), the more shocking the better, to show their parents that they had minds of their own.

All the old struggles over expressing love and anger reappear as new issues. For example, "What do you have to do to be loved," "To keep love," "To show love," "What do you do with angry feelings?" All of these questions have to be worked through with family and friends. In the process, the adolescent begins to develop more consistent concepts of relationships and styles of expressing feelings. Thus, the adult personality is beginning to form and emerge.

In the process of gaining independence, the adolescent probably needs to reject the parents' values and to reformulate his or her own value system. Unless this happens, the adolescent's parents remain with him or her forever in the form of the conscience programmed in during childhood. A teen-ager needs to rework these previously accepted values to fit with the values he or she wishes to adopt for today and tomorrow. The adolescent will probably reject his or her former values at first, pointing out contradictions in the parents' values. He or she may feel that "no one over 30 can be trusted." The adolescent may challenge his or her parents for giving conflicting messages (e.g., "What do you mean, all people are created equal—you get mad at me if I date someone who's Jewish [or Protestant, Catholic, Black, White, Hispanic, Oriental]"; "Why should I be honest— you cheat on your income tax"; "Why shouldn't I drink [or smoke]—you do").

This interim "vacuum," when old values are rejected and new ones have not been established, can be upsetting. Some adolescents temporarily take refuge in religion or in a "prepackaged" system such as the Boy Scout oath and laws. For others, their peer group provides this interim system. Closed cliques (e.g., the "in" groups) often set rules about all kinds of behavior—how to dress, who to talk to, who is "in," and who is "out."

Slowly, the adolescent begins to blend many different values from all kinds of sources into his or her own existing values. By young adulthood, a new conscience, or superego, is established. The compatibility and flexibility of this new superego strengthens one's ability to handle and express feelings and emotions in relationships. All through life one's superego will have to be able to change and grow in order to accommodate new life situations.

As the adolescent begins to feel independent of his or her family, and as the family supports and encourages this emerging maturity, the question of the three- to six-year-old is heard once again—"Who am I?" The answer, of course, can no longer be "just like mommy (or daddy)."

Identity

The second developmental task of adolescence, establishing one's *identity*, begins at this point. Becoming a "chip off the old block" isn't enough and can be too restrictive. Unlike the child, the older adolescent will select characteristics from many people—religious leaders, teachers, neighbors, relatives, parents, friends, maybe even famous people—blending certain of their features with her or his own to become a unique new person. This new person, or identity, is not one's final self, but it forms the basis of what one will become. One's identity must be reworked throughout life as roles change. One must adjust to becoming a graduate, a spouse, a worker, a parent, a grandparent, or a retiree.

Each generation and each culture exerts different social and cultural pressures on human beings. The child growing up in the Victorian era heard very different messages from the outside world than did one growing up in the "wild" decade of the post-World War twenties. The adolescent growing up in the post-Vietnam War world of the eighties and nineties experiences different social and cultural standards than her or his parents did. Let me note once again that it is crucial for parents to understand and accept that their adolescent lives in a different world than they did as adolescents and their child's adulthood will be different than the parent's experiences.

The total developmental process that begins at birth culminates in an identity for each person. If your child successfully masters all of these tasks, he or she will have a successful functional identity with healthy and positive feelings about himself or herself. If any tasks are not successfully mastered, this identity can be restrictive or dysfunctional.

Intimacy

The adolescent has one remaining task to master. Until this time, relationships have been primarily based on a child-adult model.

Now the adolescent or young adult has to learn to relate successfully to other people, and eventually to one other person, as an equal, on a one-to-one basis. This kind of relationship is often referred to as *intimacy*. The task starts in late adolescence, but it is not complete until young adulthood.

When people relate in a dependent-independent mode, they need and depend on significant and more powerful people, like parents. When you are young, you may very well feel as if you and your parents are one. This is intimacy, but not a workable kind of intimacy in an adult world. In an adult intimate relationship, in the independent-independent mode, each person depends on the other. However, even though each loves, leans on, and needs the other for his or her emotional well-being, neither loses his or her boundaries. At all times, each can still function well independently. This is a goal that most of us work on all our lives and few of us achieve with total success. But, because it represents the best that human beings can make of their adult relationships, it makes a fitting close for the discussion of normal development.

7

Psychosocial Problems for the Child with Learning Disabilities

THE CHILD OR ADOLESCENT with learning disabilities plus possible Attention-Deficit Hyperactivity Disorder (ADHD) has more than school and classroom problems—he or she has total life disabilities. As I discussed in Chapter 3, the same disabilities that interfere with reading, writing, and arithmetic also interfere with emotional and social development or cause emotional and social problems. Some infants may have difficulties from the earliest stages of development. Some children may struggle, unable to move forward through critical stages of development. Still others may develop within normal expectations, showing adequate progress at first, then be set back by the stress of entering school or reaching a grade in school where they cannot succeed.

Problems in Early Stages of Development

Infancy may be very difficult for the child who will have learning disabilities. Although these disabilities will not be apparent until later in life, some of these problem areas can affect the child from birth. As discussed in Chapter 5, the hyperactivity, distractibility, and impulsivity of ADHD might be apparent from birth.

It is not uncommon for parents to report that their child has been irritable since birth. The child never slept or slept for brief periods of time only. He or she was colicky and feeding was a chore. The baby was difficult to calm or comfort. For some parents, these behaviors did not improve until age three or four; and for others, these behaviors remain as behavioral characteristics throughout childhood.

These subtle, invisible, neurologically based problems can have a significant impact on the earliest parent-child bonding and interactions. (One mother's experiences will be described in Chapter 9.) Babies with motor problems will be more floppy and poorly coordinated. Poorly coordinated infants also may have difficulty sucking and eating. Infants who are hyperactive thrash about, their constant activity creating constant problems with care.

We do not know yet what the full impact of perceptual disabilities may be during the early months of life. Could visual or auditory perception problems be present at birth? Could such disabilities interfere with critical visual and auditory inputs that are needed to orient the child to the world or to bond with a parent? Could they also have difficulty with smell or taste? If so, how might this affect the child's early development? Could these difficulties affect or delay the establishment of *basic trust?* Parents who had irritable and difficult infants will say yes.

In Chapter 3, I discussed Sensory Integrative Disorders. Infants with these difficulties may be sensitive to touch. They do not like to be held, and often cry and thrash. The more the parent cuddles to comfort, the more they cry. Soon, some parents learn to place the baby on a pillow and to hold the pillow or to lay the baby in the crib and prop up the bottle. Since most physicians do not know about tactile sensitivity, parents are not believed. They are told that they are too anxious and must learn to relax. Fathers, who often come home late and who may be too uncomfortable to play with the baby, do not experience the same reactions and may reinforce the physician's beliefs. All of this leaves the mother confused, deprived of the desired interactions with her baby, and feeling inadequate.

If these invisible neurological difficulties affect the infant, what about the parent? Mothers and fathers often feel helpless and inadequate. They try hard to comfort and please their infant, but nothing works. They get little sleep and may become frustrated and irritable with the infant. Neither the infant's nor the parents' state of functioning help in the bonding and enjoying of this baby.

Children with the problems described above can have difficulty with separation. Mastering separation requires at least two things. First, the child must feel secure enough to venture out and explore the world. Second, this world must be attractive and fun enough to make the child want to stay out there and engage with the people in it. The child with learning disabilities plus possible ADHD may have difficulty interacting, communicating, or doing what other children are doing. He or she may find the outside world stressful and retreat back to the inside world. Parents sense this discomfort and lack of success and intuitively reach out to comfort. If either or both situations occur, the mastery of *separation* will be delayed.

The result may be a child who prefers to stay at home. When things don't work out in day care or nursery school, the child resists going, or, if forced to go, avoids the other children or interacts poorly with them. As these children struggle to master separation, you may see the negativism, the power struggles, the need to control, and the difficulties with relationships that were normal for age two persisting into ages three, four, and beyond.

What about the next stage, *individuation?* If the child is having difficulty with other children, with play activities, and with preschool situations, the steps in development that are normal for individuation will start late and may last long after the appropriate age. Other children will have long since outstripped the child in their emotional maturity. Even after age six, he or she may continue to be fearful or may try to divide adults and other children, or avoid certain activities for fear of being hurt— problems that normally occur between ages three and six. When these immature behaviors still take place in kindergarten or in the first and second grades, teachers quite understandably become angry. Classmates, too, tend to fight with the child.

Unless the disabilities have been recognized and helped, boys may have a special problem becoming "just like daddy." For example, the son who does poorly in games and sports may become insecure and prefer staying home with his mother. The father may be disappointed that his son is not doing what boys are supposed to do and lets his son know it verbally or nonverbally. The son senses the message and feels that he cannot be what his father wants. Father may get angry at the mother, blaming her for making his son a "sissy." Father is angry and disappointed; mother is angry and hurt; and, the child struggles to find a way to master individuation. He often cannot fully succeed and feels less confident in himself.

Some children master each stage of development more slowly than most. They may enter the latency period and grade school with some weaknesses in their *psychological foundation*. Each new task causes stress, which in turn causes a temporary retreat to earlier behaviors. The child with problems may now consistently lag behind. A break in development or a retreat to an earlier behavior can happen at any stage along the way, even into adolescence. Some children will have so much difficulty reaching these landmarks in psychosocial growth that professional help will be needed. It is critical, should this be necessary, that the mental health professional recognize the child's underlying neurological difficulties and the effects that these have had on parenting and on the child's development.

Let me illustrate these difficulties with growing up by sharing an interview with an 11-year-old boy. The session was taped. His words are noted; mine are in parentheses:

> I'm smart but in an L.D. program because I'm socially disturbed. I don't like to be around other people—only my parents. Maybe I'll be a bachelor. I pretend the kids are not there—only the teacher. Why can't I just be with my parents and never marry? Just stay with them. Why would any girl want to marry me. . . . I'm not strong. . . I don't like myself. I'm always sad and depressed. I'm different from everyone else. I don't like sports but I'm curious about science, but I don't learn. I don't like getting into trouble like they do.

> (You say you are smart.) No. I got a D; therefore, I'm not smart. . . . (What is the solution?) Suicide, but I don't want to kill myself. I just don't like me and people don't like me.

> I'm always depressed. I stay by myself and ignore others. My mother and father think I'm exaggerating. I try to get them to understand. (Whom do you turn to?) Nobody. I think my parents like me but no one else likes me. (Who loves you?) No one loves me. (And you?) I don't like me. I think the world would be better off without me. (Therefore, you want to die?) If I did not wake up one day, people would be happy. My class would have a party.

(How long have you felt this way?) Since a baby. I was never sure that my parents liked me or loved me. Why should they love me? I'm not special. I'm just a normal dumb sixth grader. (You are their son.) I think that they wanted someone different. (Who?) One who is smart; who listens and does not talk back. I'm the opposite.

(What makes you happy?) I never accomplish anything to be happy about. I'm nobody special. I'm not the Prince of England. I would like to stay home and have a private tutor.

I don't care what happens to myself. If I get sick, no one cares or if I get hurt. (Wouldn't your mother?) Maybe about the doctor's bills.

(Life appears to be so miserable for you.) No one ever liked me.

This child is depressed with a low self-esteem and a poor self-image. He shows difficulty with basic trust, separation, and individuation. The following explores the emotional problems that can result from unrecognized or recognized but incompletely treated learning disabilities plus possible ADHD.

Emotional Problems

I find it helpful in understanding children with learning disabilities plus possible ADHD to realize that they have had only one brain all of their lives. They don't know that it is different from anybody else's brain. People yell at them, telling them to sit still, to pay attention, to keep quiet, and to speak up. They cannot understand, either, why they are more active or distractible or why they have more difficulty with the school work. They try just as hard to learn. Why don't they succeed? Their experiences confuse and frustrate them. Why do they constantly fail? Why are they constantly embarrassed? Is it any wonder that they develop emotional and social difficulties?

The special education team points out that Billy has visual perception or visual motor problems. These learning disabilities interfere with his mastery of reading and written language skills, they say. The special education team is used to focusing on problems such as this. But, what about Billy on the playground who misses the ball because his eyes can't tell his hands what to do?

How do the other kids react to Billy's clumsiness and poor performance? How does Billy feel when he is the last one to be chosen when the kids pick sides? And, what about the physical education teacher. He or she may not have been part of the school meetings about Billy's learning disabilities or may not understand the effect of these disabilities on his sports abilities. This teacher might yell at Billy or tease him in front of his classmates.

So it is with Allison. Educational and language evaluations identified her as having auditory perception and expressive language problems. Based on this information, the school developed a specific educational and language therapy program for her. But is that enough? What happens to Allison when she is with her friends? She misunderstands what they say and responds wrong. Her friends think she is not paying attention or is dumb. They exclude her from their games. Furthermore, although someone explained her auditory and language difficulties to her teacher, no one ever explained them to her parents and siblings. They, too, get angry with her for "not paying attention." What does this do to Allison? How does this shape her friends' reactions to her? How must she feel in the family? What does she then think about herself?

All too often such problems are not correctly diagnosed. Even more often, they are not communicated to all of the people who must know. The child goes on experiencing repeated frustrations and failures. Finally, he or she develops emotional problems and is referred to a child and adolescent psychiatrist such as myself or to other mental health professionals for an evaluation. It is essential to distinguish between a child whose emotional problems are *causing* the school and academic difficulties and a child whose emotional problems are the *consequence* of these school and academic difficulties. I cannot stress this point too much. Painfully too often, mental health professionals see the smoke and miss the fire. They see the surface behaviors but do not see the underlying learning disabilities and possible ADHD that are causing the behaviors. The child is seen as primarily emotionally disturbed and the parents are often seen as dysfunctional. Each may be true; however, the reasons for this end result are not purely psychological.

Let me illustrate this important point by describing an all too common situation that results in a referral to me. A child starts school. He or she begins to fall behind and struggle. The school uses their "magic cure" by keeping the child back. Now, he or she is a head taller and a year older than classmates. His or her friends have moved on to the next grade. The child feels dumb and embarrassed. The next year he or she does not do better. The child begins to feel frustrated and angry. Soon, he or she may begin to act out in school and/or at home. Throughout this time, something predictable is happening at home. If there are two parents, I am willing to bet that one parent believes that the best way to help this child is to be firm and strict and the other believes that the best way to help is to be understanding and permissive. Thus, the parents begin to clash with each other. Eventually, the principal calls the parents in and says, "Your child is not learning. It is clear that he or she has an emotional problem, probably because of your marital problems. Get him or her to a mental health professional."

If you are smiling as you read this because you have been there or you are there, don't let it happen. At the risk of being accused of being repetitive, it is critical to clarify if your son's or daughter's *emotional, social, and family problems are causing the school and academic difficulties* or whether these *emotional, social, and family problems are a consequence of the school and academic difficulties*. Each is a totally different situation and requires a different approach to help.

As you read about the kinds of emotional problems children with learning disabilities and/or ADHD can develop, think of your daughter or son. If you recognize any of these symptoms or behaviors and you have not already asked for help, discuss the situation with your family doctor or with a mental health professional.

Withdrawal

Some children deal with frustrating life experiences simply by trying to avoid stress. This type child uses a withdrawal reaction to avoid any potentially frustrating or uncertain situation by drawing back from it and becoming passive. He or she becomes unavailable for learning.

An example of withdrawal can be seen in eight-year-old Bobbie. Because of her unrecognized learning disabilities, although she had a superior intelligence, Bobbie had failed often and was currently starting second grade for the second time. When she was asked what she did in school when she couldn't do her work, she replied, "When I was younger I used to crumble up my paper and cry. . . . Then they teased me and called me a cry baby. So, I decided that school was no fun. . . . Since I couldn't leave, I sat and pretended that I was home in my room with my dolls. . . . I made up stories and had a good time." Bobbie's teacher complained that she would "daydream the day away if I let her." This teacher saw her as immature.

Regression

Other children avoid stress by retreating to an earlier stage of psychological or social development. Earlier behaviors or immature, infantile interactions, things you think the child has completely outgrown, recur. For example, the parents of seven-and-a-half-year-old Debbie complained that their daughter had been happy and normal until she entered kindergarten. As the mother explained it, at this point "she had a change of personality. She had trouble keeping up with the other children. In first grade she just didn't learn much so now she's repeating first." The father added, "Home life is terrible. We yell at her all the time. Since school began this year, she's gone backwards, acting like a baby and talking like a baby. . . . It's impossible. . . . She won't listen and tunes me out. . . . She's begun to wet her bed for the first time since she was three. . . . She even eats with her fingers." At a therapy session, Debbie talked about school. "I have trouble because I don't understand the work, especially reading and math. . . . It's hard and I can't do it. . . . The teacher yells at me all the time. . . . Maybe I'm just not as smart as the other kids."

Displacement and Projection

Children may try to avoid the stress, the conflicts, and the feelings of frustration and worthlessness by displacing the reason for this failure onto something else. Some develop fear reactions. Their overall, school-related feelings seem to take on specific meaning. Rather than experiencing a general anxiety or depression whenever she or he is in school, the child develops a localized fear that can be named. For example, Eddie became afraid of a particular child on the school bus who always teased him. Once this fear crystallized, he could make sense out of the feelings he had when he woke up to go to school. When this happens, the child feels no better, but at least he or she does not have to endure the nameless fears and general anxiety that go with his or her unexplained and upsetting school failures.

Some children focus their anxiety on bodily functions. A child may develop stomachaches, lower abdominal cramps, headaches, diarrhea, or frequency of urination or bowel movements. These complaints often occur only in the morning of a school day and rarely on weekends, holidays, or during the summer. These children have to leave class to go to the school nurse or to go home. As with any physical symptoms, the discomfort is real. The pain goes away when the child is allowed to stay home, not because she or he was faking, but because the stress has been relieved. Katie, who was around seven at the time, once explained, "Sometimes I get into trouble because I forget to do what the teacher said or I erase too much. . . . The teacher yells at me and I get scared. . . . Then my stomach starts to hurt and I have to go to the nurse." Similarly, Franklin woke up each school day with severe stomach cramps and vomiting. His mother kept him home from school and the pains usually disappeared by noon. A complete medical workup found Franklin perfectly normal. He must have guessed why he was brought to see me. His first words were, "I know my stomach trouble is because I'm afraid of school. . . . Only it really does hurt . . . no kidding!"

Other children may explain their anxiety by focusing on their increasing awareness that something must be wrong with their bodies. They have heard parents, teachers, and doctors talking about their brain or their "nervous system" and they have been through countless examinations and tests, so, they express their worries by being hypochondriacal (e.g., "My back hurts," "My head aches," "My knee feels funny"). Sometimes this concern with their bodies extends into a general concern with body image or body damage. At times these complaints become a complete rationalization for failure: "I can't help it if I made a mistake. My arm hurts today."

Children might also avoid stress by becoming paranoid and projecting their feelings and thoughts to others. Teachers, classmates, books, desks, all get blamed. Everyone is out to get them or to show them up. For example, when Joe was 10 and in a special class, he had frequent episodes of explosive behavior. He hit people, yelled, and threw things. His usual explanation was that someone was talking about him or making a face to try to get him into trouble. At home he refused to go out and play because the neighborhood children were always talking about him. A review of his school history revealed that two years earlier he had been a sad, withdrawn boy. One year ago he was described as an angry child who continually criticized himself. A psychiatric evaluation found that he was certainly not psychotic. This was simply his latest in a series of attempts to cope with his problems by blaming others in a paranoid manner.

Children may use their diagnosis as the excuse for their problems. They have heard everyone use various labels to explain everything about themselves. Such a child may explain, "I'm brain damaged (or learning disabled) so I can't do that."

The child also might generalize the disability into a sense of total worthlessness. "I'm just no good. I can't read." For example, when confronted by a teacher with an error on a math paper, Suzie responded, "I can't do that. I'm a retard." Likewise, 12-year-old Tommy explained why he didn't have friends: "I'm brain damaged so I can't catch a ball too good. All the kids play ball and since I can't play, I don't have any friends."

Poor Self-Image and Depression

Some children with learning disabilities plus possible ADHD do not develop psychological systems that are competent enough to help them handle the pain of frustration and failure. As a result, they may experience a true sense of depression. Failures, inadequacies, and poor interactions with peers and significant adults leave the child feeling angry and devalued. Younger children who are often unable to experience this depression internally, may express their feelings by being irritable and aggressive toward everyone. Older children may exhibit classic symptoms of depression. They appear to be sad, cry easily, and may have trouble sleeping and eating. Sometimes the child turns so much of his or her anger inward that she or he becomes self-destructive or suicidal. David, an 11-year-old boy with learning disabilities and a long history of failures was referred for evaluation because of his overly polite, passive manner. During the evaluation he described himself as a "bad troublemaker." He went on to say, "I'm stupid and I can't do anything right." This, of course, was in marked contrast to his usual overly serene behavior. He added, "I get so mad with myself when I make a mistake, I send myself to my room. . . . Sometimes I punish myself by making myself go to bed early or

by finding my favorite TV show and not letting myself see it
. . . Sometimes I get so mad I slap myself."

With some children, their conscience, or superego, takes on a punitive tone and prevents them from accepting praise. They feel that they are so bad they do not deserve such praise. If a teacher compliments a piece of work, the child feels compelled to destroy it. If a parent compliments the child, he or she might act terrible until the parent yells or enacts a punishment.

When children keep these anxieties and feelings of worthlessness inside, they understandably develop a poor self-image. The child sees him- or herself as an inadequate, bad, worthless person who can't do anything right. Feedback from the outside world often encourages this self-image and, at the very least, does nothing to help correct it. For example, Ronnie, a markedly depressed 10-year-old boy with such feelings had been hyperactive since birth. Ronnie was always all over the place, his mother reported. "All he ever heard from me was 'no' or 'don't' or 'bad boy.'" Ronnie was kicked out of nursery school for being a "monster." He grew even wilder in kindergarten and was no better in first and second grade. Still undiagnosed, he repeated second grade, started third, and was then suspended from school. He had never known himself to be anything but bad, dislikable, inadequate, and stupid. The fact that he was finally found to be very bright, have learning disabilities and ADHD, didn't change his self-image.

No one can talk these children out of their self-assessments because the self-image results from a collection of real experiences. They can improve, however, when they begin to see the changes that come with appropriate help and when they begin to master learning and behavioral tasks.

Arthur is another example of poor self-image and depression. Now 12, Arthur had been diagnosed at age 5 as having learning disabilities and ADHD. He was placed on medication (the use of medication for ADHD is discussed in Chapter 14) and received several years of intensive special educational therapy as well as psychotherapy. When Arthur eventually went back to a regular sixth grade class and did well, he reminisced with me:

> Remember when I was at the special school and you kept telling me how smart I was? . . . I thought you just wanted to

make me feel good because I couldn't read or do anything. . . .
I almost gave up and felt that I would just never make it. . . .
Then one day something clicked and I started to read. I *really
read*. . . . Then I started to do math. Boy, I could really learn
just like you told me. I must have grown five years that first
week I started to read.

Other Common Defense Mechanisms

When some children have difficulty dealing with anger, they
may choose an indirect way of showing it. One such style is
called *passive-aggressive*. The child's behavior is not actively aggressive in and of itself, yet the child makes everybody angry
with him or her much of the time. Dawdling and always being
late are good examples of this. While supposedly getting
dressed, for instance, the child may play with his or her clothes
or with toys until a parent becomes furious. The child then looks
up in bewilderment and says, "Why are you so mad at me? I
didn't do anything." A special education teacher once said to me
of such a child, "He was so cooperative and helpful and sweet
that I felt like bashing him in the teeth."

Other children become *passive-dependent*. Initially, the
child avoids failure and unpleasant feelings by staying out of the
situations that could result in failure. But this passivity can expand into a veritable lifestyle. He or she avoids taking any initiative in anything and minimizes getting involved in everything.
A truly helpless child arouses sympathy in adults. The passive-
dependent child's behavior often makes people angry because
the helplessness appears to be deliberate and contrived.

Another common approach some children use to handle
stress is what Dr. Richard Gardner, a child psychiatrist, labeled as
"clowning." Clowning is usually very successful. The child learns
what to do to the wrong person at the wrong time to disrupt the
lesson plan or to be kicked out of class. Clowning serves several
functions. It can be a way of controlling feelings of inadequacy—the child clowns around to cover up feelings of worthlessness, and depression. By playing the clown or freak, the
child seems to be saying, "They call me a clown or a freak, but
that's only because I choose to be one. I really can turn it off if
I want to, but it's too much fun this way." If the child succeeds
in this behavior, he or she disrupts the lesson plan or is told to
leave the group, thus avoiding the academic work, and therefore

the failure. Clowning behavior may win a certain measure of peer acceptance. Suddenly the child everyone teases is the class hero because of what he or she did. The clowning behaviors are reinforced.

In some schools, the "punishment" for being sent to the principal's office is well worth the effort—no school work, talking to the secretary, delivering messages, or playing with the typewriter. After four years of special education and psychotherapy, Jack returned to regular classes and was doing well. He saw me and I asked him to describe what he remembered about his previous experiences in regular classes. "Boy, were those teachers stupid. Anytime it was my turn to read or do anything I had trouble with, I would tease another boy or joke around. It worked great. I got sent out of the room." Then he added, "Only you got me to see that I was the stupid one. . . You can't get help if you're not in class and I sure didn't want to spend the rest of my life in a special class."

Children with ADHD with impulsivity may develop an *impulse disorder*. The normal child learns with age to delay longer and longer between the initial impulse to act and the actual behavior, gradually building on past experiences to choose an appropriate behavior. The ADHD child, however, may remain explosive or aggressive and have temper tantrums. For example, a classmate hits Johnny or hurts his feelings. Most children would know to wait until they are on the playground and then, when the teacher was not looking, "accidentally" trip this child. But, Johnny, with an impulse disorder, does not stop to think through options. He instantly yells or hits.

Some children with impulsivity show other behaviors that are reflective of impulsive thinking. They may bedwet, steal, play with fire, hoard food, or eat excessively. It is not fully understood why these behaviors are seen with more frequency with children who are impulsive, but they are.

Occasionally children with learning disabilities appear to act *overly mature*. Faced with feelings of being different, inadequate, and fearful that no one will like them or take care of them, these children decide to grow up quickly. They also sense that they are not making it as a child with other children and guess that it would be safer to be an adult. Often they have a compelling need to be in control and become upset if they cannot control every situation. This controlling behavior might be their way of coping with a world that they experience as out-of-control. It might be a way of becoming an adult-like person and taking control of the world. They look, act, and relate to others like serious adults. This behavior may pay off. Adults compliment them and spend more time with them. Chuck is an example of overmaturity. His parents described this seven-year-old boy as not needing anyone to take care of him. Chuck was totally independent; in fact, he took care of everyone else in his family and his school class. He enjoyed most having discussions with his teacher. He had no sense of humor and was described as a "perfect little man," completely self-sufficient. In a psychiatric diagnostic session, Chuck's fantasy and play reflected great concern about dependency needs and a fear that no one would meet them. So he had to take care of himself. Chuck denied his anger and his wish to be taken care of; he used all of his emotional energies to maintain his protective facade.

Social Problems

All of the emotional problems discussed to this point profoundly affect a child's social relationships. A few other special types of social problems also deserve mention here.

As discussed throughout this book, some children have difficulty because their learning disabilities interfere with peer activities. The visual-motor problems that affect certain sports and the language problems that interfere with communications are examples. One result of such problems is avoidance of peer interactions and activities.

Some children will prefer to play with younger children because they cannot handle the interactions or participate in the activities of their own age group. They intuitively seek out an age group whose skills they can manage. A boy of nine might have visual perception, fine motor, and visual-motor disabilities, but good strengths in auditory perception, language, and gross motor areas. He goes out with his classmates but finds he cannot play baseball or basketball well enough to keep up. Then he learns that five- and six-year-olds do a lot of calling to each other and prefer running, climbing, and riding bikes. These gross motor activities and interactions he can handle. In addition, the younger children look up to him while his peers avoid or tease him. Thus, he spends more time with the younger children.

Another special social problem relates to difficulties in reading social cues or in learning social skills. It is not understood why these problems exist; however, they are very common. Most children learn very early in life to "read" body language, facial expressions, or tone of voice, and to adjust their behavior accordingly. For example, a child of three years knows when he or she is outside playing and mother yells to come in, that the tone of her voice either means you can ignore her for a little longer or you had better come in quickly. This child can "sense" a parent's emotional status by body language and know whether to approach or avoid this parent when he or she comes home from work. Many children with learning disabilities do not pick up the subtle and not so subtle messages—facial expressions, body postures, tones of voice—that suggest that they need to react differently or change their behavior. They don't back off. The joking around goes too far. Feelings get hurt and tempers may flare. They miss the cues that nonverbally say "Enough!"

In Closing

The pain that children can experience because of their frustrations and failures is real. Unattended to, it can have a major impact on personality development. Without help, these feelings and thoughts can shape behavior both for the present and the future. Let me illustrate with another clinical example.

Bob's parents were concerned. He was eight years old and had just completed second grade. He had done poorly in first grade, not learning to read or print well. During second grade he made some progress in reading but was not yet up to grade level.

"He seems intelligent," his mother reported. "But, Bob's so angry and unhappy. He's a perfectionist and gets upset if he can't do his school work." The consultation with me followed a conference requested by the principal. The principal spoke of Bob's high anxiety level in school and his poor self-image. The principal thought that he had an emotional problem and needed psychotherapy.

Bob's father said that Bob set very high standards for himself. "If he cannot do things, he says he is no good or stupid. Now, he's so afraid that he won't do well that he avoids trying any new activities."

When I went out to the waiting room to greet Bob he stood up and shook hands. He was a very serious and tense child who behaved more like an adult than an eight year old. As we entered my office, I tried to help him relax by encouraging him to choose a toy or game to play with and by chatting with him about general things. He went through the motions of setting up some toys but preferred to sit on the floor with me and talk.

The following is an excerpt from a tape recording of this session. Throughout this session Bob was verbal and serious and showed signs of being tense (e.g., twisting his fingers, frowning).

(Tell me about school.) I don't like to make mistakes. (Oh.) I get angry and frustrated. (What do you do?) Sometimes I feel like crying but I tough it out. (You can't cry?) The kids would think I was a baby. (What else do you feel?) I get angry with myself. I say I'm dumb or stupid or can't learn. (How do you feel when you say these things?) Bad. I'm just a jerk. (What do you do with these feelings?) I distract myself until they go away.

(Bob, why do you think you feel this way?) I don't know. (Could it have something to do with school?) I don't read or do math too good. (And the other kids . . . ?) They do it easier. (When you say that you look upset.) Yeah.

(What else happens in school?) I get scared sometimes that the teacher will be angry with me. (I see.) If she doesn't like my work she sends me back to do it again. I get mad because I did my best. (What do you do?) I distract myself and push it out of my mind. Then I do the work. (How do you push away such angry feelings?) I get busy with the work. (Don't you feel like yelling or throwing something, or . . . ?) No, that would be bad.

(You know, Bob, I get the feeling that you don't like yourself too much.) There's nothing to like. (You mean you cannot think of anything about yourself that is good?) I guess. (You guess?) Well, sometimes I think that Mommy wanted a girl because they don't cause so much trouble as boys. But, they may want a boy to carry on the family name. (So, you may not like yourself and now I hear you say that maybe your parents don't like you either.) Sometimes I think that.

(You know, Bob, I think the real problem is that you don't like yourself.) Yeah. (And, you look so sad right now. How long have you had such feelings and thoughts?) I think they started in first grade. (Tell me about it.) I couldn't do some of the work. The teacher use to make me do it again. The other kids got smiles from the teacher. I just got disappointed looks.

(What do you think was the problem in first grade?) I don't know. (You seemed to have trouble doing the school work.) Yeah. (You know, Bob, I've worked with other boys and girls with problems like yours. Sometimes they worry that their problems are because they are bad and being punished or because there's something wrong with their head or maybe because they're dumb or retarded. I wonder what kind of thoughts you have.) I do think about these things. (You look so sad when you think about these things.) Maybe. Sometimes I think that maybe I'm retarded. (Retarded?) Yeah. (That would be pretty upsetting to think that you were retarded.) Yeah. (Maybe we had better find out what the problems are so that you won't have to worry about things that may not be true.) I'm just too dumb to learn anything. (I can see why you might think that way. I'd like to find out what it is so that we can do something about it.) I can't do anything right.

Last year at the pool I hit my head a couple of times. (And, maybe that caused the problems?) Maybe that's why I'm so dumb. (I don't think that's the reason you're having trouble in school. But, then, I guess it's hard for you to believe me.) There's no hope for me.

At this point in the session I put Bob in my lap and held him. He finally began to cry. I reassured him that I would help him and his parents to solve his problems in school so that he could like himself again. I told him that I thought he was a pretty nice kid and that it hurt me to see him in such pain.

Formal testing identified Bob's visual perception, sequencing, visual memory, and fine motor disabilities. There was wide inconsistency on the subtests of the IQ test. Bob was of high average to superior intellectual potential. Special education interventions were developed for third grade; his teacher would be briefed.

But the damage to Bob's self-image and psychological development had already been done. He was sad, hurting, and in need of help. Psychotherapy was begun, but not for the reasons given by his principal. He was not primarily emotionally disturbed and therefore having trouble in school. He had learning disabilities and his trouble in school caused him to be emotionally disturbed.

This therapy, however, would not be successful without the special education interventions in school. How could I help him rethink his self-image and feelings about himself if he continued to have failing experiences in school?

8

Psychosocial Problems for the Adolescent with Learning Disabilities

IF YOUR SON'S OR DAUGHTER'S learning disabilities were first recognized in childhood and he or she received the help that was necessary, you are ahead of the game. Adolescence is a stressful time, but it is less so if the basic educational, social, and family supports are in place and you can build on them. If your child's difficulties were not recognized until a major behavior problem surfaced in middle/junior high school or high school, your task is going to be much more difficult. With the adolescent's problems compounded by late diagnosis and by the physical changes of puberty itself, it is even more critical to move in with a full team evaluation and a comprehensive intervention program that addresses each area of identified difficulty.

During adolescence, the fact that a learning disability is a total life disability takes on even greater meaning. It affects every kind of life involvement and interaction. Adolescents whose problems were recognized and treated during childhood must now handle new challenges. Those youngsters whose problems went unrecognized until adolescence have a double problem—they must deal with their existing disabilities while trying to compensate for the academic and emotional price they have already paid.

The adolescent with learning disabilities has special problems. Early adolescence is characterized by a strong need not to be different. The person who, as a child, cooperated peacefully with a special education routine may, as an adolescent, suddenly refuse to continue to take part in the special classes or tutoring and insist on being in regular classes. He or she may refuse to continue taking medication. You may have to come up with some creative compromises: switching special tutoring or other remedial help to an out-of-school, and therefore less public, setting or allowing the youngster to administer his or her own medication rather than going to the school nurse.

Adolescence is a time of rebelling against rules and authority figures. It is an especially difficult period of time for an adolescent with learning disabilities. As parents, you will often be in no-win situations. If you insist that your son or daughter act his or her age, your adolescent suddenly acts like a five year old. If you baby her or him, your adolescent suddenly erupts in anger, complaining that you are treating him or her like a child. If you back off and leave him or her alone, your adolescent accuses you of not caring. If you give them adult-like freedom or responsibilities, he or she abuses these privileges then gets angry if you take them away. My best advice is to accept the fact that you cannot win. Talk through this whole matter frankly with your adolescent and try to communicate and struggle through the issues together. If the rebelliousness gets out of hand, you may need to seek professional guidance.

Developmental Stages

In the Western world at least, emotional stress is to be expected during adolescence. The adolescent with learning disabilities has even more emotional problems than the normal adolescent. I have already emphasized the importance of distinguishing between emotional, social, and family problems that are *causing* the academic difficulties and those that are the *consequence* of academic difficulties. The learning disabilities have resulted earlier in frustration, failure, and behavioral problems. Now the behavior problems that resulted may have taken on a life of their own, growing to such proportions that they have made the adolescent unavailable to school participation and learning. Both areas of difficulty—the learning disabilities and the emotional problems—must now be resolved.

In addition, leftover problems from infancy or childhood may resurface. We have reviewed the normal developmental tasks of adolescence: moving from dependency to independency, establishing one's identity, learning intimacy. Adolescents with learning disabilities are more likely than most to have trouble in each of these areas.

Independence

Becoming independent, or separating, means going out from the family and realizing successes and positive experiences on one's own. An adolescent who is insecure, has a poor self-image, and does poorly with his or her peers may not be able to move away from his or her family comfortably. Instead, some adolescents simply embrace their dependency, turning away from outside companions, into the home, and putting on an appearance of being content, even preferring, to be alone or to watch television. Others find these excessive dependence feelings upsetting and fight them, internally or by lashing out at others. Negativism, power struggles with adults, and unacceptable clothing, hairstyles, and choice of friends are often ways of expressing one's fear of and discomfort with dependency. Although you may find all of these behaviors quite irritating, don't be completely turned off. It is extremely important that you understand, maintain communication, and try to help your adolescent.

As you try to help your adolescent through this struggle for independence, keep in mind his or her specific strengths and weaknesses. For the youngster to find out that one can and must succeed on one's own, you must work together to maximize successes and growth-producing experiences. You may have to rethink chores. You will also want to work with the adolescent in selecting after-school activities, sports, or jobs very carefully.

Adolescents with learning disabilities face special problems with their friends. If your daughter or son understands what she or he can and cannot do well and feels comfortable talking with you about these things, you can work together to map out special strategies that will increase the probability of success.

For example, Cathy, who was 15, wouldn't go out with her friends to get a snack after school or out to a restaurant on the weekends because she had difficulty reading the menu and was embarrassed. We discussed this problem in family sessions. Cathy's sister suggested that she pretend she didn't know what she wanted and wait until last to order. This would enable her to listen to the other's orders and to pick from among their choices. Her father suggested that he could copy the menu from the local fast-food places and other possible restaurants so that she could practice reading them at home. She tried both approaches right away and they proved helpful. Later, as she became more comfortable with her friends, she shared her problem with a girl to whom she felt particularly close. This friend understood and began to help too. When the gang was at a restaurant, her friend would turn to Cathy and say, "Gee, I can't decide if I want a pizza, a meatball sub, or spaghetti. What do you think." Ideally, Cathy would feel comfortable sharing her problem with all of her close friends. Thus, each would understand and help her.

You probably never stop to think how many situations call for quick facility in reading, but they are everywhere: one must be able to read street signs or maps, bus stop signs, TV listings, the movie guide, or a marquee. If your adolescent has a reading problem, it is essential that you all come up with imaginative suggestions for handling it.

Understanding and acting on spoken instructions is another skill that everyone must have to get along in daily life. If you can't comprehend what you are told, your opportunities for action and for learning are limited. Here again, if your adolescent has this problem, some creative solutions are in order.

Rico, who is 17 years old, had auditory perception and auditory short-term memory problems. He went for his driver's license test. He knew how to drive, drove well, and passed his written test with ease. There he sat behind the wheel waiting for the road test. His father got out of the car, Rico slid behind the wheel, and the examiner got in beside him. The examiner said, "OK son, listen to me. See that white line? Pull out, then bring the car to a complete stop at the white line, then turn left and go to the stop sign. Now, do it." Rico misunderstood some of the directions and could not remember all of them. He failed the test, not because he was a poor driver but because he had learning disabilities.

Rico's father suggested that he speak to the examiner and tell him about his learning disabilities. He thought that perhaps the examiner would give Rico written instructions or break down the instructions to shorter steps. Rico, however, refused to be treated differently. That night he and his father worked out a compromise. They went back to the test site, talked with several people after they had completed the test, and learned the routine. Rico's father wrote it out, step by step, and Rico memorized it. He reapplied for an appointment and took the test again. The examiner could have been talking in Greek. It did not matter. Rico knew the demands and successfully passed the test.

Whether the task is using public transportation, learning to shop, cooking, handling money or a checkbook, driving a car, or interacting with friends in everyday activities, work with your adolescent to develop strategies for coping with the tasks that he or she finds difficult. Building on strengths and compensating for weaknesses is critical because a sense of self-confidence, self-image, and finally, a sense of independence are all based on these small and large successes. No one can write an instruction booklet for *your* family. In fact, no one really can tell your son or daughter the best way to do activities—the disabilities to be overcome are theirs as are the tasks to be accomplished. But, you can help in every way possible as they "write their own book."

Before leaving the theme of dependency and independency, let me discuss one other concern. Your son or daughter should be receiving special education help. This help might be provided by each teacher, by resource room professionals, or by private tutors. All too often, these professionals contribute to the adolescent's feelings of dependency. They are given exercises or assignments and asked to do them. They are asked to show their homework and then helped with the areas of difficulty. They are passive and the special education professional tells them what to do. Not uncommonly, the reasons for the help are not discussed. There is a big difference between a tutor saying, "I want you to do these worksheets for me today" and a tutor saying, "Look, we know you have difficulty with visual figure-ground and that when you read you often skip words or lines or read the same line twice. I want you to work on these exercises that will help you minimize this problem." The first statement is an adult-to-child, let me tell you what to do, situation. The second statement is a colleague-to-colleague statement that respects the individual and helps him or her understand him- or herself.

This understanding of self is crucial. Unless the adolescent understands his or her areas of disability and ability, he or she is unable to take an active role in problem solving. As the adolescent moves through high school and beyond, it is essential that he or she understand his or her brain and how it works. This individual must know his or her strengths and weaknesses so that he or she can clarify problem areas and creatively work at solving them. What a difference between a teenager walking into the tutor and sitting down, waiting for instructions, and a teenager who walks in and says, "My science teacher lectures all of the time and I can't get everything down fast enough. Can you help me solve this problem?"

Another theme is equally important. We often want our adolescents to feel good and not be overwhelmed by their learning disabilities. So, professionals and parents make comments like, "You just learn differently and we will help you learn how to learn differently" or "Since the teachers are making adjustments and you are getting tutoring, you will do as well as your friends and only have to work as hard as they are." No. Don't mislead your son or daughter. Having a learning disability is a disability. The only way to prevent it from becoming a handicap is by hard work. Thus, this hard work will take more time. You can offer empathy and hugs. You can be supportive and be sure he or she gets the right help. But, the bottom line is that your adolescent will have to understand and accept that he or she will have to work harder and longer to be successful. They will have to see work as acceptable and, maybe, pleasant.

Let me illustrate this important concept by describing a 17-year-old high school junior named Jimmy. I had worked with Jimmy and his family since the third grade, primarily helping them learn what is in this book. Jimmy understood himself and what he had to do to succeed. He had accepted his responsibilities. He requested a meeting with his new English teacher during the few days before school started in the Fall. At the meeting he started by saying that he had personally selected him as his English teacher. He did not do this to impress the teacher or to win favors. Jimmy had learned how he learned best. He knew that he did best with teachers who were organized and who taught by discussion in class more than by using worksheets and the book. At the end of the tenth grade he asked all of his friends in eleventh to describe each English teacher. He picked the one who was best for him. His parents made sure he got this teacher.

Next, Jimmy said, "You may not remember, but I got the reading list from you last June. I have a reading problem and cannot read very fast. But don't worry. Over the summer I read the first four books on the list so that I won't fall behind. Also, one of the books is by Shakespeare and I know it will be hard for me to understand; so, I've ordered it through the books-on-tape service. One favor, though; when I read outloud, I sometimes mispronounce words or skip words. Would you please not call on me to read in class unless you tell me the day before so I can practice." He went on to say, "One other favor. I have a written language problem. At home I use a word processor. But in class I need more time on tests. Could I have untimed tests. I am willing to come in early or return after school to finish and I promise not to cheat."

What tremendous understanding Jimmy has of himself. What awareness of what it will take for him to do well. He has learned what he must do to succeed and he is motivated to do all that it takes. But, there is another advantage to Jimmy being his own advocate rather than a parent. It would be a hardhearted teacher who would say no to Jimmy's needs. What would have happened if Jimmy's mother had come in to say the same things. The teacher might have said, "Look, I have 25 students in each of five classes a day. I can't do all of these things. Either your son will have to make it like the other kids or he needs to be in a special class." or "Jimmy is in eleventh grade. You have got to get off of his back and let him grow up."

When they are children, parents need to be assertive advocates. As these children move into adolescence, parents must help them learn to be their own advocates. Without this ability, this adolescent will have difficulty moving into adult life, whether it is in college, on the job, in the military, or in a trade training program.

Identity

Once some beginning sense of independence has been achieved, the great task of adolescence is that of finding identity. This is difficult at best in a world where value systems change, career opportunities vary, and options unpredictably expand and diminish. The adolescent of today—as of any day, for that matter—questions some of the current "adult values," wonders what you have done to make the world the mess it is in, and shares in rather more than less uncertainty about the future.

Much of this is just like what you experienced when you were an adolescent. But in some ways, the world that today's adolescents face is quite different from that which you encountered. Sexual values and the importance of relationships have changed. College no longer "guarantees" the opportunity for social and economic advancement. Family life has become and will continue to become more mobile. Almost 50 percent of children and adolescents today live in single-parent or remarriage families. In terms of future jobs, productivity may be much harder to identify with a person's individual effort and input. More and more, education and technical knowledge is essential for success.

Under these uncertain circumstances, what kind of identity can an adolescent establish if he or she feels like a failure at school, with friends, or within the family? Any learning disability only exacerbates the problem. Such adolescents can hardly be blamed if they remain immature and child-like in their behavior. They may be bland and passive, showing no personality, or they may be quite unstable, constantly changing their minds, not knowing what or who they want to be. But if they cannot be blamed, they cannot be excused. With the proper help in school and understanding, support, and help at home, these problems can be worked out. If not, professional help will be needed.

We have said that adolescence is a time when being different is not tolerated. Being just like everyone else in the peer group is a criterion that must be met before a sense of difference and a pride in individual differences can emerge. This emerging sense of identity as a person, of course, is a big step toward growing up. However, learning disabled youngsters are already different and their social problems are innumerable, especially where their peers are concerned. They may have difficulty taking part in sports, dancing, and most other activities in which their peers are involved. They often lack social skills. Making small talk, maintaining eye contact, listening to others, waiting for someone to finish talking before they speak—all of these abilities are critical to social acceptance. Your adolescent may have mastered none of them. He or she may misunderstand what is said, make inappropriate remarks, or forget what a conversation is about. He or she may be bossy, aggressive, and belligerent, or so quiet, shy, and passive that he or she fades away in any group.

None of these behaviors leads to easy peer acceptance, and instead of pushing in the right directions, some adolescents withdraw into the house, content with television, listening to the stereo, or reading. Others will be so desperate for social acceptance that they may be vulnerable to peer pressure and act inappropriately, getting into trouble. Some may move into using alcohol or drugs because "their friends" do. Girls may become sexually active in an effort to get attention and "love." Boys may try acting "tough," hanging out on the fringes of a gang or become a follower, getting involved in petty crime.

None of these problems are easy to solve. Fortunately, most children cope with adolescence well enough to make it. Some, however, remain misfits until—and even after—they become adults. Often, situations improve as adults. The stress of school may be past history. The pressures and demands on adults are different. The nonathlete or the quiet person may be more valued, or valued for different qualities.

As parents, the best you can do is understand that your adolescent is going through his or her first identity crisis. If you try to understand the problem, it may lead to an understanding of the behavior. Help your daughter or son seek out activities, sports, and other programs that offer her or him the best chances of success. Keep communication open and set up some systematic way that you can work together on solving problems.

Many adolescents, in fact, will find techniques that they can use to help themselves. They can be very creative in finding activities at which they can succeed or ways of relating to classmates or friends. Encourage their explorations and growth.

I cannot think of a better example than Ron. He had just about every type of visual perception, organization, sequencing, gross and fine motor problems possible. He had been in a self-contained special education school since his early grade school years. In tenth grade, he started in a small private regular high school. His family and I worked together during this year. Ron was determined to make it. He negotiated with each teacher to get the accommodations he needed. He worked three to four hours each night to accomplish work that most of his classmates did in only two hours. Every assignment was carefully organized. If he had a report to do, he would block out specific time, often weeks earlier, for library work, reading time, outlining time, writing and rewriting time. For lengthy reports he dictated to his mother who then typed the material.

Ron was making it. He was bright and got good grades.

Toward the end of the year his English teacher asked each student to write an "autobiography" that could be given to the eleventh grade English teacher as an introduction. But, let Ron tell his own story. Note his self-confidence and learned ability to problem solve, compensate, and cope in his following composition.

I look at Ron and I see a young man with a great deal of will-power. One can see this in my drive to overcome the limitations that impede my learning. This is also seen in my capabilities and successes. I am what is frequently referred to as learning disabled.

The first thing one sees about me are my many limitations. One of my learning limitations is that I cannot spell. Although I have tried for many years to learn, through memorization, key words, phonetics, and other teaching devices, I cannot spell. I remember taking a spelling achievement test year after year and staying at the same grade level.

The next limitation I have is that I cannot write legibly, even to myself. For instance, I remember taking a biology test, putting down what I knew were the right answers, and getting the paper back marked 10 of 25 and "can't read." Another limitation that affects my schoolwork is that I cannot calculate quickly or write quickly, even illegibly.

Some of my limitations have nothing to do with school, but concern my athletic ability. I cannot hold a canoe paddle correctly and coordinate the movements of my arm so that the canoe does not go in circles. I cannot coordinate between the sight of the incoming ball with my eyes, the level of the bat, and the swing of my arm. Consequently, 9 times out of 10, I miss the ball completely. This problem manifests itself on the other side of the batter's box as well. I can keep my eye on the ball, follow the ball, see the ball come to me, put out my glove and miss the ball from 3 to 9 feet.

I try to overcome my limitations through coping with them. With spelling, as previously described, I cannot learn how to spell. Even using a dictionary is hard for me because I cannot figure out the first two letters of a word. I find that the best way to cope with the problem is to inform teachers of it and whenever possible, have someone who knows how to spell around. As for handwriting, although I have tried to produce a form of legible script, under the careful and patient tutoring of many, I found that this is next to impossible and my writing looks like a cross between chicken scratch and arabic. Therefore, whenever possible, I type my papers, thus eliminating the necessity for legible handwriting. To cope with my problem in calculating, I use a calculator, thus eliminating any careless arithmetic errors or c.a.e.'s as they are called. I remember going to my math teacher after class one day and saying, "I can do this work; I understand the concepts; but, I just cannot physically do the computations."

As for my athletic coordination, I try the best I can. I remember being out on the lake one day, alone in a canoe. A brisk wind arose and I was trying to go from one side of the lake to the other in a perpendicular line to this wind. This situation was made doubly frustrating because I knew I should point the canoe upwind of where I wanted to go, but could not manage to keep it pointed in that direction. I try to cope with my problems playing baseball by going out to the field when no one is there, tossing the ball as high as I can and trying to catch it.

Despite my limitations, I have many capabilities and have had several successes. I have an ability to grasp the general concepts which a teacher is trying to explain. I have been able to write essays and papers that are clear and concise. I can learn from my mistakes and form constructive criticism of my work. And, if genuinely interested in a subject, I will try to find the most information I can about it. I also have a good memory and retain factual information. I am highly motivated to get things done not only on time, but early, if possible, and am equally highly motivated to learn.

My successes are many. These include my schoolwork, where I usually get either A's or B's, of which I am very proud, and fighting my own battles with teachers to make them understand my limitations. I have some sports-related successes, also. These include my sailing ability, which enabled me to pass the sailing requirements for a patch at a summer camp I attended. At the same camp, I learned to become a fair shot and passed the four lowest shooting levels in a relatively short time. And if I couldn't paddle a canoe, I developed an ability to row, a simpler and more enjoyable form of human powered water activity.

My most recent success at school includes surviving, if just barely, a rather confusing three days with a science teacher, thanks to the help of an English teacher, and surviving by not going crazy at the thought of what I cannot do.

Recognition of my capabilities has led to an urge to overcome my limitations and has produced many successes. I admit, however, that I could not have succeeded without the encouragement of many people.

Let me amplify Ron's next-to-last paragraph, the one about surviving. His science class went on a one-week trip to a nature facility. Each day the staff lectured on different topics. Ron wanted to learn, but he could not write as fast as the speaker spoke. Soon, he was lost and couldn't understand the demonstrations or the assigned projects. For example, "Now go out into the woods and look for examples of the symbiotic relationship I just described." He asked his biology teacher for help. She sent him to the instructor. The instructor seemed puzzled and didn't know what Ron wanted. By the third day Ron was so frustrated that he stormed out of the class, muttering to himself about the stupid teacher. He walked off into the woods, angry at himself for being so unable to handle the situation. Why hadn't he explained his needs to the instructor? What would he do if he didn't learn everything? How would he ever make it in college with all that lecturing? All his old doubts and fears resurfaced. After a time he decided he needed help. He went to his English teacher, someone he felt close to and trusted, and explained his problem. His teacher went with him to the instructor and discussed the problem. The English teacher agreed to take notes for Ron who was then freed up to listen. The rest of the week went well.

This story of Ron was in the first edition of this book. I can now give you a follow-up. He finished high school and went to an excellent college that understood people with special needs and provided the necessary services. Ron began to take his lap computer to class to take notes. He graduated with honors and at the time of this second edition is in law school and doing well.

As you watch your adolescent grow up, talk to other parents whose children have had similar problems, to your family doctor, and to the special education professionals at your school. If your adolescent is having more trouble than you can manage, don't hesitate to seek professional help.

Intimacy

Most adolescents slowly work on and through the tasks of moving toward independency and developing a beginning identity. The task of intimacy begins in late adolescence, but is really worked on more in early young adulthood. The high school senior may begin to experience "being in love" with someone who makes him or her feel good and may begin to learn the sharing and intradependency of intimacy.

If your son or daughter has a poor self-image and low self-esteem, dating and close relationships may not be possible. If he or she has poor social skills and difficulty making or keeping friendships, dating and close relationships may not be a possibility. The longer the limited successes or isolation exist, the greater the problems become. First, class friendships develop and reputations are established. Even if changes take place, it is hard to undo one's reputation or to break into the system.

Second, with each month the social problems exist, the adolescent loses that much more experiences; thus, he or she falls even further behind in social comfort or in mastering social skills.

There are no simple answers. Sometimes psychological help is needed. You might seek opportunities for social contact that have a potential of being successful. Initially, try finding activities that are centered around a topic or task rather than social interactions. Maybe a computer club, nature club, or volunteer work group sponsored by the school or your religious organization. The focus will be on what is learned or done rather than on talking or interacting. Ideally, this activity should be adult-supervised rather than peer-supervised. Your son or daughter will begin to be part of a group activity without having to be accepted or successful with group interactions. By using the adult leader plus problem solving, he or she might begin to feel more comfortable and successful around peers. Encourage going and practicing relating to the others in the group. At a minimum, he or she will have a positive group experience. All the better if he or she gains some confidence and social abilities. At the best, a friendship might be started because the friend is not from the school where his or her role and reputation are known.

Attention-Deficit Hyperactivity Disorder in Adolescence

About 50 percent of children with Attention-Deficit Hyperactivity Disorder (ADHD) will continue to have this disability as adolescents. The same treatment approaches will be needed. Medications will still be part of the treatment plan. School understanding and accommodations will still be necessary. The special difficulties with the adolescent who begins to resist taking the medication was discussed earlier.

It is critical that medication coverage be considered for every aspect of the adolescent's life when the hyperactivity, distractibility, and/or impulsivity interferes with success. These problems are apparent in school. They might interfere with family relationships, peer interactions and activities, and sports or other activities. This concept will be discussed in more detail in Chapter 15.

Girls who are only distractible might not be recognized until high school. They are quiet and do not get in trouble. They are seen as average students. Their friends call them "airheads" or "space cadets" but accept them. No one observes the distractibility and short attention span. Once diagnosed and treated, remarkable improvement is noted. She becomes more organized and capable in school. She talks in a more sophisticated way. She relates better with everyone. If your daughter has learning disabilities and has struggled each year, or if teachers still complain that she does not pay attention (maybe because she is just too social or "boy crazy") or does not complete work, consider the possibility of distractibility. Remember, you do not have to be hyperactive to have ADHD.

Treating the Learning Disabilities in Adolescence

If learning disabilities have gone unrecognized and untreated, the adolescent is likely to develop psychological difficulties. Some adolescents may lie about and avoid homework. Some will try to convince you (and themselves) that they could be successful but that they just don't care about school. Some will act out in school, cut classes, or get into trouble with school rules. Some of these young people who need special help, sadly, get the message that the school does not want them and they quit. I call them "school pushouts" rather than school dropouts. The school so neglects and abuses them that they give up and leave. Once out from under the pressures of school, they may settle down, get a job, work toward a high school equivalency, and move on with life. For many, without professional help, they will carry their problems and difficulties into adulthood.

Learning disabilities are life disabilities. They will continue into adolescence. Thus, it is critical that you continue to work with your school for the necessary services. Don't let the school offer a watered down approach. It is very easy for the school to give up on continued remedial and compensatory efforts and shift totally into accommodations. The students are then given less demanding classes. Teachers work around the reading, writing, math, or other problems. Your son or daughter might graduate, but he or she will not have the necessary skills and education that will be needed for life. If you live in an area where the school system puts its emphasis on grade school and provides minimal services by high school, you may need to seek private help. Become an advocate for the programs that your child or adolescent needs. If your son or daughter needs such classes, doubtless others do as well. Even if you can afford the private help that is necessary to supplement the deficiencies in your high school program, don't be content just to continue that way. Get together with other parents or parent groups and try to push your school to develop appropriate programs within the school.

If your adolescent's learning disabilities were not diagnosed until high school, he or she will need intensive special education interventions. In addition to needing remedial, compensatory, and accommodation programs, he or she may need help in filling in deficiencies from the past. He or she probably has major gaps or holes in basic knowledge that have to be addressed. If your child did not learn that $2 + 2 = 4$ in elementary school, he or she will not be able to understand that $2a + 2b = 4c$ in high school. The same may be true for basic grammar and punctuation rules.

As graduation gets closer, you and the school professionals will have to assess the future. Where is your son or daughter, academically? Where can you expect him or her to be by graduation? Should you encourage a college and, if so, what kind of college? If not college, should you encourage technical school, vocational training, joining the military? Discuss these concerns with the school professionals and/or private consultants. Make sure that your son or daughter participates in the process and the decisions.

If college is the best direction, know that there are many excellent two-year and four-year colleges that will accept students with learning disabilities. Learn how to select the correct school based on the services that are provided and learn how best to apply to maximize the possibility of acceptance. Accommodations may be needed for taking the Scholastic Aptitude Test (SAT). It is possible to take the SAT and the Achievement Test (AT) untimed and/or with a preceptor to read the questions and/or to write the answers. The college may have to look at a broader picture than SAT scores and grade point average. Your child may need a college that offers tutoring, liaison with faculty, and a resource center. Competent, motivated people with learning disabilities can go as far with their education as they wish. It takes work—more work than the average student—but it can be done. Programs and resources are available today for colleges, graduate schools, and professional schools.

It all boils down to this. As your son or daughter gets older, he or she must begin to accept some and later most of the responsibility for his or her own life and well-being. As self-image and identity emerge, that advocacy becomes inescapable. No one else is on the front line, and no one else knows better what he or she needs. You must help your adolescent to learn to speak for her- or himself and to fight for what is necessary. You cannot do your adolescent's job for him or her any longer and high school is a good time to face this and help with the transition toward adulthood.

I gave an example of a high school student earlier. Let me end this chapter by sharing another example.

At 17, John was a senior, in regular classes, but taking two hours a week of private special education tutoring. John had been in special programs since the fifth grade. He was a bright young man with learning disabilities in the visual perception, sequencing, and written language areas. His oral reading ability was at about the fourth grade level. He had learned to compensate and was successful.

When he began his senior English class, he met with his

teacher and explained what he could and could not do. He requested permission to have more time when taking written tests in class. He explained that he would get his homework in on time because he would take the extra time at home and would use the computer. He did not, he said, want to turn in unfinished tests in class, however, and he volunteered to come in early or come back during lunch or after school to finish them. He asked to be trusted to not cheat or pass the questions on to others. He also requested that he not be called on to read out loud in class and explained why.

As the semester progressed, the teacher allowed for the accommodations, except for one. The teacher had the students read literature assignments and write reports on these assignments. John did his assignments and did each well. Each week, however, the students had to take turns reading their reports out loud in class. John was not excused. At first, he memorized his reports. In class he pretended to be reading as he recited his material. As you can imagine, this soon became a major time drain and it seemed counterproductive to John. So he stopped memorizing his written work and approached his teacher again to explain his wish to avoid reading in class. The teacher insisted that John read and John firmly refused.

He worked hard and got an A on each report and on each exam. In spite of this, he received a B at the end of the first marking period. At this point, he called me for advice and we worked out a strategy. He asked if I would come with him when he went to implement our plan. I told him that I would role-play the situation with him and help him in any other way I could, but that it was time for him to fight his own battles. I assured him that he could do it.

John requested a conference with the teacher and the principal. He started the meeting by telling the principal that he had received a B in English. Then, he asked the teacher what grades he had gotten on each report and test. The teacher acknowledged the A's. John opened a folder and showed the principal these reports and exams. Then he asked the teacher why he received a B rather than an A as an overall grade. The teacher replied that the grade was also based on class participation. When John asked for clarification, the teacher admitted that John participated in class discussions but that he refused to read his reports in class.

Calmly—we had rehearsed this before—John asked the teacher if he was aware that he had learning disabilities and, specifically, a reading disability. The teacher said that he knew of this but thought that if John wanted to be in a regular class, he had to be able to be like all the other students. John took a deep breath and said, "I wish to advise you that if you do not change the B to an A, I will file a legal suit against you for discriminating against the handicapped based on Section 504 of the Rehabilitation Act of 1973."

That night John called to brag. He got his A. He was pleased with his grade and with himself. I was delighted with the confidence he had gained and the growth that his behavior reflected. Yes, his parents could have done it, maybe better, certainly in a more indirect style, but John needed the experience of fighting for what was right for him and he got it.

9

Family Reactions to the Child or Adolescent with Learning Disabilities

WE HAVE DISCUSSED AT some length the problems that children and adolescents with learning disabilities and/or Attention-Deficit Hyperactivity Disorder (ADHD) have in their relationships with people both outside and inside the home. The emotional and social problems of family members who not only want to, but have to deal productively with their daughters, sons, brothers, and sisters with these disabilities also deserve special attention. I would like to start with a discussion of the normal reactions of parents and siblings, then go on to look at the larger problems that arise when perfectly normal feelings linger too long or become too extreme, thus becoming abnormal and possibly harmful.

When one member of a family suffers, everyone in the family feels the pain and reacts to it, sometimes with nearly equal distress. Parents, brothers, sisters, grandparents—each is part of this human system within which the child or adolescent with learning disabilities lives and grows. Everyone in the family needs to understand the full range of problems the child or adolescent has if anyone is to be of help. Everyone needs to understand her or his own reactions as well, and sometimes this is a painful and difficult process.

After your child or adolescent has been through an evaluation, someone on the evaluating team should explain the findings to you. The child, too, should know and understand, to the degree possible, the results of the findings. Sometimes the evaluator routinely takes care of this. Rarely, however, does anyone, including the parents, explain the findings to sisters, brothers, and other family members. Yet, it is imperative that everyone connected with the child know about and understand the problems.

As parents, you undoubtedly had difficulty accepting that your son or daughter was different, that something was wrong. You may have experienced, or may yet experience, a series of reactions not too different from the grief reaction that people have when someone dear to them dies, although this grief is of lesser intensity. In a way, this reaction is very valid. Initially, you might fear that you have to "give up" a part of your child, or at least your ambitions for the child that you fear may never be realized. As we talk about these reactions, don't become distressed. These feelings are not only normal, they are to be expected.

We shall go on to look at many of the problems that increase the stress that the family already feels about the basic situation. If you recognize that any of these are serious problems in your family, you would do well to consult your family physician or a mental health professional. Above all, don't feel ashamed to discuss feelings that may seem "selfish" or "unworthy" to you. These problems are real and your feelings are genuine. You must look at them squarely and deal with them. Keeping a stiff upper lip, or denying that they exist, only makes things worse for you and for your family.

I recently evaluated a 10-year-old boy who had a major behavioral problem with his family. When I met with the parents to review my impressions and recommendations, I started by saying, "You know, I hate to say this, but, now that I have gotten to know your son, I must tell you that if he were my son I would have killed him by now." Mother burst into tears. She was so relieved to hear that someone else could be as angry at this child as she felt.

Normal Parent Reactions

It should not surprise you that in addition to being mothers and fathers, parents are also human beings. They have their own feelings and thoughts. They usually have mates with whom they enjoy intimate relationships, relationships that are often hard enough to manage successfully without additional family stresses. Having a child with a disability stirs up feelings and thoughts, fears and hopes for which most people are unprepared. These reactions affect both the parents as individual people and as a couple.

At no point is the stress greater than when the diagnosis is made—this is the moment when parents feel the first rush of anguish, fear, helplessness, anger, guilt, shame—all at once. Nothing can describe the thoughts going through a parent's head as he or she rides home from the school or the doctor's office after the first conference. No sensitive professional should ever describe a child's problems to a parent without acknowledging these feelings and ending with a positive course of action such as "and this is what we will do about it."

Unfortunately, not all professionals are this sensitive. Some play what I call the "Ha, Ha, you have leprosy" game. They throw out a lot of labels, banging a parent over the head with "Your child is disabled or . . ." and then say goodbye. Out the parents go, overwhelmed, with little understanding, hope, or direction to take.

Denial

The initial phase of the grief-like reaction to the discovery of a learning disability and/or ADHD, as with other grief reactions is often *denial.* "It can't be true . . . the doctor must be mistaken." Or, "She only saw him for an hour; I don't believe it." You may doubt the competence of the bearer of such news and want to punish him or her. Frequently parents seek other opinions. Getting other evaluations can be useful. Unfortunately, "doctor shopping" for someone who will tell you what you want to hear does not do anything productive for your child.

Another form of denial is the "cover-up" reaction. One parent, usually the mother, wants to "protect" the other parent by not sharing the results of the studies or by minimizing the problems. Some parents successfully cover up the fact that the child is in a special school program for years. Sadly, the mother or father who is uninformed about the child's true abilities often continues to build up unrealistic expectations and demands results of the child that the child cannot possibly produce. The child, seeing through this cover-up, perceives the true reason for it: "They can't accept me as I am; they have to pretend that I'm different than I really am." This often makes the child quite understandably angry or sad, and he or she usually has difficulty accepting himself or herself when parental acceptance is not perceived.

After the Denial

Once a parent can "look" at the problems, he or she may feel overwhelmed with feelings of helplessness. How could this have happened to me? Why me? What will we do? Often, there is an effort to find an explanation for the helplessness. Somehow, if a reason can be found there might be some control over "it" happening again and the parent does not feel as helpless.

It is not uncommon to wonder if the problems were caused by someone else, resulting in anger. The other possibility is that the parent is the blame, resulting in anger against oneself or guilt. Lets look at these feelings and reactions.

Anger

A period of anger commonly follows the denial stage. Parents may direct this anger inward, against themselves; or project it outward, blaming the other parent or any other outside source. Upon learning of a child's disability, it is normal to feel anger. Other sentiments, such as "Why me?", "How could God do this to me?", "How could I have done this?", "How could *you* have done this?", or "We never should have had children!", are often expressed. This anger might be projected to people outside of the family. This reaction will be discussed later.

Guilt

Parents may turn their initial anger inward, attacking themselves rather than the problems. Often they feel depressed. Associated with this reaction may be feelings of guilt. It is a very short step from "How could I have done this?" to "It's all my fault." The parent may berate her- or himself with statements such as "God is punishing me because . . ." or "I didn't follow my doctor's advice," or "I've been given this extra burden to prove my worthiness."

As discussed above, for some people, feeling guilty and/or depressed represents an attempt to establish control over a situation that they perceive as basically hopeless and out of control.

If a parent can lay the blame or attribute the cause to himself or herself, that person then conquers the situation by explaining it, however erroneously. The logic is that if this happened for a reason—on account of something one did—and if one does not practice that transgression again, then nothing like what has happened will happen again.

Just as the child who feels depressed tends to become quiet and to pull away from people, so the depressed parent becomes isolated. If this depression is allowed to continue, the parent may withdraw from the child or the other parent at just the time when one or the other, as well as the other members of the family, need that person the most.

If initial anger has been displaced outward, the parent enters into a pattern of blaming or attributing the fault to someone or something outside of herself or himself. Like the guilt reaction, blaming an outside agent at least places responsibility *somewhere*, and this too protects one from feelings of helplessness. The parent may blame the physician because "He didn't get to the hospital fast enough," or "I told her I was in labor, but she wouldn't believe me and I almost delivered in the car," or "If the pediatrician had come out to see him rather than prescribing over the phone, he wouldn't have had that high fever." A person may generalize this reaction to all professionals, who then become "bunglers," "incompetents," and "charlatans." Statements such as "It's the school's fault," "She's just a young, inexperienced teacher," or "He's just a rigid old teacher" are also common. The teacher, doctor, or whoever is the butt of anger probably never hears these complaints. But the parent may never allow the child to forget them. Reactions such as these undermine the child's faith in and respect for the very people he or she must turn to for help and hope.

Some parents attempt to suppress their guilt or their need to place blame somewhere else by overprotecting the child. The most normal, human thing to do when a youngster is hurting is to reach out and try to protect her or him. This is necessary and helpful. But one's goal must be to protect the child only where she or he needs protecting and to encourage the child to grow where he or she does not need protecting, even though that may be painful. A blanket of overprotection covers the child's weaknesses, but it also smothers the child's strengths. Not only does overprotectiveness keep a child immature and delay growth in areas where that is possible, it also makes a child feel inadequate. He or she knows what's happening. For example, when everyone else has a chore to do but your daughter does not, when everyone takes turns clearing the table but your son never has to, that child will very probably conclude, "See, they agree with me—I am inadequate." Such children may be poorly coordinated or unable to concentrate for any length of time, but they are as sensitive as you, and maybe more so.

Most parents do work through these normal denial, anger, and guilt phases. When they do, they gradually become strong advocates for their children, mobilizing their energy in constructive ways.

Pathological Parent Reactions

The most common pathological parent reactions include chronic denial, chronic anger, and chronic guilt.

Chronic Denial

Some parents cannot give up their denial. They continue to "doctor shop" in a continuing search for the doctor with the magic answer or magic cure or for someone who will say that nothing is wrong with their child. Such parents greet the newest professional on the block with flattery and praise, criticizing the many doctors, educators, psychologists, and psychiatrists whose opinions they have rejected. Ultimately, the new "hero" too is rejected and then attacked. As their frustration grows, they hop from one promised cure to another, often becoming the victims of those who capitalize on people in distress. This hopeless "shopping," of course, deprives the child of time that should be spent in constructive programs and the valuable therapy that he or she needs.

The chronic denial reaction has other potentially serious consequences. Because each "authority" fails, she or he must be downgraded when the parents move on to the next one. The child picks up the message not to have faith in anybody in any professional capacity. This faith and trust is absolutely necessary in order to have hope, and hope is absolutely necessary if one is to work toward overcoming the handicap. And, as I said before, the child also picks up that subtle but clear message: "We can't accept you as you are. We must find someone who will tell us that you are not the way you are." The child hears, knows, and reacts with anger, shame, and a conviction of inadequacy.

Chronic Anger

If parents do not resolve their initial anger and learn to handle it, they may continue to project it. With this attitude, nothing can go right. Someone is always wrong in their minds: "After all this time and money, you haven't helped my child. How come?" Or, to the child: "After all my efforts, why can't you learn anything?" Such parents, miserable themselves, are almost impossible for professionals to work with—or for a child to live with.

Chronic Guilt

When a parent handles his or her unresolved guilt by becoming overly dedicated to the child, that parent is apt to be covertly furious about it. What comes across in public is the dedication: "No task, no trip, no expense is too great to help my child." What comes across behind the scenes is the anger at having to do all of this, and at having to give up things. Occasionally, a parent becomes a professional martyr. He or she never lets anyone forget how great the effort, how selfless the sacrifice. The surface behavior may be sweet and admirable, but somehow the child picks up the bitter parallel message: "Look how much I do for you, you ungrateful, good-for-nothing child. You're worthless to begin with, and you show no appreciation."

A parent may handle unresolved guilt by withdrawing from other social and/or family contacts and totally dedicating himself or herself to the child. Some parents carry this to the point where they have almost no energy left for relationships with the other children in the family or with their spouse. Taking care of the one child's needs becomes so demanding that the person is too worn out and weary to meet the needs of the other children, to participate in social activities, or to continue intimate relations with his or her spouse. The result is a dysfunctional family and, probably, a strained marriage. And, once again, often the anger at this state of affairs is not openly discussed between the parents but displaced onto the child who is seen as the cause of it all.

For other parents, the normal initial reaction of overprotecting the child might become a lifestyle, one which both prevents growth for the child and the parents and increases the child's feelings of worthlessness. Under these circumstances, the child can easily become infantilized. Occasionally overprotective behaviors may stem from a parent's attempt to cover up feelings of his or her own inadequacy as a person and a parent. People with low self-esteem and feelings of worthlessness may achieve feelings of being wanted and needed by deluding themselves that they are "all the child has in the world." When the child's existing immaturity and feelings of incompetence lead to failure, he or she naturally retreats back into the home. The overprotecting parent sees this and feels even more justified in moving in and protecting some more. A self-defeating cycle begins to repeat itself, the child increasingly realizing that she or he is helpless without the parent, and the parent reinforcing the notion that the child cannot survive without him or her.

In Summary

It is expected that parents will experience the normal denial, guilt, and anger following the confirmation of their child's or adolescent's disabilities. It is not expected that these difficulties will continue and become a chronic pattern of functioning. If you see yourself or your spouse in these more chronic descriptions, consider getting help so that the difficulties can be handled. This assistance will make the parent feel and function better, as well as the child or adolescent.

The Reactions of the Other Children in the Family

As discussed earlier, when parents suspect a learning disability and become concerned, they usually take their son or daughter to one or more specialists. Finally someone explains to them what the problems are and what needs to be done about them. At some point, someone probably sits down with the parents and "interprets" the findings. Occasionally, but not often enough, someone sits down with the child or adolescent and explains to him or her what the problems are, what the events of treatment will be, and why. Almost never does anyone explain any of this to the child's brothers and sisters—yet, as part of the family, they need to know. *When one member of a family hurts, everyone feels the pain and hurt.* When the siblings are left in the dark, what are they supposed to do? How might they react?

The reactions of your other children may be made worse because you expect more of them than you expect of yourselves. The child or adolescent with learning disabilities and/or ADHD is very good at getting parents frustrated and angry. One parent may yell or hit; another parent might cry, withdraw, or pout. Your other children get just as frustrated or angry. Yet, if they yell, hit, cry, withdraw, or pout, they are often punished or told they may not act that way. They are human, too. They are entitled to the same feelings you have. You cannot tell them not to have these feelings. You cannot tell them not to role model their behaviors after their parents. You must acknowledge that they have normal and expected feelings and help them learn what to do with them. If they cannot act like their parents, teach them an acceptable way of expressing their feelings.

If the two parents disagree on parenting styles or discipline methods, the stress and conflicts between the other children and the child with the disabilities can cause major stress between the parents. This problem can be even worse if there is a divorce and the children spend time in two different families, each with a different style of responding.

Your other children and adolescents might struggle with many different feelings as they live with and try to cope with their sibling who has the problems. Let me review some of these reactions.

Anxiety

Some siblings become very worried and feel *anxious*. This is especially true in families where the cover-up is on and little, if anything, is said. For example, a sibling might ask, "What's wrong with Jimmie?", to which his or her parents say, "Oh nothing special . . . it's OK." Yet the sibling sees the parents taking Jimmie from one place to another, and hears words like "brain damage" or "Where are we going to get the money for all of this?" The brother or sister sees mother or father upset, maybe in tears, maybe angry. Aware that something is wrong but not knowing what it is, the sibling's imagination may take over. Frequently the brother or sister fantasizes worse things than those that are real. Then he or she worries. I have heard brothers and sisters say, "Will he live? Is he going to die?", "Will it happen to me?", or "If it's not important, why all the whispers and hush-hush?" Your other children must have clear information at a level that each can understand and all of the facts that are needed in order to understand.

Anger

Brothers and sisters may become *angry*, fighting with the child who has the problems or with their parents. If double standards are in effect, you can be sure they will notice them and become angry. For example, "How come I've got to make my bed and she doesn't?", "He broke my toy and you didn't do anything", "Why is it that when I do something I get punished and when he does the same thing I am told that I have to be more understanding?" Similarly, the amount of time and energy that the parents spend with the child who has the disabilities may make the other children very jealous. Taking the one kid to special tutoring, special programs, and doctors, leaves little time or energy available for the others. This child demands most of the spare time to be spent on his or her homework, leaving little time for the parents to help the others. So much money may be spent on this child or adolescent that everyone else has to do without or vacations have to be compromised. One can't really blame the siblings for complaining.

Furthermore, these children will undoubtedly have to take some teasing at school. Such comments as "Hey, how's your dummy brother?" or "Your sister sure acts funny . . . she's so gross . . . is she a mental case?" can be heard. Anyone, and especially a child, is embarrassed by such comments and gets angry. Even at home, a normal sibling may not feel safe. Parents insist that they let the child with disabilities who has no friends play with their sibling's friends when they come over, and they act foolish, embarrassing the sibling. Your other children may stop bringing their friends home for fear of what their brother or sister will do. Some will do everything possible to be at a friend's house as much as they can.

Guilt

Sisters and brothers may feel guilty, too, particularly about their anger when the verbal or nonverbal message from their parents is "He can't help it," or "It's not her fault." This is a hard message to swallow for someone who has not yet gained a lot of perspective on life. Or, a brother or sister may secretly think, "I'm glad it's not me," then feel guilt and/or shame for thinking such thoughts.

Acting Out

Because of these feelings of anger or guilt, a brother or sister might *act out* against his or her sibling with the disabilities. They may tease and provoke the child to encourage misbehavior, or they may do something themselves, then set up the child as a scapegoat. They are so frustrated and angry, and they are told that they cannot show their feelings, so they get even in these ways. As the parents punish the child with the problems, the siblings feel revenged. Sometimes normal siblings set up the child with disabilities to look or act bad simply because they think that the worse their sister or brother looks, the better they look.

Covering Up Success

A normal sibling can also negatively affect the child with disabilities. It seems to be the plight of children with handicaps that a younger brother or sister is not only supernormal and delightful but precocious, quickly passing him or her academically and socially. This hurts. Yet, in all fairness to the other children, they must be encouraged to live up to their potential. They deserve encouragement and praise. Do not hold back or minimize praise for fear of hurting your son or daughter who has learning disabilities. They have to learn to cope with reality.

There is no way that you can prevent some or all of these feelings from surfacing in your family. None of your children were born self-denying, altruistic models of charity. Besides, all of these feelings, provided they are kept within limits, are normal and can be handled. The more you are aware of your behavior and the more you try not to have double standards or expect more from your children than they are capable of doing, the less there will be difficulties. The only way to forestall the worst of this anger among your children is by first giving them all of the facts, then letting them know that it is safe and acceptable to discuss with you what they are thinking and feeling, and finally, answering their questions rationally and honestly.

None of this will be easy, but you are their parents too. In Chapter 15, I will suggest ways of handling unacceptable behaviors within the family. If you see that you need help in explaining your situation or if you feel that the family is not functioning well, don't hesitate to ask someone for help.

An Example of Normal Family Reactions: Danny

I first saw Danny for an evaluation at age three. I followed his progress and worked with the family off and on for the next 10 years. I still keep in touch with the parents. Shortly after the initial evaluation, his mother began a diary. Initially she tried to reconstruct her experiences with Danny from the time of his birth. I have interwoven Danny's clinical picture with excerpts from that diary. Mrs. S. writes exceptionally well, often eloquently, but don't mistake this for a fictional account. As she confronts and finally begins to bring the various stages of her despair under control, you will be struck by the truth and validity of her account. Perhaps you will share her tears and pain because you have been there also.

Pregnancy

Mrs. S.'s third pregnancy, after two sons, one four years old, the other two, went without complication. Her comments reflect the anticipation with which both parents greeted this child.

A 3rd son? What a joy, what a delight, such pride for the Father—what pleasure for the only woman—the queen in a household of adoring men. The other 2 are dark-haired and dark-eyed like Mom and Dad. The 3rd is a unique one with his blue eyes and strawberry blond hair. Grandma says he was meant to be a girl. Everyone agrees, "Well, if you had to have a 3rd son, at least he's different." We didn't realize at that time just how different he was.

Danny had the advantage of being the 3rd child. By the time a 3rd is born all of the anxieties implicit in the care and handling of a normal infant have vanished. No more fits of panic when the baby cries unexpectedly. No more wringing of hands at the first sign of a sniffle or loose bowel movement . . . just a placid, cool, nonchalant parent juggling baby on one arm, holding middle brother with the right hand, pulling the wagon laden with sand box toys with the other, calling to the oldest son to look both ways while crossing the street on his bike. The combination of self-confident Mother and animated, stimulating surroundings are calculated to make this 3rd baby so happy, so comfortable, with none of the pressures or tensions that the other 2 had to endure. "They bring themselves up, these 3rd children do. He'll be your easiest," assured our pediatrician.

Delivery and the First Year of Life

Danny's delivery was normal, with no reported difficulties, and his physical examination prior to discharge from the hospital was also normal. Mrs. S. quickly noticed, however, that he was different from the other children—irritable, overactive, unable to focus. Feeding him was a problem, and often accompanied by his vomiting. The pediatrician treated him for colic. Danny also had trouble getting to sleep, and he often slept only three to four hours at a time. Sometimes he cried and thrashed about for 30 minutes to an hour. Holding him did nothing to comfort him. Several other early suggestions of neurological difficulties were present. Danny's skin was overly sensitive to touch, and he persisted with a tonic-neck reflex beyond the early weeks of life (i.e., when his head was turned to the side, the arm on the side he faced pulled up).

Mrs. S. reported that from the start, Danny didn't like her. When she picked him up, he cried; the more she cuddled him the more he cried (the tactile sensitivity). When she turned his head toward her nipple, he pushed her away (the tonic-neck reflex). She felt helpless, inadequate, angry, and guilty. She did not yet understand, so she blamed herself.

> Well then, why did he cry so much? Why did he squirm in your arms as if pleading to be released to the security of his crib? Why the endless bouts of vomiting, before, after, during his meals? Why not the same show of pleasure at being rocked and played with like his brothers? Why no "coos" or "goos" or babbles or giggles? Where was this joyous, relaxed, happy 3rd baby syndrome?

> By the end of Danny's first year of life, I attempted to review all of these statements regarding the easy routine with 3rd baby—the enjoyment I was supposed to be savoring through him—the idea that "he's your last so lap it up" sort of notion.

All I could come up with was a dull ache in the pit of my stomach. Why isn't he fun for me? Why doesn't he return my love? Why no give-and-take between baby and anyone? His constant crying and whining, his discontent and apparent discomfort, convinced me that he must be in some physical distress. That question, along with his persistent vomiting, brought me to the pediatrician who assured me that he was fine. I must relax and learn to loosen up. That along with a little sympathetic support was supposed to reassure me.

But the dull ache in head, heart, and stomach persisted. Why the relief for me at Danny's bedtime? Why the feeling of incompleteness when he was around and the feeling of solidarity and wholeness without him?

My growing conclusion was that there must be something wrong with me to result in this personality conflict. I was perplexed by my feelings of guilt in relation to this child, because if that were my pattern, why wasn't I feeling guilty in relation to my other children? I realized later that my guilt originated from ambivalent feelings toward him—feelings of love and hate, of sympathy and anger, of concern and fear. The insecurity that my relationship to him created inside of me resulted in feelings of self-doubt about my capacity as Mother and in regard to my own emotional stability which had never been in question.

My loneliness while submerged in these feelings was intense. In spite of a good marriage and a loving husband, I was alone. Many of these feelings and observations were not shared by my husband who wasn't with Danny as much as I, who never saw him vis-a-vis his age peers and who by virtue of a very placid, calm nature had a greater capacity to accept a wide diversity of behaviors. Every attempt I made to acquaint him with my concerns was met with assurance that Danny was fine—perhaps a little immature, but fine. The family reminded me that I was older when I had him—perhaps two kids had been enough, all of this being after the fact. All I was left with were doubts, fear, and anger directed toward myself and toward this creature who was the source of all my problems.

In looking back over Danny's first year of life, as well as those of others like him, it is difficult to pinpoint just what impact his neurological disabilities had. Auditory perception disabilities were later diagnosed. What effect did they have on his orienting to sound or on his learning to relate to or attach to his mother? What effect did his auditory figure-ground disability have? Could Danny orient at all to his mother's voice? What must the world be perceived as when being held is experienced as uncomfortable or painful? Mrs. S. describes her frustrations, confusions, and ambivalent feelings toward the developing relationship with her infant son. Could Danny's feelings have been any less troubled?

Years One and Two

Danny's language development was delayed. On top of everything else, he now became frustrated by his inability to communicate his needs. His gross motor development was delayed also, resulting in very slow mastery of sitting, standing, walking, and running. He was hyperactive and distractible. He did not outgrow his tactile sensitivity and became defensive to touch, avoiding too much body contact. Possibly because of these neurological problems, he had trouble dealing with separation. Both parents found handling Danny overwhelmingly difficult. With no information and no reassurance from her pediatrician, Mrs. S. continued to search within herself for an explanation.

> By 13 months of age a lock on his bedroom door was required to keep Danny protected from his own enormous fund of aimless energy which was consistently directed toward destructive pursuits. Perhaps his resentment at being locked in or an increasing hyperactivity was the cause of the extreme havoc he wreaked on his surroundings. Linoleum was lifted up off the floor of his room. Pictures in their frames were torn down from the walls, window shades were replaced because they were ripped up. A rocking chair was used to bang against the wall, thus creating dents in the plasterboard. A harness held him down in his high chair and one was used in the stroller when he was reluctantly wheeled away from his exhausted Mother by an equally reluctant babysitter. And all the time I'm thinking what is wrong with me that I have created this child who I wish I never had.

> The more I disliked him, the more he clung to me, the less able he was to let me go, thus causing horrendous scenes at

my departures, serving to increase my guilt, and self-blame. "When I leave he gets so scared. Therefore, I shouldn't leave. But, if I don't I'll go mad. So, I'll leave but he'll scream and I'll feel so awful." This internal dialogue characterized every separation we were ever to endure.

His constant aimless running resulted in many falls and bruises, the worst of which was a collision with Danny's nose and the dining room table. Sutures were required for that accident, which was followed by several other close calls, all a result of his hyperactivity and poor coordination. Along with this went the assaults by Danny upon anyone who dared get physically close. Once he was seated on my lap I would in a 5-minute period of time receive several blows to my jaw from the unpredictable banging of his head. His frantic squirming discouraged me from holding him or cuddling him. Kicks on knees and in stomach, little hands pushing my face away from his—so many efforts to keep me away—all added up to one conclusion. He doesn't love me and I don't love him and it's my fault and it's unnatural and wrong and I wish I didn't have him and I've ruined my life forever. And yet, there he sat with his sad blue eyes and his confused forlornness. He was as unhappy as I was and I had to find out why.

Year Three

Danny's gross motor problems persisted. He began to develop language, but he often appeared to misunderstand or to respond in ways that made little sense. His parents felt that his thinking was more concrete than his brothers' had been at the same age. He developed fears of unknown places and of new objects. His separation problems persisted. Although toilet trained for bowel functioning by age two-and-a-half, he wet the bed at night (i.e., *nocturnal enuresis*). He started nursery school.

At last Danny was three. A new era was ushered in by his enrollment in a nursery school—relief for Mommy and some friends (please God, some playmates) for Danny. But more importantly, at last some objective feedback from emotionally uninvolved teachers who see normal three-year-old kids all the time. No more would I have to rely upon Dad's calm assurances, upon Grandmother's accusations, upon my own frantic self-inquiry.

Several months passed before the teachers decided that it was time to confront me with reality. Danny was not involved with the other children, they reported. Furthermore, he was tense, frightened, highly distractible, and most of all, very unhappy. It was with mixed feelings that I received this news. On the one hand I was very upset to hear my worst suspicions confirmed. On the other hand I was relieved to hear that someone else saw the same thing—that my sanity and clear vision need not be held in doubt any longer. Most of all, I was grateful for the sense of purpose and motivation that this shared awareness endowed me with.

It was at this point that the parents brought Danny in for consultation. In the course of the evaluation, his pediatrician and a pediatric neurologist, as well as a special education professional and a speech and language therapist saw him. I did the child psychiatric and the family evaluations. The concluding diagnoses included:

1. Specific learning disabilities: auditory perception, sequencing, abstraction, auditory memory, gross motor, and demand language disabilities.
2. Hyperkinetic Reaction of Childhood (the term in use then for what would now be ADHD), manifested by hyperactivity, distractibility, and impulsivity.
3. Sensory Integrative Disorder, manifested by tactile sensitivity and defensiveness.
4. Emotional problems: separation anxiety, fears, poor peer relationships.
5. Family problems: overwhelmed, frustrated, helpless feelings by parents.

Also noted was the perseveration and the bedwetting. This was seen as another reflection of a dysfunctional nervous system.

The following treatment plan was recommended and implemented:

1. Special education and language therapy in a therapeutic nursery school for children with learning and language disabilities.
2. A trial on medication to minimize the hyperactivity and distractibility.

3. Preventive family counseling focused on educating the parents about their child's disabilities and their role in helping.

The medication, Ritalin, significantly decreased the hyperactivity and distractibility. It also stopped the bedwetting. (I have seen this effect of Ritalin with many children and wonder if the bedwetting might be a reflection of the impulsivity. Perhaps, once the impulsivity is treated the bedwetting stops.) The parents learned to use deep touch stimulation when holding Danny, lessening his tactile sensitivity and, thus, his tactile defensiveness. He adapted to the new therapeutic nursery and slowly his language improved. The long process of special education therapy began.

Mrs. S. describes the evaluation and its impact. Her awareness of her feelings and the shift in her ways of handling them reflect the counseling.

It was these feelings that enabled me to have Danny evaluated. He was seen by many specialists, each seeming to focus on one part of his problem. By the end, all the parts came together and presto—a diagnosis—something to grab hold of— something to explain it all and most of all a means, a method, a way to help.

Danny's neurological impairment caused perceptual problems which resulted in learning difficulties, we were told. His restlessness, his dislike for being touched and touching, his chronic unhappiness, and frustration all could be explained by this syndrome. The cause of it was unknown. So who could be blamed? There was a way to help him . . . please tell us how? There is a way to handle him at home that will make him feel good and happy and worthwhile . . . please tell me and I'll try. It will take time but he'll get better . . . or will he??? How great!

So, with all this, I gazed upon my neurologically impaired Danny, lifted my eyes to the heavens and whispered, "Thank you. It's not as serious as I thought. Thank you. There is help available. Thank you. He will in time get better. Thank you, again. You are not a crazy, unlovable, unnatural Mother. Thank you; thank you; thank you!"

But if that's the case, why didn't anyone believe or support me? Why was I kept in this state of anxiety and fear all these years? Where were the experts or even the loved ones? Why didn't they trust me? Why didn't they hear? And so once again I was angry—a state that was becoming second nature to me—descriptive of my mood and personality.

The anger directed itself inward then because it was futile and uneconomical to express it, I became sad, depressed, forlorn. In short, I felt pity for myself. Why did it have to happen to me? What did I do to deserve this? How will I ever find the strength to endure? How can I be a Mother to this poor, defenseless child? Days of brooding were to follow. I was caught up in a grief reaction that was all-consuming. I accused everyone of being unable to understand what I was going through. In a way I was trying to say, "Look how I am hurting. Won't someone take care of me and see how much I am caring?" The only problem with this behavior, I soon determined for myself, was that it accomplished nothing positive nor worthwhile, and, furthermore, it led me to feel unattractive and selfish.

As soon as this awareness surfaced, a new era dawned. Self-indulgence, once completed, paved the way for the realization that Danny and I were going to be involved with one another for many years to come and that I'd better come to terms with his problem and begin to work on it with him so that both of us could be happier than we were. Thus, I allowed myself to become informed by the professionals, comprehending the "whys" and learning the "how-tos." With this knowledge came understanding, and with this understanding came coping, and with this coping came a growing sensitivity toward his positive changes and progress. This encouraged me to continue with renewed courage and with expectations for Danny, based on the reality of the situation.

No longer was there room in my rationale for unproductive self-pity, brooding, or accusations. I realized that the effects of this attitude would result in more problems. Let's then acknowledge that we have a problem. Let's not be afraid to label it, to explore it, to learn about it, to deal with it, and to accept it.

Years Three through Twelve

Although Danny remained in special education programs through the fifth grade, by the fourth grade he was in a regular education program, receiving special education and language therapy one hour a week each. He remained on Ritalin. His parents worked closely with his school programs and his teachers throughout the years. They carefully selected those peer activities and sports that tended to build on his strengths rather than to magnify his weaknesses. Each year brought successes and new challenges. Mrs. S. reflected on these experiences:

> But, does acceptance defend a Mother against uncomfortable feelings? Does she ever adjust to the situation and simply continue her day-to-day existence, giving minimal thought or worry to this part of her life? The answer for this Mother is a resounding NO!
>
> The process of adjustment is an ongoing one. On his bad days I feel bad. Back creeps the old sense of fear and foreboding. On good days I feel hopeful and perhaps a trifle excited at the glimpse of health and wholeness I see under the surface. On most days I feel the responsibility of another day. I decided that I will try to begin at his beginnings—to love him, to accept him right where he's at. I realize I must plan according to his needs at that moment and with this comes the task of ignoring some of my own. No one can do that without feeling some anger.
>
> And what about the feelings of deprivation when you see how poorly he measures up to his age group, and, as he grows older, how poorly he stands in relation to children even younger than he? What of the feelings you get when you see him rejected by children and adults alike because he can't relate in the expected, conformist manner? What of the embarrassment you feel when his problems result in antisocial behavior in public? What kind of excuses do you force yourself to fabricate to ease your self-consciousness? What do you say to family when they assure you that all he needs is some discipline and he'll fall into line? The disruption he causes in the tempo of family life—the interference with certain pleasures arouses anger, deprivation, and guilt. And how about the emptiness in your gut when you catch a glimpse of his inner world of confusion and loneliness? How does that make you feel?
>
> With all of these feelings resurfacing with every new situation, how can one ever expect to be adjusted? The only answer I

have found is to make room for the feelings, to accept them—not to luxuriate in them, but not to deny them . . . to say them out loud to yourself or to whoever is unafraid to hear them. This paves the way for a stronger, more positive relationship with Danny.

The way I relate to Danny becomes reflected in the way he sees himself. If I allow his problems to scare me, he too becomes scared. Communicating to him that he is worthwhile and loveable and that I have hopes for him enables him to face his future with hope and courage. This places a great responsibility on me, but it is the only chance any of us have for a good life. If we have hope for Danny, he will have hope for himself.

I still wish I had three perfect sons. I occasionally indulge in that "wouldn't it be lovely" fantasy. I have come to treasure in the other two what many people take for granted. I have a great investment in them but I do in Danny too. It is an investment imbued by the implicit faith I have encouraged myself to have in him and in me. It will take a long time and it will be difficult, but I have hope that it will work.

Current Progress Note

When the first edition of this book was written, Danny was in the eighth grade. Academically he was doing well. His peer relationships were limited and best handled one at a time. He related well to his parents and brothers but was described as "a little aloof" with others. He continued to need the medication. His psychological functioning was age appropriate.

As I prepared the second edition, I called Danny's mother. He is about to enter his senior year at an excellent college. Academically he is doing very well and has a B-plus average. He has learned to be very organized and efficient. His major is music. Danny's mother reflected that music had always been his "salvation." He is good and can escape into playing for hours at a time. At this time, he plays the keyboard, composes, and records his music. He is well-respected as a musician.

He still has social difficulties. He has friends, but no special friend. He has girls who are friends, but he has never had a girlfriend. He still does not have a good sense of humor and, although much improved, he does not pick up many social cues. Yet, he has completed three years of college and is comfortable.

She ended our conversation by saying, "He's a real sweetheart, a lovely person. Yet, he is never going to be perfect . . . I hope he will not be a lonely person." Although she agreed that he had accomplished far more than any of us dared to wish for when he was three, four, or five, the worry about the future never ends.

PART THREE

Diagnosis

10

The Evaluation Process

AS I HAVE STRESSED throughout this book, the child or adolescent we are discussing has a group of problems that often are found together: learning disabilities, Attention-Deficit Hyperactivity Disorder (ADHD), other neurological problems, plus secondary social, emotional, and family problems. Thus, to evaluate this person fully, a team effort is required. This team might work in a medical setting, in a mental health facility, as part of your educational system, or in a private practice model. Your family physician might be part of this team, might be the one who requests the evaluation, or might have nothing to do with the evaluation.

It is difficult for one person to evaluate your son or daughter and clarify the areas of difficulty. Before you initiate an evaluation or agree that the school can do the studies, you need to know at least two things: (1) who will see my child or adolescent, and what will he or she do; and, (2) who will coordinate the evaluation, integrate the findings, and present them to me?

Most often, the school becomes concerned and initiates an evaluation. Ideally, the school special education team will collect information from parents, family physician, and anyone else who has worked with or known your child. Be forewarned that you may have to push assertively for the necessary studies, then work hard to be sure that each person involved communicates with each other. Don't let each person send you a report, expecting you to understand the results and to integrate the information from each professional. One hopes that all will interact. If they do not, however, you must insist that they come together to form a working team.

I hope we have passed the time when children who do not succeed in school are routinely kept back. Repeating a grade may be appropriate for some children, but it should not be implemented until enough studies have been done to understand why a child is not learning. A child with a learning disability who is kept back, but who gets no additional help the second time through the grade, may do no better during the repeated year. Do not let the authorities at your school force your child to repeat a grade unless they have done an evaluation to show why the difficulties have occurred and how a repeated year will help. Don't casually accept such comments as "immature" or "needs another year to grow." Unless they know why your child did so poorly and have specific rationale for such an action, think before you respond. If your child is immature and under-achieving and you agree to repeating the year, press for him or her to receive special education services during the repeated year.

I would like to discuss where to go to get an evaluation, who should be involved in doing it, and what you should expect from it. Such efforts might be with your public school, a private organization, or a group of private practitioners. I shall also suggest ways to prepare your child or adolescent for such an evaluation. In Chapter 11, I will go into more detail about the specific studies done by each evaluator and show you how to understand the findings.

Where to Go to Get the Evaluation

Your first option should be your school system. If you are in the public school, you are entitled to a free assessment. If you are in a private school, your public school is required under law to provide a free assessment. Your first step is to talk to the principal. If you are in a private school, talk to the principal of the public school your child would have attended. In most public schools, the principal initiates bringing in the special education diagnostic team to evaluate students in need. If the principal disagrees or refuses to forward the request, seek guidance from a consultant, perhaps a special education person in private practice. You can appeal above the principal, but you need to know how to do this in your school system.

If you want to have a private evaluation, find out who to

contact by discussing your concerns with your family doctor, with other parents, or with members of parent organizations (see Appendix at the back of the book). In many communities, there are private diagnostic services that have the full complement of professionals that are needed to do the evaluation.

The Evaluation Process

An evaluation should have three parts: the planning, the assessment (i.e., testing, observing, interviewing), and the interpretation of the findings. First, of course, the parents should know who will see their child or adolescent and why. The child must also know why he or she is being evaluated and what to expect during the testing. When the planning phase begins, the team members or primary coordinator should decide what questions need to be asked and who should try to answer them. For example, why is this child not mastering reading? Why is she or he so distractible with a short attention span? Why does he or she get into so much trouble in school?

During the evaluating phase, several different people see your child or adolescent to conduct formal studies. One person may observe him or her in school and/or get information from the classroom teachers. Someone will meet with the parents to inquire into past medical, developmental, and psychosocial information and to explore the current problems in school and at home. Other specialists (itemized below) will also observe and test the person. Finally, the information and impressions that result from these multiple studies must be pulled together and synthesized. The questions must be answered. One person may share these conclusions and recommendations in an interpretive session with the parents or each specialist may summarize their findings. Later I will describe the way I prefer these interpretive sessions to be conducted.

Several professionals are involved in the team evaluation. An educator with a graduate degree in special education, preferably in the area of learning disabilities—the *special educator*— will evaluate your son or daughter to determine if learning disabilities exist, and, if so, in what areas. (These studies are done by doctorate-level psychologist in some states.) This person also explores learning strengths and approaches for intervention in problem areas. These studies determine your child's or adolescent's performance level in certain skill areas like reading or math.

If these studies show difficulties in the auditory perception and language areas a *speech and language pathologist (or therapist)* may do additional studies to clarify these difficulties and to explore possible treatment approaches. If the special educator's studies suggest difficulties in the gross and/or fine motor areas, an *occupational therapist* may do further studies and suggest other interventions.

A doctorate-level psychologist (*clinical psychologist, school psychologist*) evaluates and studies the child or adolescent to clarify several issues. Does he or she show evidence of an emotional problem? If so, what is it? What is his or her level of intellectual functioning? What are her or his approaches to organizing, thinking, and problem-solving (often referred to as *cognitive style*)? Often, the results of these tests do not provide a true reading of your child's abilities. The learning disabilities or ADHD interferes with certain test performances and, thus, may lower the scores. Once the psychologist takes this into account, however, the test results do tell us where the child currently is functioning and what his or her potential might be.

Sometimes a neuropsychologist is asked to participate in the evaluation. Neuropsychological studies explore the same areas as the clinical psychological evaluation but with more focus on brain function and dysfunction than on educational strengths or weaknesses.

A *physician* should do a complete physical examination. In some instances a *neurologist* or *pediatric (developmental) neurologist* may examine the child or adolescent. A brain-wave test (i.e., electroencephalogram or EEG) or other diagnostic studies may be done. These studies should not be done routinely. Usually they are done only if there is a history of or suggestion of a seizure disorder or if there is another specific concern. If a hearing problem is suspected, an *audiologist* and/or a physician specializing in ear, nose, and throat disorders—an *ENT specialist* or *otolaryngologist*—may be called in. If a visual problem is suspected, an *optometrist* or a physician specializing in eye diseases—an *ophthalmologist,* may participate.

The mental health professional who sees your child or adolescent may be determined by who is available within the system doing the assessment or by the suspected problems. Your son or daughter might be seen by a *school counselor, social worker, psychologist, psychiatric nurse, general psychiatrist,* or a psychiatrist who is specially trained to evaluate and treat children and adolescents—a *child and adolescent psychiatrist.* This specialist assesses the person's level of psychological and social functioning as well as explores for evidence of emotional conflicts, stresses, or disorders. This person may not be the same mental health professional who meets with the parents or the family to explore past history and current concerns.

The special additional issues involved in diagnosing ADHD will be discussed in Chapter 12. At times, other special studies might be used.

Ideally, the full team then meets to discuss their findings, to establish a clinical impression or diagnosis, and to develop a treatment plan. One or more members of this team should meet with the parents to share the findings. Later, someone should meet with the child or adolescent. Ideally, someone should meet with the family to explain the findings and recommendations.

As parents, you must be sure that you understand all of the findings, and you must be comfortable with the recommendations. At a minimum you should have clear answers to the following questions:

1. Does my child have learning disabilities? If yes:
    ~ What are his or her learning disabilities?
    ~ What are his or her learning strengths?
    ~ How far behind is he or she and in which areas?
    ~ What plans do you have for helping?

2. Does my child have ADHD? If yes:
    ~ Why do you feel he or she has this disability?
    ~ Who will direct the treatment?
    ~ If medications are recommended, who will work with us to understand this approach to treatment? (The issue of medication will be discussed in detail in Chapter 15.)

3. Does my child or adolescent have emotional or social problems? If yes, what are they?
    ~ Why do you think they exist? (Be sure that the professionals are distinguishing between emotional and social problems that cause academic difficulties and emotional and social problems that are a consequence of academic difficulties.)

~ What do you recommend we do about these problems?

4. Do we have family problems? If yes:
   ~ What are they?
   ~ What do you suggest we do? (If no one sees the effect of the problems on the marriage, siblings, or general family functioning, say so now and ask for help. If doing so would be uncomfortable in front of the people present, seek out someone later and discuss this.)

5. Who will coordinate all of these recommended actions and who will be sure that everyone involved communicates with each other? (If no one is named, pick someone yourself and ask if he or she will accept this role.)

6. How will we assess progress and when should we meet again to look at the progress and to plan ahead? (Don't leave with a vague answer. Try to set a general time; for example, we will meet again in 60 days.)

Preparing Your Child or Adolescent for the Evaluation

When an evaluation is in order, your son or daughter must know why it is being conducted, who he or she will see, and what will be done. Be as honest and direct as possible. You might say, for example, "You have been struggling in school. I know you want to do well. We are having these studies done to try to understand why you are having so much difficulty and what we can do to help." By doing this, you are saying that you understand his or her frustration and unhappiness, that you share these feelings, that you want to understand why the problems exist, and that something can be done to correct the problems and make things better. The words you choose to get this across will depend on your son's or daughter's age and your style of relating to him or her, but the message should not vary: We care about you. You are hurting. We must do something to help. There is help and hope.

If possible, make a list of each person who will see your child or adolescent. Identify who each is and what each will do. If you do not know these answers, find out. You might explain:

Educational testing : This is not like a school test. There may not be right or wrong answers. The test will help us understand how you learn best and where you have trouble learning. The results will help us plan a way to help you if you do have learning problems. There is a characteristic of these studies that needs to be explained. In order to find out where your son or daughter is performing in different skill areas, it is necessary to present successively more difficult tasks until he or she fails three consecutive questions or tasks. Explain this concept and stress that he or she should not get upset or discouraged if it appears that he or she is making lots of errors. Explain that the tests are designed to have this happen.

Psychological testing: The psychologist will talk with you and do different tests. These tests will help us understand how you learn and how you solve learning and life problems. Yes, an IQ test may be done to help us understand why you might be having difficulties. Stress that no one thinks he or she is dumb or mentally retarded. We know he or she is smart. The test is needed as part of learning how he or she learns.

Mental Health evaluation: No formal tests will be done. A person will talk with you. You might play with games or toys while talking (for younger children). He or she knows about learning difficulties and about the worries and problems people can have when they are not doing well in school. Add that you do not think he or she is crazy. However, you see that he or she is frustrated and unhappy and this specialist can help the family learn what can be done to help. If the professional is a physician—for example, a child and adolescent psychiatrist—and your child is young, you might want to reassure that unlike the family doctor, this doctor will not give shots.

Special tests: If special studies are to be done, like brain-wave studies, ask the person who will be doing them to help you explain what will happen and why the studies are to be done.

Never surprise your son or daughter by keeping him or her in the dark or by tricking him or her into seeing someone. Your youngster has a right to know what is going on and why. If he or she refuses to participate in any part of the evaluation, ask a member of the team or the person he or she is upset about seeing how to handle this resistance.

I remember arranging for an evaluation for a 16-year-old girl who had struggled in school all of her life. She was sent to see me because of behavioral problems. I suspected learning disabilities. She refused to take the tests. Finally, she agreed to do all of the studies except the IQ test. It took several sessions of work with her before she was able to put into words her fears. "All of my life I have feared that I was retarded. I believe my parents kept telling me I'm smart because what kind of parents would tell their child the truth if she was retarded. Now I feel almost safe because I know it is just a fear. If I take *that* test and find out that I *really* am retarded I could not live with myself. I would kill myself." She was finally able to handle her fears and take the test. I made special arrangements. She could not tolerate waiting weeks to get the results. What we worked out was that she came to my office first. I walked her to her car so that she could drive to the psychologist. We planned in advance for her to return to my office as soon as the testing was done. The psychologist agreed to score the test immediately and to call me. By the time she got to my office I was able to give her the results. She was of superior intelligence but had strong suggestive evidence of significant learning disabilities.

After the Evaluation

Once you, the parents, understand the results and recommendations, you should see to it that the person who was evaluated also knows what they are. If you feel capable of sharing this information yourself, you might try it. Preferably, however, one of the professionals who participated in the evaluation should meet with this child or adolescent and review the findings and recommendations. I have made this point so many times that you might accuse me of being redundant. But, I cannot stress too much how critical it is for the person with the disability to understand himself or herself.

At some point the rest of the family should be fully informed. Sisters, brothers, grandparents, aunts, and uncles will want to know what the results show and what will be done to help.

I cannot overemphasize that the evaluation is only a start. You must follow up on every recommendation to make sure that everything agreed upon continues to be done. Even when the school has done the evaluation and started a program, you must monitor it to see that everything that was agreed upon is offered and conducted. Frequent contact is needed and usually you must initiate it.

You must also be sure that everyone involved in the treatment process communicates with each other. The regular classroom teacher must know what the special education teacher is doing. The doctor prescribing medication for the ADHD must get feedback from you and the school. And don't forget to talk about all of this with your son or daughter. How do they feel things are going? Is the help useful? Their opinions are critical and they must feel that they are respected and part of the process.

If things do not get better or if they get worse, talk to the teacher or special educator. When a school year comes to an end, request a meeting to review progress and to make plans for the next year.

Being a constant advocate is hard work. You cannot rest. No one can be as motivated and concerned as you, the parents. Your task is not only essential, it is unavoidable.

11

The Evaluation Procedures

NOW THAT WE HAVE LOOKED at the evaluation as a process, I would like to review each part of this process, focusing on particular types of studies and tests that are conducted. The more you know about these procedures, the more intelligent a consumer you can become. You cannot afford to sit through meetings with professionals while they speak in their professional tongue and be lost. You must know the information that allows you to be an informed consumer.

Hopefully, your knowledge will be used to help you better understand your son or daughter and how to help. At times, this knowledge might prevent a professional from misdiagnosing your child. Or, at the least, it is your way of communicating that you are knowledgeable and that you will not accept everything said just because it is said. You do not have to become a professional; however, you can learn enough to be intelligent about that profession. Let me illustrate. A psychologist reports to you, "Your son has an IQ of 106 and he is about at grade level. I do not know why you are so concerned." Having read the reports, you reply, "But, his Verbal IQ is 128 and his Performance IQ is 97 and the subtest scatter is from 7 to 15. How do you explain this? Yes, his Full Scale IQ is 106, but doesn't this suggest that he has a learning disability?" You are not letting someone reach an incorrect conclusion. And, you are saying that you are an informed consumer and an assertive advocate for your child and you want answers and help.

In the first edition of this book I listed specific tests in each category. I found that some tests stopped being used and some tests were revised. In addition, each year a new test came out.

My list was quickly out of date. In this edition, I will list the more traditional tests. If your son or daughter is to have a test you do not know about, ask questions. What does it measure? How are the results given? What do the results mean?

The Psychoeducational Evaluation

The primary purpose of the psychoeducational evaluation is to identify your son's or daughter's areas of learning strength and any learning weaknesses or disabilities. The major goal of such testing is to bring to light what can and should be done to intervene in these areas of weakness and disabilities and to establish a special school program that can help the child to overcome, compensate, and/or accommodate for these difficulties.

The studies might be done by a special educator, psychologist, or both. In general, there are three areas that are assessed:

1. Intelligence
2. Achievement levels in school skill areas
3. Specific areas of learning strengths and weaknesses

Intelligence

The first task is to assess a child's potential for learning. The IQ test used to accomplish this may be given by a trained special educator or psychologist. These studies have been very politicized in certain states. Specific IQ tests have been banned in certain states. Alternative assessments may be used.

The two most frequently given tests of intellectual ability are the Stanford-Binet and the Wechsler Intelligence tests. The Wechsler tests come in three different units: the Wechsler Pre-School and Primary Scale of Intelligence (WPPSI), the Wechsler Intelligence Scale for Children (WISC), and the Wechsler Adult Intelligence Scale (WAIS). Several screening tests are also used to determine who might need more extensive studies. Each is timed so that a standardized score for the person's age can be determined.

1. *The Stanford-Binet Intelligence Scale* is for age two to adulthood. It emphasizes verbal responses more than nonverbal. Thus, if a child was tested on the Stanford-Binet Scale when he or she was a preschooler, then on the Wechsler scale several years later, the two IQ scores may not be comparable.

Your child might appear to have dropped in IQ, especially if there are motor problems.

2. *The Wechsler Pre-School and Primary Scale of Intelligence* is for ages four to six-and-a-half and measures verbal and nonverbal reasoning and perceptual motor abilities.

3. *The Wechsler Intelligence Scale for Children* is for ages 6 through 16 and measures general intelligence. Five parts measure verbal abilities and five parts measure nonverbal, or performance abilities. These two scores are combined to produce a full-scale score.

4. *The Wechsler Adult Intelligence Scale* tests verbal and nonverbal intelligence of adults aged 16 and over. If your adolescent is 16 to 18 and in high school, this test must be conducted. Thus, he or she is scored based on adult standards. Sometimes it is helpful if the psychologist also scores the results by specific age.

These intellectual assessment tests provide more than an IQ score. Equally important, the results assist in the diagnostic process. Children and adolescents with learning disabilities will do well on the parts of the test that utilize their areas of strengths, but do poorly on the parts that touch their areas of disabilities. When the differences in the separate subtest scores (called *subtest scatter*) are compared with the rest of the results of the educational evaluation, the picture of the learning disabilities and the reasons for poor classroom performances become clearer. For people with learning disabilities, the IQ test in isolation cannot be used. The scores simply do not truly measure intelligence. The subtest scores do, however, help to identify areas of weakness and do suggest intellectual potential.

The Wechsler Intelligence Scale for Children (WISC) is used so frequently, and the subtest results can provide such meaningful information, that we should look at this test in more detail.

The WISC has a *verbal* and a *performance*, or nonverbal, part. Each part has five basic subtests:

WISC Verbal Scale
~ Information test
~ Comprehension test
~ Similarities test
~ Arithmetic test

~ Vocabulary test
~ (A Digit-Span test can be used)
WISC Performance Scale
~ Picture Arrangement test
~ Picture Completion test
~ Block Design test
~ Object Assembly test
~ Coding test
~ (A Maze test can also be used)

Each subtest measures a different intellectual function or *cognitive style*. Each score is based on the expected normal performance for a person of similar age. Each area of function, and therefore each score, can be affected by learning disabilities or ADHD, as described below.

Information (verbal). This subtest measures the amount of general knowledge a person has acquired both in school and as a result of life experiences in the family and elsewhere. Children with learning disabilities who do poorly in school have picked up a lot of general information in the classroom and outside of school and may do well on this subtest.

Comprehension (verbal). This subtest measures abstract thinking and one's ability to comprehend concepts. It may measure basic native intelligence that is separate from learned knowledge.

Similarities (verbal). This subtest measures abstract thinking by asking how things are alike or different. This test, like comprehension, may measure basic intelligence separate from learned knowledge.

Arithmetic (verbal). This subtest measures one's numerical reasoning ability by using verbal problems; that is, story problems written out in words. The expected level of performance is based on grade-level knowledge. Thus, if a child is behind in math (or, because of being in special education classes has not had the same level of math as others), the score on this subtest will be influenced.

Vocabulary (verbal). This subtest requires a child to define or explain the words given. It measures general exposure to vocabulary as well as to words learned in school.

Digit-Span (verbal). This subtest requires a child to remember a series of numbers. For example, "I am going to give you three numbers. I want you to wait until I tell you to answer and then give them back to me." Later, "I am now going to give you three numbers. When I tell you to, give them back to me in reverse order." Thus, this subtest measures auditory short-term memory.

REMEMBER: If your son or daughter has any language disabilities, the scores on these verbal subtests might be influenced because he or she did not understand the instructions or could not express the answers. If he or she has auditory distractibility, the scores on these tests might be influenced because he or she may have had difficulty attending and staying on a task.

Picture Completion (performance). This subtest requires the ability to analyze a total picture and to identify what is missing. The child has to find the missing part and identify it or place it into the total picture. Thus, this subtest measures the ability to look at a whole concept and break it down into its parts.

Picture Arrangement (performance). This subtest requires the ability to pick up social clues in order to help place a series of pictures in their proper sequence of events. For example, there might be four pictures like a cartoon strip. If placed in the proper order, they would show one picture of someone walking up to a car; one of this person getting into the car; one of this person starting the motor; and then one of this person driving away. The pictures are mixed up on the table. The child must understand the social context to respond correctly. Thus, the subtest measures the ability to place parts of information into a whole concept, using social cues.

Block Design (performance). With a set of blocks available, the child must look at a picture of a design, then put the blocks together to make that design. The child must analyze the whole complex picture, then break down the pattern into its parts so as to know which blocks to use to reconstruct the pattern. The subtest measures, in part, the ability to break a concept down into its parts and then to rebuild the concept.

Object Assembly (performance). This subtest presents the parts of an object (e.g., a person) that the child must put together. This calls for abilities opposite to those needed for picture completion or block design. Here the parts must be analyzed and then put into a whole concept.

Coding (performance) A code is given (e.g., 2 = *), then a sequence is given. The child must use the code to decode the sequence. For example, the alphabet might be listed. Next to each letter is a symbol. Then, a message is written using the symbols. The message must be decoded. Since this subtest is timed and the better one can remember the code the faster he or she can go, it measures visual short-term memory.

REMEMBER: If your son or daughter has visual perception, sequencing, organization, visual-motor, or motor disabilities, he or she may do poorly on some of these subtests. If he or she has visual or auditory distractibility, the subtest performance may be affected.

Each subtest requires different abilities and accomplishments. Some require auditory skills and others require verbal skills. Some require basic knowledge and others require acquired knowledge. This acquired knowledge might be learned in or out of school. Some tests require short-term memory, sequencing, integration, or abstraction ability. Some require language skills or visual-motor, gross motor, or fine motor skills.

Children with learning disabilities may do well on those subtests where their problems do not interfere, and their scores in these areas should suggest their intellectual potential. They usually do not do as well on those subtests that demand performance in their area of disability. These scores, perhaps, best reflect how the child is performing in the classroom.

ADHD can affect the child's scores. If the child is hyperactive, he or she might do less well on the performance tests that require concentrated motor coordination. If he or she is distractible, the test results might reflect more the inability to focus and stay on a task than true ability. If he or she is impulsive, the first answer that occurs might be said or used. Planning ahead, such as with the blocks, might be difficult.

For example, suppose 12-year-old Tom has good auditory perception, auditory sequencing/abstraction/organization, auditory memory, and expressive language skills. However, Tom also has visual perception, visual sequencing/abstraction/organization, visual memory, fine motor, and visual-motor disabilities. He has been in special education classes. His WISC scores might be:

Verbal IQ	128
Performance IQ	88
Full Scale IQ	108

To say that Tom is of average intelligence (i.e., an IQ of 108) is misleading and incorrect. What can be said, perhaps, is that he shows evidence of superior intelligence based on subtest scores where he had no disabilities (verbal). He is bright, but frustrated in school because of his disabilities. In most school efforts requiring visual and motor skills, he probably performs at a below average level.

Let me go through Tom's test results to illustrate how to understand the scores. The numbers in the middle column below are his subtest scores. These scores are based on charts standardized by age. In general, a score of 10 is average.

Test	*Score*	*Possible Meaning*
Verbal Tests		These are in areas of his learning strengths.
Information	14	Suggests a child of superior intelligence who is learning through school and general life experiences.
Similarities	15	Suggests a child of superior intelligence with good reasoning and abstraction abilities.
Arithmetic	9	Suggests that the level of math learned in special education programs was not at the expected (sixth grade) level.
Vocabulary	17	Suggests a child of superior intelligence who is learning through school and general life experiences.

Test	*Score*	*Possible Meaning*
Comprehension	13	Suggests a child of high-average to superior intelligence.

His Verbal IQ score is 128, in the superior range. Yet, note his lower math score, probably because of his learning disabilities and his being in a special education class. This score of 9 is averaged with the others in establishing his Verbal IQ; thus, his true verbal intelligence is probably higher than 128.

Now, lets look at Tom's performance scores.

Test	Score	Possible Meaning
Performance Tests		These are in areas of his learning weaknesses.
Picture Completion	8	Probably his visual perception and visual-motor disabilities interfered with this task. He scores in the low-average range.
Picture Arrangement	10	This is an average score; yet, for a boy of his superior ability, it would be seen as underperformance. Probably his visual perception and sequencing problems interfered with performance.
Block Design	7	This low-average to borderline score probably reflects his visual perception, visual memory, and visual-motor disabilities plus his anxiety with timed tests.
Object Assembly	10	This is an average score but an underperformance for him. The same learning disabilities probably interfered.
Coding	3	The anxiety plus his visual perception, visual memory, and visual-motor disabilities combined to result in a performance that would be scored in the retarded range.

His performance IQ scores at 88, the low-average range. Perhaps this score reflects his level of performance in the classroom with timed and written tests and reading requirements. It in no way reflects his level of intelligence.

The Full Scale IQ scores at 108 or average. In no way does this truly reflect his intelligence.

These scores suggest a boy of superior intellectual ability who has learning disabilities that interfere with certain test performances, resulting in lower scores on some subtests. These lower scores suggest the types of problems he might have in school. The difference between his intellectual ability and his school performance may explain his frustrations and poor self-image.

Never let someone give you only an "IQ score." You must look at the full test and the scores on each subtest. To say that Tom was of average intelligence (IQ 108) would be inaccurate. For the school to design an appropriate program for him based on the average IQ rather than based on his superior IQ potential would be equally wrong. Only a full understanding of all the test results and their meaning can lead to a proper interpretation and to appropriate program planning.

Achievement Levels

Once the intellectual assessment is measured, it is necessary to compare this with the true performance to see if the student is achieving or underachieving. Standardized achievement tests are given by the special education person to measure where the child or adolescent is performing in different academic skill areas. The results may be presented either in terms of grade-level performance or in terms of percentile level for one's age. Percentile levels compare your child's performance to all other children in his or her grade or to his or her age. If one performs at the 75th percentile, for example, it would mean that 25 percent of children in his or her grade (or age) would perform better than he or she does.

It is important to understand the difference between the demands of these tests and the demands of the real classroom. Some children or adolescents will do well on a reading comprehension test that requires them to read a paragraph and then to respond to verbal or written questions. However, in the real world where they have to read pages and pages of material, their level of comprehension might be very much lower. The same might be true with arithmetic. The student might be able to do well on the test because the demand is for the answer and he or she can do it in his or her head. But, in the classroom the child must write out each step and show how he or she got the answer. Here, the child's visual perception, visual sequencing, visual short-term memory, or written language disabilities might interfere.

In general, these tests measure four areas of achievement:

Reading: Reading tasks measure the ability to decode familiar and new words as well as nonsense words. Next, there is an assessment of reading comprehension. Finally, there might be an assessment of the ability to use the information obtained in the written task.

Writing: Writing tasks measure the ability to write (i.e., form, space, print versus cursive). Next, there is an assessment of spelling, grammar, punctuation, use of capitals, and quality of language (i.e., syntax).

Math: Math tasks measure basic math knowledge as well as knowledge of math skills for each grade level. There might be an assessment of the child's ability to apply math skills to new tasks.

General Knowledge: These tasks measure level of general knowledge acquired for each grade level.

Let me briefly describe the most popular tests used today. As I noted at the beginning of this chapter, your son or daughter might be given other, perhaps newer, tests.

Metropolitan Achievement Tests. Used for grades one through eight, this test is given to a group of children at the same time. It assesses levels of achievement in a wide range of language and arithmetic skills. Because it is given in a group setting, ADHD can affect the results.

Peabody Individual Achievement Test. This test is used for ages five to adulthood to measure general academic achievement in reading mechanics and comprehension, spelling, math, and general knowledge.

Stanford Diagnostic Achievement Tests. Used for grades 1 through 12 to assess mathematics and reading skills, this test also provides instructional objectives and suggestions for teaching.

Wide-Range Achievement Tests. Used from kindergarten through college, this test covers oral reading, spelling, and arithmetic computation. Scores are by grade level for each skill.

Woodcock-Johnson Psychoeducational Battery—Tests of Academic Achievement and Interest. Used from pre-school through adult level to measure achievement in reading, math, written language, and general knowledge, these tests also assess the level of academic versus nonacademic accomplishments.

Specific achievement tests relating to reading, spelling, writing, written language, arithmetic, and oral language are available. The results of these tests may be expressed as a grade equivalent or as a percentile ranking. These tests are also used to assess strengths and weaknesses in order to plan remedial instruction.

Specific Diagnostic Test for Learning Disabilities

If a discrepancy exists between a person's intellectual ability and his or her performance level, one must find out why. Several broad-based tests assess each aspect of learning, looking for input, integration, memory, and output abilities and disabilities. Each school system has its own preferred or required battery of such tests; thus, I will not try to discuss any specific one.

If these diagnostic tests show areas of disability, further studies might be done to focus in more detail on a specific area of disability. There are tests to assess auditory perception, visual perception, visual-motor integration, memory, expressive language, and motor (written language) skills.

The completed evaluation should clarify the areas of learning disabilities as well as the areas of learning ability. The results should lead to recommendations for the appropriate academic program, including the type of program and the specific services that are needed.

It is important to understand the difference between the diagnosis of a learning disability and a school system concluding that a particular person is "eligible for services." In the public school system, a child or adolescent could be found to have a learning disability but still not be eligible for services. Eligibility is based on the concept of *discrepancy;* that is, the extent that the individual is behind for his or her age and grade. Each school system has its own criteria for how far behind someone must be to be eligible for services. This concept will be discussed in Chapter 19, on legal issues.

The Mental Status Evaluation

The mental status evaluation is done by a mental health professional who is trained to work with children and adolescents. The assessment should focus on several levels of psychological functioning and on the interrelationships among them.

The *intrapsychic* assessment notes the issues of emotional conflicts that are faced by the child or adolescent and the coping techniques (defense mechanisms) that he or she has called into play in order to deal with them. The clinician will note whether the areas of concern and conflict as well as the behaviors are age-appropriate or not.

The *interpersonal* assessment focuses on the child's or adolescent's styles of interacting with parents and other adults and with siblings and peers. Conclusions will tell whether these styles of interacting are positive or negative, helpful or not helpful, successful or not successful.

The *behavioral* assessment tries to clarify which behaviors the child is using because they have become learned patterns of behavior through selective rewards (reinforcement) or nonrewards by the parents or others, or because they have been modeled for the child by others.

The *systems* assessment focuses on the child's or adolescent's roles in the family as well as in other important systems—the school or the neighborhood. The clinician determines how the roles that the child plays in one system influence or interact with the roles he or she plays in other systems. Are the behaviors that are observed in school a reflection of family stress or a cause that contributes to family stress?

These mental status evaluations might take place in the mental health professional's office with the child, the parents, and/or the family. If direct observation of the school experiences is not possible, teachers' reports will be reviewed.

If, at the end of the evaluation, the clinician concludes that the child has social, emotional, and/or family difficulties, the next clarifying step is to determine if these problems are caused by or made worse by the learning disabilities and/or ADHD. If the problems are due to frustrations, failures, and school stress, no treatment should be started until the necessary special education programs are in place or, if present, the ADHD is treated.

These social, emotional, or family problems may have started as a consequence of learning disabilities and/or ADHD. If they now seem so ingrained that they have a life of their own, the clinician may recommend individual, group, behavioral, or family therapy, or some combination of these. I will cover these treatments in more detail in Chapter 15.

The Medical Evaluation

Your family physician must make sure that your son or daughter has no physical difficulties. Other professionals will examine him or her if any hearing, vision, eye muscle imbalance, or other difficulty is suspected. A neurological evaluation may be requested if there is a specific concern or if your school system requires such an evaluation.

If the history or observational information suggest that a seizure has occurred or a seizure disorder is suspected, a full neurological evaluation is done. Several types of seizures are possible. *Grand mal* seizures (generally called *epilepsy*) are characterized by major convulsions, with intermittent spasms of all body muscles, followed by a jerking motion of these muscles. After the seizure, the child is asleep or lethargic. When he or she wakes up, the child is confused, disoriented, and has no memory of the event. During a grand mal seizure some people lose bladder or bowel control. Many report a brief sensory experience, or "aura," prior to the seizure. *Petit mal* seizures are brief attacks, with momentary loss of consciousness often associated with symmetrical jerking movements of the eyelids or some other part of the body. Sometimes no muscle activity occurs, just the brief loss of consciousness. He or she probably will not fall over or fall down. Once the episode ends, the child is alert and has no memory loss except for the short span of the seizure. *Psychomotor* seizures are accompanied by attacks of a wide variety of confused behaviors. Explosive, aggressive actions may occur. The sufferer is confused and disoriented after the episode. A child might have a *focal* seizure, which is characterized by convulsions confined to a single limb or muscle group, or to a specific type of sensory disturbance.

After the Evaluation: A Final Note

Once again, let me stress that you must learn everything you can about the evaluation. And, you must share these facts with your son or daughter as well as with the rest of the family.

Of equal importance, insist on a written report of each evaluation as well as a summary report of the findings and recommendations. Read each report and be sure that you understand what is written. If you find something written that is different from what was said verbally, question the professional. Be assertive. You must understand the information.

Keep a file of all evaluations that are made. Keep notes of each meeting. This information will be useful in the future, should further evaluations be needed.

12

Evaluation
for ADHD

AT THIS TIME THERE ARE no formal tests to establish the diagnosis of Attention-Deficit Hyperactivity Disorder (ADHD). There are no specific physical findings or blood, urine, brain imaging, electroencephalographic, or neurological findings that establish the diagnosis. There are excellent rating scales that can identify if the child or adolescent is hyperactive, distractible, and/or impulsive; however, these rating scales may not differentiate between ADHD and other possible causes for these behaviors. The best diagnostic technique is the clinical history. This clinical history must include observational data from the school and the family.

As discussed in Chapter 5, there are many possible causes of hyperactivity, distractibility, and/or impulsivity in children and adolescents. In addition, many individuals with ADHD also have a learning disability. Furthermore, certain types of learning disabilities can result in hyperactive or distractible behaviors. The evaluation process must include a consideration of all of the possible causes of the observed and reported hyperactivity, distractibility, and/or impulsivity.

Perhaps the reason that too many children and adolescents are diagnosed as ADHD is that this "differential diagnostic" thinking is not done. A teacher tells a parent that a child cannot sit still and/or cannot stay on a task. The parent goes to his or her physician who prescribes medication. The assumption is that all children who are hyperactive and/or distractible have ADHD. In order for you to work closely with the professional evaluating your son or daughter for ADHD, I must review the other possible causes of these behaviors and the approach that should be used to establish the diagnosis.

The "Official" Criteria for ADHD

The official guidelines used by physicians to diagnose ADHD is from the official classification system, *The Diagnostic and Statistical Manual of Mental Disorders* (published by the American Psychiatric Association; see Appendix for address). The current edition is a revision of the Third Edition; thus, you will hear of "DSM IIIR." Don't let the title of the manual upset you. ADHD is identified as a psychiatric disorder and, thus, listed in this manual. According to these guidelines, to be considered as having ADHD, your son or daughter must meet the following three criteria:

1. A disturbance of at least six months during which at least eight of the following are present:
   a. Often fidgets with hands or feet or squirms in seat (in adolescents, may be limited to subjective feelings of restlessness)
   b. Has difficulty remaining seated when required to do so
   c. Is easily distracted by extraneous stimuli
   d. Has difficulty awaiting turn in games or group situations
   e. Often blurts out answers to questions before they have been completed
   f. Has difficulty following through on instructions from others (not due to oppositional behavior or failure of comprehension); for example, fails to finish chores
   g. Has difficulty sustaining attention in tasks or play activities
   h. Often shifts from one uncompleted activity to another
   i. Has difficulty playing quietly
   j. Often talks excessively
   k. Often interrupts or intrudes on others; for example, butts into other children's games
   l. Often does not seem to listen to what is being said to him or her
   m. Often loses items that are necessary for tasks or activities at school or at home; for example, toys, pencils, books, assignments
   n. Often engages in physically dangerous activities without considering possible consequences (not for the

purpose of thrill-seeking); for example, runs into street without looking

2. Onset before the age of seven

3. Does not meet the criteria for a Pervasive Developmental Disorder (a more serious psychiatric disorder)

I believe that there are difficulties with the DSM IIIR criteria. First, each of the above behaviors could be caused by an emotional problem, a learning disability, and/or environmental influences. Second, recent research suggests that ADHD may be but one aspect of a group of *Attentional Disorders*. Thus, a broader clinical concept may be needed. However, for now, DSM IIIR is the official diagnostic manual and the criteria listed are used by physicians.

As much as I do not like to admit it, there are pediatricians and other family physicians who do not fully understand ADHD. It becomes critical that you understand what it is and is not so that you can work with (perhaps, at times direct) your physician in the evaluation process. Therefore, I will go into more medical detail than might be needed for parents.

The Differential Diagnostic Process

The three presenting behaviors are hyperactivity, distractibility, and/or impulsivity. Let's look again at each of these behaviors before focusing on the possible causes.

Hyperactivity

As discussed earlier, most hyperactive children and adolescents are not running around the room or jumping on the furniture. They appear to be fidgety. Their fingers are tapping; their pencil is moving; their leg is swinging; they are up and down from their desk or the dinner table. Something is always in motion. Parents may report that the child is equally restless at night, moving about the bed. With adolescents, the fidgety behaviors may be less apparent; however, they are there.

Distractibility

It is important to look at the many reasons for distractibility. I think of two general groups: internal distractibility and external distractibility.

Internal Distractibility
- ~ Daydreaming
- ~ Auditory Perception Disability
- ~ Cognitive Dysinhibition

External Distractibility
- ~ Environmental Overload
- ~ Attention-Deficit Hyperactivity Disorder

Daydreaming is not uncommon with children and adolescents. For example, a student may escape into his or her thoughts and then realizes that he or she has not heard a word the teacher was saying. The teacher might comment that this student is not paying attention. The daydreaming might reflect family or other stress, an emotional disorder, or the excitement of an event (day before a holiday or vacation).

Auditory perception disabilities were discussed in detail in Chapter 3. If a child or adolescent has such a disability, he or she may have difficulty with an auditory figure-ground problem. That is, if there is more than one sound in the environment (e.g., students talking, activity in the hall, teacher talking), he or she may have difficulty knowing which sounds to listen to. The teacher might be into his or her third sentence before the student with this disorder realizes that the teacher is talking and attends. By then, the student is lost and is described as not paying attention. Another auditory perception disability is an auditory lag. These individuals need to concentrate on what they hear for an instant longer than others before it is understood. Thus, at any time they are concentrating on what they just heard while trying to hold on to what is coming in next. They cannot keep up this process, thus they miss parts of what is being said. The teacher reviews a lesson plan. As soon as he or she is finished, this student asks a question that the teacher just discussed. He or she is accused of not paying attention.

Some individuals have difficulty inhibiting their internal thought processes. There is no established term for this difficulty. I call it *cognitive dysinhibition.* Their internal thoughts protrude into their conscious behaviors. They are in class and suddenly start to talk about something that appears to be off the topic. For example, younger children might suddenly start to talk about dinosaurs or space. Or, they might begin to laugh or become paranoid because of their internal thoughts. This disorder is most often found in a more serious psychiatric disorder called Pervasive Developmental

Disorder. Before this disorder is identified, the child might be described as someone who is distractible and who never stays on a task.

The best example of an environmental overload occurred when many educational systems decided that the "open classroom" would create a more stimulating environment for learning. For many normal students the noise and multiple auditory inputs created distractibility. They could not pay attention to their teacher or to their work. The stimulation of the many workstations both in their classroom and in adjacent spaces often became visually overstimulating and caused distractibility. These students did not have ADHD, but they appeared to be distractible.

For some students, sitting next to a window that is open or to a door that is open to the hall can be distracting. For other students, a classroom that the teacher cannot control thus, one that is noisy or has students moving around, can be too much of a sensory overload to permit attending to a task. The same situation might exist for students who like to do their homework in the family room with the television playing and siblings running around or talking.

Impulsivity

Impulsive behavior is described as the inability or difficulty with stopping to reflect before speaking or acting. Thus, the child or adolescent with a problem with this behavior interrupts the teacher or parent, answers a question with the first thought that occurs, or says things and then is sorry he or she said it as soon as it is said. This individual might get frustrated or angry and yell, throw something, or hit someone. He or she never learns from experience because to learn from experience one has to stop and think about past experiences and consequences before speaking or acting. The impulsive child or adolescent does not have the luxury of the time to think first.

Impulsivity is characteristic of many psychiatric disorders and can reflect immaturity, anxiety, depression, or learned (and possibly rewarded) behavior. This behavior might reflect an immature or dysfunctional nervous system. One such dysfunction is ADHD.

Differential Diagnosis
Emotional Issues

Anxiety

The most common cause of hyperactivity, distractibility, or impulsivity with children, adolescents, and adults is anxiety. Anxiety can be a reflection of psychological stress or conflict or reflective of a specific psychiatric disorder. If these behaviors are a reflection of anxiety, the diagnosis is not ADHD. When someone is anxious, he or she can be restless and motorically active. For children, motor activity might be the primary way of reflecting anxiety. In addition, when one is anxious, it is difficult to pay attention. A child might daydream or might try to watch television or read a book. However, it is difficult to stay on the task or to pay attention to what is heard, seen, or read. Anxiety can cause an individual to be irritable and to appear to be impulsive.

Depression

The next most common cause of hyperactivity, distractibility, or impulsivity with children, adolescents, or adults is depression. The depression might reflect a psychological conflict or stress or might reflect a specific psychiatric disorder. If these behaviors are a reflection of a depressive process, the diagnosis is not ADHD. Depression can be expressed at all ages and may be reflected in an agitated or withdrawn form (i.e., *psychomotor retardation*). If agitated, the individual may be restless and active. He or she will have difficulty concentrating or staying on a task. Some may be irritable and act impulsively. If in the withdrawn phase of depression, the individual might feel so involved with his or her feelings and/or thoughts that he or she has difficulty paying attention to what is going on or with communicating with people.

> Chris was 10 years old and in the fifth grade when I was asked to do a consultation. He had been in individual and group therapy for two years because of his emotional problems. He was unhappy in school and not doing his class or homework. A psychological and educational evaluation was done by his school system 18 months earlier that showed evidence of visual perception, visual motor, and fine motor difficulties. However, the evaluation team concluded, "His weaknesses were not great enough nor his skill levels behind enough to qualify for services."
>
> A review of his school records plus the history provided by his parents revealed that he had been labeled as hyperactive and distractible in preschool and kindergarten. The first grade

teacher described him as overactive and unable to stay on a task. The second grade teacher made the same comments. Third grade was described as terrible. He got into fights, disrupted the classroom, and did not complete his work. Fourth grade was similar. He was falling further behind in school skills and strategies. The teachers blamed this on his behavior and his "refusal" to sit still or pay attention.

The history added to the diagnostic process. Chris was adopted by this family at age four and one-half. He had been in a foster home for one year prior to this adoption. He had been removed from his mother because her boyfriend had sexually abused him. Mother was neglectful and often left him alone. The social agency history reported that mother had used alcohol and drugs during this pregnancy. Chris had been placed in individual and group therapy to help him cope with his past. All of his academic and behavioral problems were seen as secondary to his emotional problems.

During my psychiatric assessment sessions with Chris, he spoke openly of his past. He knew about it and felt that he no longer worried about it. "I talked it all over in my therapy. It is behind me and this is my family now and forever. I like them." I could find no evidence of emotional conflicts related to his past. He did speak of his frustrations in school. He did not like school and he knew he was not as smart as the other kids. Chris was aware that it was difficult to sit still in class. He also was aware of his easy distractibility by any noise or activity. He blamed the fighting on the other kids teasing him.

He showed a chronic and pervasive history (as far as such a history could be obtained) of hyperactivity and distractibility. Thus, the diagnosis could be ADHD. The pregnancy history of alcohol and substance abuse might support a neurological problem manifested by ADHD and learning disabilities. However, the other history suggested that he was still dealing with what is called a "Post Traumatic Stress Disorder" related to his early childhood history. The hyperactivity and distractibility might be a reflection of his anxiety and/or depression.

After discussing the issues with his therapist, I presented the diagnostic questions to Chris and his parents in a family session. We agreed to a trial on medication to help clarify the issues (medications are discussed in Chapter 14). He was started on Ritalin (generic name: methylphenidate), 5 mg three times a day. From the first dose, he became calmer, less distractible, and better able to stay on a task. All of his teachers and his parents noticed the significant improvement.

After several contacts with his school system, he was identified as learning disabled and placed in a special education program. With this change in program and the use of the medication, the fighting and other behavioral problems at school stopped.

Behavioral Issues

It is estimated that about 50 percent of children who meet the DSM IIIR criteria for ADHD will meet the DSM IIIR criteria for other behavioral problems—called *Oppositional Defiant Disorder* or *Conduct Disorder.* Similarly, most children who meet the criteria for these disruptive behavioral disorders will meet the criteria for ADHD. The critical question for the mental health professional is whether these are separate disorders that coexist in the same child (called *comorbidity*) or whether they represent different clinical pictures of the same underlying difficulty.

This issue is confused further by referral bias. If the definition of ADHD is established on the basis of the behaviors of children evaluated in mental health facilities or by mental health professionals, then it is likely that the most obvious behaviors will be focused on and the diagnosis will be an Oppositional Defiant Disorder or a Conduct Disorder. This result will have the effect of a self-fulfilling prophecy by further encouraging educators to see the child or adolescent as only having an emotional problem.

Recent research supports the belief that ADHD should be identified as separate from Oppositional Defiant or Conduct Disorders. Evidence shows that children can have any of these disorders alone, but that they are more likely to occur in combination with each other. Each must be clarified and the treatment plan must address each disorder. To focus on the other disorders and not treat the ADHD will not be successful.

Since you will hear of these two disorders and, possibly, your son or daughter will be labeled as having one of them, I need to go into more detail on each. Again I will use the guidelines in DSM IIIR, since these are the ones used by professionals.

Oppositional Defiant Disorder

The essential feature is a recurring pattern of negativistic, hostile, and defiant behavior that has become developmentally stable for at least six months. These symptoms must be present to a degree that is excessive or deviant for the child's mental age.

The DSM IIIR diagnostic criteria for an Oppositional Defiant Disorder are:

1. A disturbance of at least six months during which at least five of the following are present:
   a. Often loses temper
   b. Often argues with adults
   c. Often actively defies or refuses adult requests or rules; for example, refuses to do chores at home
   d. Often deliberately does things that annoy other people; for example, grabs other children's hats
   e. Often blames others for his or her own mistakes
   f. Is often touchy or easily annoyed by others
   g. Is often angry and resentful
   h. Is often spiteful or vindictive
   i. Often swears or uses obscene language
2. Does not meet the criteria for Conduct Disorder, and does not occur exclusively during the course of a psychotic disorder or significant depression.

Conduct Disorder

It is not uncommon for a child to be diagnosed ADHD in early childhood then as Oppositional Defiant Disorder in later childhood and, finally as Conduct Disorder in late childhood or early adolescence.

The DSM IIIR criteria indicates that the essential feature of this disorder is a persistent pattern of conduct in which the basic rights of others and major age-appropriate societal norms or rules are violated. It is usually pervasive, occurring in school, the community, with peers, and at home. Physical aggression and physical destructiveness are more common in this disorder than in an Oppositional Defiant Disorder.

The DSM IIIR criteria for Conduct Disorder are:

1. A disturbance of conduct lasting at least six months, during which at least three of the following have been present:
   a. Has stolen without confrontation of a victim on more than one occasion (including forgery)
   b. Has run away from home overnight at least twice while living in parental or parental surrogate home (or once without returning)

    c. Often lies (other than to avoid physical or sexual abuse)

    d. Has deliberately engaged in fire-setting

    e. Is often truant from school (for older person, absent from work)

    f. Has broken into someone else's house, building, or car

    g. Has deliberately destroyed others' property (other than by fire-setting)

    h. Has been physically cruel to animals

    i. Has forced someone into sexual activity with him or her

    j. Has used a weapon in more than one fight

    k. Often initiates physical fights

    l. Has stolen with confrontation of a victim; for example, mugging, purse-snatching, extortion, or armed robbery)

    m. Has been physically cruel to people

2. If 18 or older, does not meet criteria for Antisocial Personality Disorder.

Neurological Factors Other than ADHD
Learning Disability

One type of a learning disability, an auditory perception disability, was discussed earlier in this chapter. A child or adolescent with such a disability can appear to be distractible. Other types of learning disabilities might make it difficult for the student to understand, organize the work, or complete assignments. The student might appear not to be staying on a task when the real issue is that he or she is on a task but cannot do the work. If the student with a learning disability does not understand the work and cannot do the work, he or she may become anxious. This anxiety can cause hyperactive or distractible behavior. In this case, it is the anxiety caused by the learning disability that is causing the behaviors and not ADHD.

Sometimes the diagnosis of ADHD is correctly made and the student is started on the appropriate medication. The hyperactivity and/or distractibility decrease. However, the associated learning disability may not have been diagnosed. Suddenly, the student can sit in class and attend to his or her work; however, he or she does not understand the work and cannot do it. He or she becomes anxious and starts to fidget or to daydream. The teacher might believe that the medication is no longer working. It is important to understand that even ADHD children or adolescents on the proper medication can become anxious or depressed.

Sensory Integrative Disorder

As discussed in Chapter 3, some individuals with a learning disability also have a Sensory Integrative Disorder. To quickly review, these individuals have difficulty receiving and processing perceptions that are needed to orient and use their body in space. The three perceptions affected with this disorder are the tactile, proprioception, and vestibular systems. These individuals may be tactilely sensitive or defensive; they might have difficulty moving their body appropriately in space or in doing a task that requires muscle planning (e.g., buttoning, tying); or, they might have difficulty orienting their body to their head position. If tactiley sensitive or defensive they will be overly aware of tags on their clothes, a belt, or the texture of their clothes; thus, they may wiggle or move about, appearing to be hyperactive. They might be unsure of their body and its position in space; thus, they might move about, trying to become more comfortable. Children with a Sensory Integrative Disorder, thus, might be fidgety. In these situations, the hyperactivity and fidgety behaviors are a reflection of this disorder and not of ADHD.

Rating Scales as Part of the Diagnostic Process

Rating scales are popular when assessing children's behaviors. In addition to the clinical interview, these behavioral rating scales provide information from people who know the child well (e.g., parents, teachers). They are seen as efficient, and they are based on established norms.

The question is, what is being measured or assessed? The data from a rating scale might show the individual to be hyperactive, distractible, and/or impulsive. But, the clinician still does not know why these behaviors are present. Thus, if they are used, they must be considered as a source of observational data to be used as part of the diagnostic process but not as the diagnostic process.

There are advantages to using rating scales in clinical practice. First, there are normative data that permit the clinician to deter-

determine the degree of deviance of a particular child within the population of same-age and same-sex children. This is essential to the diagnosis of ADHD, since many ADHD characteristics occur to some degree in normal children. Second, rating scales can be a convenient means for collapsing information about a child across situations and time intervals into units of information of value to diagnosis. It would be difficult to collect direct observations of children over diverse settings and throughout several months for clinical purposes. Finally, rating scales provide a convenient means for evaluating a person's responses to clinical interventions.

Since rating scales are often used by clinicians, let me briefly review the more popular ones. If you are asked to fill out such a rating scale, be sure to question what it measures. You may need to remind the clinician that the information obtained might clarify that your son or daughter is hyperactive, distractible, and/or impulsive, but the information will not establish the diagnosis of ADHD.

Parent Rating Scales

The *Conners* series of parent rating scales have been the most widely used. There are three forms, the original 93-item version, the revised 48-item version, and the 10-item Abbreviated Symptom Questionnaire. It should be kept in mind that these scales were developed during the time that an earlier diagnostic manual was in use and the focus is primarily on hyperactivity.

The *Child Behavioral Checklist*, by Achenbach and Edelbrock, was developed in 1983 and is widely used. It has a hyperactivity factor; but, there is no factor related to distractibility.

New instruments have been developed that address the DSM IIIR criteria. Examples are the *Child Attention Problems* (Barkley), the *ADHD Rating Scale* (DuPaul), and the *Attention Deficit Disorders Evaluation Scale* (McCarney).

Teacher Rating Scales

The *Conners* Teachers Rating Scales are most widely used. There are several versions. Again, the primary focus is on hyperactivity. The Conners Abbreviated Syndrome Questionnaire, developed by Conners and Barkley, is a 10-item list; however, it assesses general misconduct and aggression rather than inattention and other specific ADHD symptoms.

The *Child Attention Problem* rating scale contains 12 items that specifically assess inattention and overactivity.

Newer Rating Instruments

The *Yale Children's Inventory* is a parent-completed rating scale that assesses multiple factors related to ADHD and associated disorders. There are 11 scales: attention, impulsivity, activity, tractability, habituation, conduct disorder-socialized, conduct disorder-aggressive, negative affect, language, fine motor, and academics. Thus, an effort is made to identify hyperactivity, distractibility, and impulsivity as well as evidence of an emotional disorder or a learning difficulty.

Diagnosis of ADHD

I have spent so much time telling you what is not ADHD. We should move on to what is ADHD and how the diagnosis is established.

The clinical history plus observational data best help the clinician establish the diagnosis of ADHD. This history is obtained from parents, the current teachers, the school records, and from other significant adults (e.g., scout leaders, religious educators). The observations should include the school and the home environment.

If the history of the behaviors of hyperactivity, distractibility, and/or impulsivity relate to specific times in the individual's life or to specific spaces or activities, consider anxiety as the possible cause. For example, Billy was never described as hyperactive until third grade, or Joan is only distractible in math class, or Bob is only impulsive after his father gets home at night. The history of the behaviors has a starting point or the behaviors appear to occur during specific times of the day.

If the history of these behaviors relates to a situational crisis or loss, consider depression as the possible cause. For example, John was never described as hyperactive until his parents separated, or Mary has become inattentive in class since her parents began openly to fight at home. These behaviors might occur following such obvious stresses as parental fighting, separation, divorce, or after the death of a family member. They might also occur after the birth of a sibling, moving to a new house, or starting a new school. The history of the behaviors has a starting point and appears to be related to a life stress.

If the behaviors began after starting in a particular environment, consider the environment. If the student has a learning disability and/or a Sensory Integrative Disorder or if the clinician suspects one of these disorders, clarify if they exist before concluding that the diagnosis is ADHD.

If the behaviors are *chronic* and *pervasive*, consider ADHD. Chronic in that they have been there forever. Pervasive in that they are there all of the time.

Chronic

Chronic behavior is illustrated in the following example. You might report that your son's teacher complained that he could not sit still or pay attention in the fourth grade class then add, "You think she has trouble, you should have heard his third grade teacher and his second grade teacher and his first grade teacher, and his kindergarten teacher. I have the only son who was kicked out of nursery school because he would not sit still during circle time and pay attention." Or, a mother might report that her child kicked more *in utero*, squirmed in her arms, has always been in motion. She might add, "He started to walk at 10 months and at 10 months, one second he would run into another room, out the door, or into the street if I was not there to stop him." She might add, "I can't remember one meal in his whole life when he sat in his seat for the entire meal." The behaviors have been present throughout the individual's life.

Pervasive

Parents describe the child's hyperactivity, distractibility, and/or impulsivity. The classroom teacher describes these behaviors as does the art, music, and physical education teacher and the lunch room monitor. The Sunday School teacher, scout leader, or tutor see the same behaviors. The behaviors are there all of the time—they are pervasive.

In Summary

All children and adolescents who show the behaviors of hyperactivity, distractibility, and/or impulsivity do not have ADHD. In reality, ADHD might be the least most common cause for these behaviors. A clear differential diagnostic process that takes into account all possible causes for these behaviors is needed before a diagnosis can be made. Since the diagnosis is made by a physician and some physicians may not know much about ADHD, you must be knowledgeable.

As with a learning disability, once the diagnosis is established, it is important to explore the impact of the ADHD on your child or adolescent as well as on the family. The behaviors will interfere with school performance. As you already know, the hyperactivity, distractibility, and/or impulsivity will interfere with family interactions and activities as well as with peer relationships and activities. The treatment plan for ADHD is discussed in Chapter 14. This plan must take into account the total child or adolescent in his or her total environment. The treatment approach must go beyond prescribing medication.

If your son or daughter has been diagnosed as ADHD only, it is critical that you consider if he or she might also have a learning disability. As you know by now, the likelihood of also having a learning disability is about 80 percent. If present, this disability must also be treated. The treatment for ADHD will not treat the learning disability nor will the treatment for a learning disability treat the ADHD. They are two different but associated disorders.

If there are emotional, social, or family problems, the clinician must try to understand the role the ADHD plus possible learning disabilities might play in causing or contributing to these problems. The treatment plan will be different if the emotional, social, or family problems are seen as the primary difficulty or if they are seen as secondary to the ADHD plus possible learning disabilities. The impact these disabilities have had on the individual and family will also be addressed with the treatment plan.

PART FOUR

Treatment

13

Your Role in the Treatment for Learning Disabilities

NOWHERE IS UNDERSTANDING your total child or adolescent in his or her total environment more important than when you are dealing with learning disabilities. As I have been saying over and over, they do not just interfere with reading, writing, and arithmetic; they interfere with all aspects of life—at home, in the neighborhood, at religious education, in sports, at clubs and other organized activities—in short, everyplace. Wherever your son or daughter goes, you must be an advocate for making the most of his or her strengths. You must see to it that your child or adolescent has as many positive experiences as possible. How do you build on their strengths and minimize their weaknesses? Who can work with you at school, at home, and outside of the home?

To start, do you know where your child's or adolescent's learning disabilities and strengths lay? If not, ask to meet with the special education team at your school or, if the evaluations were not done by the school, with the special educator who did the testing. You might review the material that was covered in Chapter 3 on learning disabilities and in Chapters 10 and 11 on the evaluation and any notes you have made on your daughter's or son's evaluation. Then contact the person or people who can help you educate yourself.

Because your son or daughter spends so much time at school and because that is usually where the special education programs are put into effect, I shall focus first on the treatment of learning disabilities in the school environment. Later, I will discuss the treatment in the home environment.

Treating Learning Disabilities in the School

Ideally your school system is as concerned as you are about developing the necessary help and the proper program for your child or adolescent. If not, you may need to push for what you need. (I discuss how to be such an advocate more fully in Chapter 19 on legal issues.)

The treatment of choice for a learning disability within the school system is special education. This statement might seem to be so obvious that it need not be noted. Yet, I find often that this obvious statement is not followed.

Depending on the school's facilities, budget, and approach to the problem, your son or daughter will be placed in a specific level of service. The names for these levels varies around the country. Descriptively, they are:

Level One: He or she is in a regular classroom and any professionals that are needed will consult with the classroom teacher.

Level Two: He or she is in a regular classroom but is "pulled out" for up to one hour of special services a day.

Level Three: He or she is in a regular classroom but is "pulled out" for up to two hours of special services a day.

Level Four: He or she is assigned to a special education program (often called a resource room) and is "mainstreamed" out to regular class activities as appropriate.

Level Five: He or she is assigned to a special education program full time. This program can be part of a regular school facility or in a special facility.

Level Six: He or she is assigned to a special education program full time. This program is in a self-contained special education school and may be public or private.

The process for establishing the appropriate placement and

services also varies from school system to school system. The names for each step will differ, but, generally, the steps are:

1. You request to the principal that your son or daughter be evaluated or the principal informs you that the school staff feels that such an evaluation is needed. (If you had a private evaluation done, the results should be given to the principal who initiates the process of review.)

2. Representatives from the school system's diagnostic evaluation team should review the concerns (or studies), talk to the appropriate teachers, and observe your son or daughter. They then set up a meeting with the parents (often called an *Education Management Team* meeting). At this meeting, the professionals agree or disagree that an evaluation is needed. If they agree, they should explain what studies will be done and why. They should set a tentative time frame for doing the studies. If they disagree, you should be informed of your right to appeal.

3. Once the studies are completed, the evaluation team meets with you to discuss the findings and recommendations (often called an Admissions, Review, and Dismissal (*ARD*) meeting). At this meeting three decisions are made, each requires your approval:
   ~ Does your son or daughter have a disability and, if so, what is (or are) they?
   ~ If he or she has a disability, what level of service should he or she have and which professionals will be involved (e.g., special educator, speech and language pathologist)?
   ~ Where will these services be provided (e.g., local school, another school)?

4. As part of this meeting, a formal *Individualized Education Program* or IEP should be presented. This plan identifies each area of difficulty, describes how each difficulty will be addressed, and reviews how progress will be assessed. (More details on this IEP will be described in Chapter 19, on legal issues.) If you disagree with any of the decisions presented in the above item #3 or with the IEP, you should be informed of your right to appeal.

If your son or daughter is in a public school, the above services are mandatory under law. If your youngster is in a private school, you have the right to request the evaluation and services from your public school.

Should you decide to provide the necessary help on a private basis by paying a special educator or other professional to work with your son or daughter, it is critical that these efforts be coordinated with the classroom teacher and with any professional within the school system who is working with your youngster.

You might decide to send your child or adolescent to a private school for students with learning disabilities. Sometimes, because of your location, you must consider a boarding school for such students. Ideally, your public school will agree to the need and fund the program. If not, you will find the financial cost high. If you want to consider a private placement and do not know where to find one, ask someone in the special education program of your school system. A list might be obtained from your local chapter of the Learning Disabilities Association (see Appendix) or you can look up specific directories in your library or order the directories of such schools from:

1. *The Directory for Exceptional Children*
   Porter Sargent Publishers, Inc.
   11 Beacon Street
   Boston, Massachusetts 02108

2. *Directory of Facilities and Services for the Learning Disabled*
   Academic Therapy Publication
   20 Commercial Boulevard
   Novato, California 94947

3. *The Schoolsearch Guide to Private Schools for Students with Learning Disabilities,* by M. Lipkin
   School Search
   127 Marsh Street
   Belmont, Massachusetts 02178

Remember that there is nothing magical about a private school. Not just any private school will do, either. A private school that provides general education may turn out to cause more stress for your child than your public school. You may get smaller classes and more structure, but with it may come a higher level of academic demand, or an excessive emphasis on grades and college preparation, and, with that, intense competition among the students.

A school that is designed and staffed to work with students with learning disabilities or a regular private school that has the resources and staff to address the needs of those students with learning disabilities is what you need. Know what you are getting. Talk to parents of children at the private school about academic demands, number of homework hours, and flexibility. Ask other parents of children with learning disabilities for advice about what to do and what not to do, and weigh their experiences when you make your choice.

If you find that you cannot get the appropriate special educational help in your school system or community, you may find yourself considering a boarding school. To me, this is always the last choice and should be considered only if it is absolutely necessary. Boarding schools can be excellent, and some have excellent special programs for students with learning disabilities. However, if your son or daughter is to live away from home, you must weigh the loss of the security and strength that the family provides against whatever your child or adolescent will gain from the programs at that facility.

If you cannot find any local programs that are tailored to help with the learning disabilities or if your child's or adolescent's behavior at school or at home is so problematic that you must consider a boarding school or residential treatment center, get the best help you can in selecting a good one, one that will be most likely to help your son or daughter.

Earlier I described the levels of programs available in the public school setting. Which one is best will depend on the degree of disabilities, his or her level of current academic performance, and availability of programs.

The best program offers what the child or adolescent needs academically, behaviorally, and socially in the *least restrictive environment* possible. This judgment has to be made for each individual. The least restrictive environment is not necessarily the program closest to a regular class program. For some children and adolescents, the least restrictive environment that will be of maximum help might be the most restrictive environment available. For example, a child with multiple areas of learning disabilities who is several years behind in basic skills and overwhelmed might feel most relaxed and safe in a small, self-contained, special education program. The freedom and rough-and-tumble of a regular classroom might be so overwhelming that he or she will be inhibited or less available to learn. In the self-contained environment, he or she might feel safe and, thus, take risk in learning.

If your son or daughter is in a regular class and "pulled out" for special services, watch him or her carefully. How much time does he or she have in the special program? Is he or she seen alone or in a group? One study looked at a group of five children with learning disabilities who were seen in a resource room, as a group, 30 minutes a day. It sounded great. They noted that on an average five minutes were lost coming in and getting settled and another five minutes were lost getting ready to leave. The remaining time had to be shared. Often, a group activity was done. Each child received a total of seven minutes a week of individualized help specifically designed to address his or her learning disability.

Another concern in the "pull out" programs is that the special education, speech and language therapist, occupational therapist or other professional work closely with the classroom teacher or teachers. Without this interaction, the classroom teacher may not know how to compensate for or accommodate to the needs of the student during the time in the regular program. Sometimes the student is expected to make up the work missed while in the special education program. He or she might have to do the work at home or during recess. Explore if you think this is fair and discuss it with the team of people who are involved. I have seen children fall between the cracks. They are pulled out each day during the time the classroom teacher does social studies. Suddenly, at the end of the year everyone realizes that the student never learned this subject. I must sound very paranoid to you. I think that public school teachers want to understand and help our children and adolescents. Sometimes "the system" or other pressures interfere. You have to be on guard to catch the difficulties so that you can speak up.

Monitor the program. In September your son or daughter is getting everything that he or she was promised in the IEP. As the school year goes on, the case load for each professional might build. Gradually, the amount of time may decrease or the number of other students in the program may increase. Ask your youngster from time to time how often he or she is seeing the tutor or speech teacher and how many other students are with him or her. If you learn that the program is being diluted, speak up. The shortage of personnel may be real, but this shortage is the school's problem. Your problem is assuring that your child or adolescent gets what he or she is supposed to get.

Don't be afraid to monitor. Keep informed. Ask if the special education person is trained and certified to work with children with learning disabilities. Expect and ask for conferences between the classroom and special education professionals on a regular basis to learn of your child's progress and problems. If you have not heard from the school professionals by early spring about planning for next year's needs and placement, remind them of the need for such a meeting.

The Regular Classroom Teacher

If your son or daughter is in the regular classroom for all or part of the day, what should you expect of the regular classroom teacher? He or she must be knowledgeable about your child's or adolescent's particular pattern of learning disabilities and learning abilities. The classroom teacher may not have the time or the training to offer remedial or compensatory therapy. The special education professionals can handle these areas. The classroom teacher must know how to build on the child's strengths while understanding, accommodating, or compensating for his or her weaknesses.

If a child had a congenitally deformed leg, no teacher would expect him or her to run on the playground as well as the other children. If a child were blind, no teacher would hand him or her a printed book to read. If a child were deaf, no teacher would explain something to the class verbally and expect this student to perform. The child with learning disabilities has problems just as significant; only, his or her disabilities are invisible. People do not believe this or they forget. They have a written language disability and lose points on a report because of the misspelling. They have a fine motor problem and are expected to copy 20 math problems from the board before they can start their math test. They have an auditory lag and are expected to listen to a lecture and take notes. Are these demands any less insensitive to a disability than the examples given for the person with physical handicaps, who is blind, or who is deaf? I think not.

The sensitive, well-informed classroom teacher can do much to help your son or daughter. If the teacher knows that the child has specific disabilities, he or she can learn the best way to teach each academic skill and subject for that individual. To do this requires a knowledge of the student's strengths and weaknesses.

The special education professional should be the one to help the classroom teacher learn how to compensate or accommodate. Let me give a few examples to illustrate. If a child is having difficulty learning to read because of an auditory perception problem, the teacher might use a multisensory approach (using visual, tactile, and other sensory inputs). If a child has a visual motor and fine motor problem but good language skills, the teacher might call on the child to answer a question in class but not ask him or her to write on the board. For the child with the reverse pattern, the teacher might ask the child to write on the board but not call on him or her to answer a question.

If the child has fine motor and written language problems, the teacher might make a copy of whatever is put on the board (or overhead projector) and give it to this student. He or she might be given more time on written tests or assignments. The teacher might give the student a copy of notes based on the lesson that was taught in class or ask another student to use a piece of carbon paper so that an extra set of notes would be available at the end of class. Build on strengths. Compensate for or accommodate for weaknesses.

Recently I went to a school for a conference. Before the meeting started I decided to say "hello" to my favorite seventh grade classroom teacher in that school. As we were talking, a young boy came by to enter the class. I knew the boy and of his demand language disabilities. The teacher called him aside and said, "Ralph, later this period I am going to call on students to answer the questions at the end of Chapter 10. I want to tell you now that I will call on you to answer question four." What sensitivity. The teacher was not going to excuse Ralph nor was he going to call on him and embarrass him. Instead, he gave Ralph the time needed to shift the knowledge from a demand language situation to a spontaneous language situation. Ralph was prepared to succeed.

The art teacher, music teacher, and physical education teacher must be educated, as well as hall or lunchroom monitors. All must know how to build on strengths and handle the weaknesses. The most frequent disaster for students with visual motor plus gross and/or fine motor disabilities is gym. A teacher with no knowledge of the disabilities might yell at the student or shame him or her in front of peers. You must not let this happen.

Your job is not to be responsible for teaching each of your

son's or daughter's teachers and aides about the learning disabilities. Your job is to make sure that the special education person or team carries out this responsibility. If you find a teacher who is insensitive and uncooperative, act on it. Speak to the teacher or the principal. Don't let your son or daughter suffer because of another person's problems.

Homework

What about homework? Who is responsible for what? What do you do when homework time is a battle zone and causing tremendous stress between you and this child or within the family?

All youngsters need help from time to time with their homework. Those with learning disabilities may need extra assistance. I believe, however, that the main role for parents is to help their children feel good about themselves. This means helping them to build a good self-image, encouraging their feelings of acceptance, seeing that they feel loved. For some children and adolescents, being able to work with their parents on schoolwork is a positive and sought-after experience. Some, however, become so dependent on parents to do the work for them that they may take advantage of the situation, and this ultimately erodes their self-esteem and your patience. Others do not like to expose their weaknesses or reveal their problems and resist help or say they don't have any homework.

If you find yourself wondering about such a problem, you may want to talk to your child's teachers as well as to your son or daughter. Let the teacher help you decide what to do. How much homework should they be doing? How much should you be helping? Don't let your child browbeat or nag you into doing his or her homework.

You might request a meeting with the teachers involved and your child. Perhaps the teacher is giving a 20-minute assignment without realizing that it takes this child an hour. Homework of necessity involves reading and writing. If these are the child's areas of weakness, what alternatives could be arranged. Maybe you need to remind the teacher that in addition to the assigned homework, he or she expects the student to complete all uncompleted class assignments. Because of the learning disabilities or the time spent in a "pull out" program, this child might have twice as much work to do at home as the other children. Negotiate solutions.

If you must help your son or daughter do homework or certain tasks and your approach only leads to frustration, speak to the special education professional. You may need to learn the best approaches to use when teaching. For example, if you are helping your daughter memorize a spelling list, should you call the words out, use flash cards, or ask that she copy them over and over. The answer is not based on what worked best for you or for another of your children. The answer might be based on whether her strength is in auditory short-term memory or visual short-term memory.

You can do some activities to help with the process of doing homework and with preparation for school that do not require sitting down and doing the child's work. Your knowledge of their strengths and weaknesses will help you individualize the help to meet their specific needs.

1. Help your child or adolescent to organize materials for school. The youngster may be keeping English papers in the math section or today's work with old returned papers. Work with your son or daughter to set up a system of organization and ask the teacher to help.

2. Some youngsters have trouble organizing their life. They forget to bring home what they need, they forget to take to school what they need, and they forget to turn in work even if they did it. They lose things, including the key to their locker. They might need an assignment book completed and monitored by the teacher. They might need a large backpack so that they can carry everything in it. They might need a second set of books assigned so that they can keep one set at home all the time. This assignment book can have two columns. The left one lists the assignment by subject or class. The right one lists what needs to be taken home for that assignment. Thus, when they go to the locker at the end of the day, they only have to run down the right column and fill their backpack.

3. You may need to set up specific schedules and tasks to help with organization. Before going to sleep each night, the backpack must be filled with everything that will be needed the next day. It is too hectic in the morning to do this. Attach little notes to remind of morning tasks—take lunch, take permission slip, take gym shoes.

4. You may need to help with time planning. Many students with learning disabilities have difficulty planning ahead. Sit down and map out a time plan. Start from the end. For example, "Your book report is due on this date." Have him or her think through with you from finish to start how long it will take to type the final draft, to go from the second to the final draft, to go from the first to second draft, to read the book. Mark off each date a task should be started and each date a task should be completed. You will end up with an organized time plan to be followed.

5. Make sure the child understands homework instructions. Memory problems, poor handwriting, or ADHD may result in an incomplete or incorrect idea of what to do at home. The youngster may cover this up by saying there is no homework or may do only part of the assigned work and believe that all of the work is done. Suppose the teacher told the class to read Chapter 6 and answer the questions at the end of the chapter. Your child, who has an auditory short-term memory problem, does not write it down. That night he or she reads Chapter 6 and believes that all of the homework is done. The next day the teacher asks for the answers to the questions and they are not done. In this instance, an assignment sheet or book may help. The child must write down each homework assignment and the teacher must initial to show that it is correct. The parent can use the list to monitor if all work is done.

6. If you feel that too much homework is being assigned, meet with the teacher or teachers. Discuss what you feel your child can handle. Work out a plan before the overload frustrates him or her and results in the child being turned off.

7. If your child has ADHD as well, distractions may be a problem when off of medication. Help find a quiet, less cluttered area with few distractions. Some find music as a background sound helpful, and some will find it distracting. In general, TV and homework do not go well together for these students.

8. You may find it helpful to set aside a specific time each day or weekend day for doing homework. Allow for time to relax, play, and unwind after getting home from school. It is difficult to spend a full day in school and then be expected

to do homework as soon as you come home. If possible, let them have some control. Sit down when they get home and help them plan out the evening. Depending on what they have to do and how long it will take, would they like to do their homework or part of it before dinner, or after dinner, before their favorite TV show.

If your child or adolescent seems to have little or no homework, while his or her teachers complain that he or she does not turn in work or comes to class unprepared, ask for a conference with the teachers and your youngster. Set up a plan with consequences. If playing policeperson each night results in battles and anger, suggest to the teacher and your child that you "resign." Work out a plan with the school that responds to him or her coming to school with work not done. Perhaps he or she will have to use lunch or recess time or stay after school to complete all homework not done on arrival that morning. At home you can say, "If you want any help, please let me know." Then, stay out of it. If the work is not done, the school will handle it. Maintain your sanity and the family's peace.

Treating Learning Disabilities in the Home Environment

You want to help all of your children grow up with a positive self-image and confidence. This is hard enough to do, but it requires even greater effort if your son or daughter has learning disabilities. Don't excuse this child from chores, even though that might be the easy way out. A double standard for this child and the other children in the family sends the nonverbal message that you too think that the child with learning disabilities is inadequate. Building on your knowledge of what the child can and cannot do, try to select tasks and activities at which she or he is most likely to succeed. This success builds confidence, and with that confidence comes increasing family and social acceptance.

Let's discuss home first, then the neighborhood, clubs, and other activities. I cannot give you a ready-made program, but I can suggest an approach—a way of thinking and problem-solving. Using this approach, you can write your own book on your own son or daughter.

Your youngster's learning disabilities will be quite apparent at home. Tell the child clearly that you understand, and make sure the child hears and believes you. Reassure your daughter or son that you are glad that she or he is getting help. Ask for the child's own advice on how you can help best. For example, when talking to a child with an auditory figure-ground problem (i.e., difficulty selecting what sounds to focus on), you may need to establish eye contact before speaking. Go into the room where the child is and call out his or her name. Speak to the child only after she or he looks up.

If your child has difficulty with sequencing (i.e., getting the steps of a task in the right order), help him or her get started. Don't do the job for the child, but help him or her get organized. To illustrate, call this son or daughter over and say, "Look, I know it is hard for you to set the table because you are confused about where to put the fork, knife, spoon, glass. So, I just drew a picture of a typical place setting. I will put it in this drawer in the kitchen. Whenever it is your turn to set the table, feel free to take it out and use it." What are you saying? You have a disability. I wish you did not but you do. I will not excuse you from life, but I will teach you a way to compensate. What a positive message to give. Similarly, suppose your young son with sequencing problems has difficulty dressing in the morning. He gets confused and often puts the wrong article of clothing on first. Lay the clothes out on the floor in the order he is to get dressed and place a favorite stuffed animal at the starting end. Then say, "When you get dressed, start at your teddy bear and work your way down." Help your child compensate. Do not do the tasks for him or her if possible and do not excuse the child from life.

One approach to this type of help is to make a list of the areas in which your child is strong and one where your child is weak. Next to each strength, write out all of the tasks that he or she is capable of doing. Next to the weaknesses, write out all of the tasks that you have noticed where a disability interferes. Then think creatively about what you could do to build on the strengths while helping to compensate for weaknesses. If you get stuck, ask the special education professional.

What household chores could he do? If your son has visual-motor and motor disabilities, you might not ask him to load or unload the dishwasher (unless you have plastic dishes). But, he could walk the dog, bring in the newspaper, take out the trash.

Sometimes you are not sure if he or she really has difficulty doing something or if he or she is just lazy or not in the mood to do the task. One rule I find helpful is to assume that he or she can do the task and insist on it. Then watch. If you find real problems, you can then move in and make adjustments.

If you would like to take an active part in helping your son or daughter work on his or her learning disabilities, consider using normal household activities to reinforce learning. I cannot write out a recipe for doing this. However, I can suggest a way of thinking and you must individualize it. Many kitchen activities, for instance, require reading, measuring, counting, and following instructions. Such activities provide good practice in these skills as well as in sequencing. Chopping and stirring make good gross motor exercises. If you want to improve auditory memory, take the person shopping with you. At first, while near the correct shelf, ask the child to pick up an item, a can of peas, let's say. Later, make it two or three items. Still later, make it an item an aisle over, then two aisles. Think of other activities that are fun, done together, and which work on weaknesses.

We have discussed chores within the house. What about activities outside of the house. What about sports, clubs, and other programs. Use your knowledge of strengths and weaknesses to select the best activity or to plan the needed adjustments for these activities. Each sport requires different strengths. If your son or daughter has visual perception and visual-motor disabilities, he or she might have difficulty with sports that require eye-hand coordination for doing such tasks as hitting, throwing, or catching a ball. Baseball or basketball might be poorly played and avoided. Look for sports that require more gross motor abilities and minimal eye-hand skills—swimming, soccer, bowling, horseback riding, sailing, canoeing, certain field and track events. The child who refuses to play baseball may excel at swimming. Let swimming be his or her area of success.

Some children and adolescents find all sports difficult. But it might be possible to improve some of the required skills through practice. Most of the kids his or her own age won't take the time or have the patience to help; however, a parent or an older brother or sister can go into the yard, or anyplace else where the other kids won't see, and practice catching, throwing, or hitting.

Because of difficulty following directions or because they

simply play so poorly, some children never learn the basic rules of a game. Once again, you or someone in the family may need to sit down and teach the child how to play baseball or hopscotch from the ground up, going back over the rules until the child catches on.

You can use this approach with all outside activities. Build on strengths. Don't magnify weaknesses. For example, picture a 10 year old with fine motor, sequencing, and visual-motor disabilities at a scout or Indian Princess meeting. Everyone is working on a project—cutting out pumpkins or drawing turkeys —and your child's cutouts or drawings are total failures. He or she cannot color and stay within the line or cut and stay on the line. Everybody laughs. Another failure and the child doesn't want to go to any more meetings. But if the activity leader had known what the child could and could not do, his or her gross motor abilities might have been used. He or she could hand out the paper, squirt the glue, smear the paste. Maybe, he or she could have been asked to read about the theme of the meeting and give an oral report to the group while they work on the motor task. On parent night, if you ask this child to demonstrate knot tying, he or she will refuse to go. But, let him or her march in carrying the flag and all is a success. Turn potential failures into successes.

When such children or adolescents go to the local youth center, don't let them wander around and select what they want to do at random. Whether they should be in arts and crafts or photography depends on what they are able to do reasonably well. Many crafts require good visual perception and eye-hand coordination; many aspects of photography involve gross motor skills. Plan ahead for all occasions. Work with the club, group, or activities leaders as extensions of yourself. Help them to understand what you want to accomplish beforehand. They can help you only if you have advocated for your own cause.

Make sure such people understand that your child does not always hear every instruction given. They must know in advance to check with the child and to repeat instructions if necessary. Your child might appear quiet or indifferent because language does not come easily. Tell this to the people in charge. You may have to explain the whole thing: your child is not retarded, bad, or lazy. The disability is simply invisible. You can and must make the instructor or activity leader sensitive to your child's or adolescent's special needs.

Don't forget Sunday school and religious education programs. Be sure that the staff knows all about him or her so that they can work with you in designing appropriate classroom and activity programs.

Choosing a camp, whether day or sleep-away, requires the same attention. You may need to consider a camp that is designed for children with special needs, or you might be able to use a carefully selected regular camp. Think about whether your child can handle a large or small camp. What strengths and abilities does the child have to have for that camp, and how do you match them with the offerings of the camp? Some camps focus on drama, arts, or horseback riding. Are these activities that will build on strengths or will the child sustain more damage because he or she cannot do these activities well. Some camps are sports-oriented and competitive. Woe to the girl or boy who has visual perception and eye-hand coordination problems and who drops the ball or misses the hit, causing the team to lose the game! But there are camps that focus on noncompetitive activities or gross motor sports. Your clumsy, nonathletic son or daughter might do very well at a camp that focuses on waterfront activities. Swimming, rowing, sailing, canoeing—all of these are gross motor activities.

Before selecting a camp, talk with the director at length. Is this person flexible? Can she or he describe programs that might work for your particular child? Don't hesitate to educate the counselors, either. They will appreciate the information, and your son or daughter will undoubtedly benefit from the understanding of such important people.

If they are going to a sleep-away camp, plan ahead for every possible problem. Maybe you need to arrange for them to call home to problem-solve. Maybe you need to ask the counselor to call if there are difficulties. If your son or daughter has major difficulties with reading and writing, corresponding will be a problem. How will he or she read or write letters? Maybe you could give this child a tape recorder and you can mail him or her a tape. He or she "listens" to your letter. Later, the tape could be erased and he could dictate a letter back. Creative problem solving before the crises can minimize or avoid the crises.

In Summary

In this chapter I have illustrated a style of thinking and problem solving. The specific examples may or may not fit your child or adolescent, but the general principles apply to every case.

It is work. You must learn more about your youngster than you may have imagined possible. You must be creative. It will take extra effort, but if you don't do it, who will?

14

Your Role in the Treatment of ADHD

THE TREATMENT OF Attention-Deficit Hyperactivity Disorder (ADHD) must involve several models of help, including individual and family education, individual and family counseling, the use of appropriate behavioral management programs, and the use of appropriate medications. Such a "multimodal" approach is needed because children and adolescents with ADHD have multiple areas of difficulty. As with learning disabilities, the total person must be understood in his or her total world.

As you understand by now, children and adolescents with ADHD might have other associated disorders such as learning disabilities, Tourette's Disorder (a chronic tic disorder), seizure disorders, or Obsessive-Compulsive Disorder. In addition, many individuals develop secondary emotional, social, and family problems. Each problem must be identified during the evaluation process and each must be addressed in the treatment plan. To treat ADHD with medication only and not address the impact the disorder has had on the parents and the family or the associated learning disabilities will not be successful.

I would like to briefly describe the educational and counseling efforts you need. If your professional does not or cannot provide them, find someone who can. Later in this chapter, the use of medications is discussed in greater detail.

Individual and Family Education and Counseling

The first critical step is to educate you—the parents—on ADHD. Next, the child or adolescent must understand his or her disability. Finally, siblings, grandparents, and other meaningful adults will need to know and understand.

Different professionals use different approaches to explain ADHD. You may find that if you have done a lot of reading, you know more than the professional you are seeing. I would like to describe how I explain ADHD and its cause and treatment to parents, children, adolescents, and siblings. The concepts and words I use are based on research. I do simplify some of the concepts by using symbolic thinking to illustrate the points I want to make. I do believe that I am providing the best information on ADHD. To make this educational process as real as possible I will write as if you were sitting in my office and I was speaking directly to you.

Let me review what the current research strongly suggests about ADHD. All of the facts are not yet in but current research does give us a lot of understanding. Your son or daughter has hyperactivity, distractibility, and/or impulsivity. We discussed earlier how the diagnosis was made based on a chronic and pervasive history of these behaviors (see Chapter 11 on evaluation). Let's discuss each behavior.

First, let's address hyperactivity. As you know we are referring to a child's fidgety behavior. What causes this fidgetiness? There is an area in the brain that stimulates muscle activity. It is in the thinking part of the brain or the cortex (called the *premotor cortex*). I call this area the "accelerator." There is another area in the lower part of the brain that decides how much of these messages will get through to the muscles (called the *Ascending Reticular Activating System*). I call this area the "brakes." Normally there is a balance between the accelerator and the brakes and the brakes appear to be the controlling factor. Children and adolescents with hyperactivity due to ADHD appear to have a brake that is not working effectively. Thus, the accelerator is not as controlled and the individual has an increased amount of muscle (motor) behavior. I will explain why we think the brake is not working well after distractibility and impulsivity are addressed.

Next to be discussed is distractibility. The type of distractibility found with ADHD makes it difficult for the individual to distinguish between relevant and nonrelevant stimuli in the environment. Thus, nonrelevant stimuli distracts him or her and the child has difficulty sustaining attention—he or she has a short attention span. The way the brain works is that when information comes into our brain through our eyes or ears it is run through what I call a "filter system." If it is important it is allowed to pass through to the thinking part of the brain or the cortex. If it is not important or if it can be handled at a lower level of the brain, it is monitored or processed at a lower level of the brain. In this way, the cortex is not cluttered with every stimulus that enters the brain. This filter system appears to be in the same lower area of the brain as is the braking system.

Let me illustrate how this filter system works. You have been in a store and many children yell mommy or daddy, yet you only hear your child. Or, if you are like me, you probably get in your car and drive home then suddenly realize that you were daydreaming and do not know how you did not get lost or hit someone. Somehow, your brain was able to monitor important information at a lower level, freeing your cortex to think of other things.

In ADHD, the filter system is not working efficiently, thus all stimuli go through the filter system and bang on the cortex, saying "pay attention to me." Your child might have more difficulty with sound input, distracted by every sound around, or he might have more difficulty with visual input, distracted by every item around him or her. I will explain why the filter system is not working well after I address impulsivity.

Finally, let's look at impulsivity. We know less about this behavior. It appears that when information is processed in the brain it first arrives at a basic "circuit board." From here it is relayed to many areas of the brain for action and then comes back to this circuit board for a reaction. It appears that this basic circuit board is not working effectively. There may be some "short circuits" causing the initial input to be responded to immediately. Your son or daughter does not stop to think before he or she talks or acts and is described as impulsive. This basic circuit board appears to be in the same lower part of the brain as the "brakes" and the "filter system." I will explain why it is not working well in a minute.

It is because these three systems are in the same area of the brain that these three, what appear to be random, behaviors (i.e., hyperactivity, distractibility, impulsivity) often are found together. What, then, causes the brakes, filter system, and circuit board to be inefficient? Current research strongly suggests that the reason is that there is a decrease in the chemical that is needed to transmit messages from one nerve ending to another in this area of the brain—called a *neurotransmitter.* The neurotransmitter suspected of being deficient is norepinephrine. We discovered in 1937 that certain medications helped to decrease these behaviors with children with ADHD. We now think we know why they work. The medications appear to increase the amount of norepinephrine at the nerve interface at this lower part of the brain. Once the amount of this neurotransmitter reaches a normal level, the brakes can work efficiently and the child becomes less hyperactive; the filter system can function properly and the child becomes less distractible with an increase in attention span; and the circuit board can operate properly and the child becomes less impulsive.

It is important for you to understand that the medications used with ADHD do not drug, sedate, or tranquilize your child. The medications make him or her "normal." It is like diabetes. When a diabetic is given insulin, he or she can function normally. But the medication does not cure the diabetes. Once the insulin is metabolized, he or she returns to being diabetic. So, too, when the proper medication is used to treat the ADHD, the individual can function normally. Once the medication is metabolized, he or she returns to being ADHD.

I agree that I am using poetic license with anatomy and physiology in the above descriptions, but parents usually have not gone through medical school, and the symbols and descriptors help to understand their child or adolescent. Once these terms have been introduced, they can be used during the treatment plan. For example, "He is still more fidgety than he should be. We may need more medication to get the brakes working better." This information also helps you understand that the use of medications is not to drug your son or daughter so that others can live with him or her. The medications help this child function normally. You need not feel guilty because you placed your son or daughter on medication.

Now that you understand that ADHD appears to be a neurological, or more exactly, a neurochemical disorder, it is easy to see why ADHD exists all of the time. As is discussed later, to have your son or daughter on medication only during school hours and school days makes no sense. Yes, the school is delighted with the change, but you and your family and the kids in the neighborhood have to live with the hyperactivity, distractibility, and/or impulsivity, causing family and peer problems.

Individual and Family Counseling

If, after the educational process and the use of proper medications, the school behaviors, family behaviors, or difficulties with peers do not improve, more help may be needed. The hyperactivity, distractibility, and/or impulsivity may be less, but the oppositional, controlling, or abusive behaviors may remain or, the "dysfunction" caused to the marriage or the family may not lessen because the ADHD is under control. Couples, family, or individual counseling may be needed.

Whichever form of clinical help is started, it is critical that the clinician consistently keep in mind the impact the ADHD and the possible associated disorders can have on both the child or adolescent and the family. If the person doing the counseling is not the person managing the medication, these two professionals must communicate so that adjustments in the medication can be made as needed.

The Role of the School

It is hoped that the use of appropriate medication will lessen or stop the behaviors of ADHD. The classroom teacher needs to understand the medications, how they work, what side effects might occur, how to observe behaviors, and how to communicate with the clinicians. The teacher must be sensitive to the child's or adolescent's feelings. He or she should not call out in front of the class, "Billy, it's time to take your pill." Or, when Billy misbehaves, call out, "Billy, did you take your pill this morning."

I would like to suggest some guidelines your son's or daughter's teacher should consider to help with the ADHD. These guidelines focus on four areas. Each, as you will see, could be used for children and adolescents with learning disabilities alike.

Establishing the best learning environment

The classroom should be modified to address the child's hyperactivity and/or distractibility. The student should sit near the teacher's desk to increase the teacher's awareness and control.

The student should be seated in the front of the class with his or her back to the rest of the class, thus, minimizing the amount of visual stimulation. The student should be surrounded with good role models, preferably students who will not get pulled into inappropriate behavior. Distracting stimuli should be minimized such as air conditioners, open windows or doors, or high traffic areas. Transitions and changes should be handled with awareness that these activities might be difficult. The student with ADHD might need more structure and supervision in the hall, at lockers, at lunch, or on field trips.

Giving instructions and assignments

When giving instructions or assignments, the teacher should maintain eye contact and make the information clear and concise. There should be a consistency with daily instructions and expectations. The teacher should be sure that the student understood the directions before beginning the task. If necessary, repeat the instructions. The student should be made to feel comfortable when seeking help. It is helpful to require a daily assignment notebook in which the student writes down all assignments each day. The teacher signs the notebook to confirm that the assignments are correct and the parents sign to show that the work was completed.

Modifying unacceptable behaviors

Rules of the classroom should be clear and known. The teacher should remain calm, state the infraction of the rule, and avoid debating or arguing with the student. It is helpful to have preestablished responses or consequences for inappropriate behaviors. The consequences should be presented quickly and consistently. It is important that the teacher avoid ridicule and criticism.

Enhancing self-esteem

Building or rebuilding self-esteem is important. The teacher should reward more than punish. Any and all good behavior and performances should be praised immediately. Ways should be found to encourage the student. If the child or adolescent has difficulty, it is important that the teacher find a way of reestablishing contact and trust so that new solutions can be found and tried.

Treatment with Medications

The use of medication to treat what is now called ADHD was first described in 1937. During that year there was an epidemic of viral encephalitis. Some of the children, as they recovered from this disease, were observed to be hyperactive and distractible. A pediatrician, Dr. Charles Bradley, tried a stimulant medication (Benzedrine) and found that the children became less active and distractible. Stimulants have been used to treat these behaviors since that time. It is important for you to understand that the stimulant medications have been used for more than fifty years. Follow-up studies into adulthood show these medications to be effective and safe, with no apparent long-term side effects.

Between 70 and 80 percent of children and adolescents with ADHD show improvement on the appropriate medication. These medications will decrease or stop the hyperactivity, distractibility, and/or impulsivity. They do not treat the learning disabilities if they also exist. For some of the children and adolescents with ADHD manifested by hyperactivity, medication can result in improved motor control and possibly in improved handwriting. The individual who is distractible might be better able to organize his or her thoughts when speaking or writing because of less interference with the thinking process. Short-term memory might improve because of better ability to stay on a task and concentrate. The individual with impulsivity might perform better because he or she can now reflect before answering a question. For the same reason, he or she might be better able to use cognitive strategies for learning. However, the basic underlying psychological processes associated with the learning disabilities appear not to be changed.

There is no established protocol for treating ADHD with medication. I will present an approach I find helpful. The protocol discussed should be seen as one possible model for thinking through each step of the clinical treatment process. Each clinician might use a variation of this model.

Clinical Premises

It is important that the necessary differential diagnostic process be considered before establishing the diagnosis of ADHD. If the clinician establishes this diagnosis, it is presumed that the behaviors are neurologically based. Therefore, since ADHD is not a school disability but a life disability, the need for medication must be assessed for each hour of each day. As stated earlier, to place a child or adolescent on medication only during school hours on school days will result in the individual doing better in school. However, he or she may continue to have difficulties within the family and in interactions with peers. To take an individual off of medication that is successfully treating ADHD and then send him or her to day or to sleep-away camp during the summer is inviting problems. The concept of "drug holidays" started with the concern that the use of the stimulant medications might inhibit Growth Hormone and, thus, growth; thus, the child needed to be off medication so that he or she could catch up with Growth Hormone. This concern started after one study suggested such a possibility. Several major studies conducted since have shown that Growth Hormone is released at night, when the child is off medication, and that there appears to be no concern with growth. Although the final answer is not available, the general view is that the clinician does not have to worry about growth problems.

Once the appropriate medication is found, several important questions must be addressed:

1. How much medication is needed per dose?
2. How frequently is medication needed?
3. When should the person be on medication?

An approach to answering these questions will be discussed for each medication currently in use.

As previously discussed, there is nothing magical about puberty for these children. The only way to determine if a child or adolescent continues to need medication is to take him or her off of the medication once or twice a year and to observe him or her to see if the ADHD behaviors return. If they do, medication should be restarted. If they do not, the medications can be stopped.

A Clinical Protocol

I find it helpful to have a format to follow in treating individuals with ADHD. In the absence of an established protocol, I will discuss the one I use as a possible way to approach treatment.

Treatment starts with one of the medications in what I call *Group One*. If these medications do not help or if the side effects create a problem that cannot be clinically resolved, *Group Two* medications are tried. If these medications do not help or only help control some of the behaviors, a combination of Group One and Group Two medications might be tried. If the patient still does not respond or if side effects require the clinician to try something else, *Group Three* medications are considered.

> *Group One Medications :* These are stimulant medications and are proposed to work by increasing the concentration of the deficient neurotransmitter, norepinephrine, at the nerve interface. Examples of such stimulants include:
> > ~ Methylphenidate (Ritalin)
> > ~ Dextroamphetamine (Dexedrine)
> > ~ Pemoline (Cylert)
>
> *Group Two Medications*: These are called *tricyclic antidepressants*. They are proposed to work by inhibiting the uptake of norepinephrine, thus, increasing the concentration of this transmitter at the nerve interface. Examples of such medications include:
> > ~ Imipramine (Tofranil)
> > ~ Desipramine (Norpramine)
>
> The tricyclic antidepressants may decrease the hyperactivity and distractibility. For reasons that are not clear, they might not be as helpful in decreasing the impulsivity. Thus, if these medications help with some of the behaviors and not with the impulsivity, one of the Group One medications might be used in conjunction with the tricyclic antidepressant.
> > > ~ Clonidine (Catapres) is not a tricyclic antidepressant; however, it may best be considered with the Group Two medications.
> > > ~ Bupropion (Wellbutrin) has been suggested as a medication for ADHD. Recent studies show it may be effective. It is not a tricyclic antidepressant; however, it does work at the nerve interface in a similar way.
>
> *Group Three Medications*: About 70 to 80 percent of children and adolescents with ADHD will respond to one of the medications in Group One or Group Two or to a combination of these medications. Twenty to 30 percent will be

"non-responders." Research to date does not clarify why these individuals do not respond to the medications. It is possible that the diagnosis is incorrect. Another possibility is that these individuals have another form of an attentional disorder. Another concept being considered is that for these individuals, the presumed neurological problems are not in or only in the Reticular Activating System. To use the symbolic model discussed earlier, perhaps the hyperactivity is not due to a poorly functioning "break" but due to increased activity by the "accelerator" in the cortex. Possibly, distractibility is not caused by a poorly functioning "filter system" but due to an oversensitive cortex. And, possibly, the impulsivity is not due to a poorly functioning "circuit board" but due to "short circuits" in the cortical areas. That is, perhaps the difficulties are not in the lower brain but in the cortical areas. Medications in Group Three are presumed to "calm" the cortex. Examples of such medications include:

~ Thioridazine (Mellaril)
~ Carbamazepine (Tegretol)

There is another small subgroup of the "non-responders" that now may begin to be clarified. There have been several case reports of young adults who were diagnosed as ADHD as children and who responded well to the use of stimulant medication for years. Each developed a full Bipolar Disorder (previously called Manic-Depressive Disorder) in his or her early twenties. In these cases, there was a family history of such a disorder. Also, the childhood descriptions included possible mood swings or changes in behavior. Since the characteristics in childhood for bipolar illness are not known, one must consider the possibility that for some ADHD and Bipolar Disorders share a common neurochemical theme or that for some, the behaviors of ADHD might be the earliest clinical evidence of this disorder. Such children and adolescents may respond very well to the use of lithium. Some children or adolescents present a complicated clinical picture suggesting multiple areas of brain dysfunction. They might show behaviors that are characteristic of individuals with Pervasive Developmental Disorder. In addition, they might have learning disabilities and/or ADHD. These individuals might show some improvement with the Group One or Group Two medications. When Group Three medications are tried, some improvements may be found as well. It is possible that for this group both the cortex and the Reticular Activating System might be involved. Using this clinical lead, the use of a Group One or a Group Two medication along with a Group Three medication may provide the best results. It is presumed that medication is needed for both brain sites.

To Summarize:

> *Group One Medications:*
> ~ Methylphenidate (Ritalin)
> ~ Dextroamphetamine (Dexedrine)
> ~ Pemoline (Cylert)
> *Group Two Medications:*
> ~ Imipramine (Tofranil)
> ~ Desipramine (Norpramine)
> ~ Clonidine (Catapres)
> ~ Bupropion (Wellbutrin)
> *Group Three Medications:*
> ~ Thioridazine (Mellaril)
> ~ Carbamazepine (Tegretol)
> ~ Lithium

Perhaps an analogy might help you understand the different medications. Picture a lake with not enough water in it. There are two ways to increase the level of water. One could pour more water into the lake. (The stimulants increase the production of the needed neurotransmitter.) Or, one could place a dam, thus slowing down the outflow—in this way, the level will rise as well. (The tricyclic antidepressants slow down the breakdown process, thus allowing the neurotransmitter that is produced to stay around longer.)

Group One Medications: The Stimulants

It is difficult to predict whether a child or adolescent with ADHD will respond better to one stimulant medication versus another. Some will respond poorly to one and have a positive response to another. Clinical findings, EEG, and neurochemical measures do not appear to be useful predictors of stimulant responsiveness. The clinician must use his or her own judgment as to which one to try first.

Each of these medications has shared unique characteristics, effects, and side effects. Ritalin (generic name: methylphenidate) and Dexedrine (generic name: dextroamphetamine) are available in both short-acting and long-acting forms. Cylert (generic name: pemoline) is only available in a long-acting form. (*Note:* Since you are probably more familiar with the trade names, I will use them when referring to the medications. However, keep the generic names in mind. If necessary, refer to the list of medications on p. 206.)

Ritalin is available in 5, 10, and 20 mg tablets and in a long-acting, Ritalin-SR 20 tablet. Ritalin-SR 20 contains 20 mg of methylphenidate and releases approximately 10 mg initially and 10 mg four hours later. Although there are references to the amount needed per kilogram of body weight, the amount needed by each individual does not seem to relate to body weight. A young child and an adult might need the same amount. The average dose is 15 to 30 mg per day in divided doses. Some individuals may require more. The Food and Drug Administration guidelines recommend up to 60 mg per day; however, more may be used if clinically necessary and carefully monitored. If the medication is rapidly metabolized and only lasts about three hours, it may be necessary to give four or five doses a day; thus, in some cases, using more than 60 mg.

Dexedrine is available in 5 mg tablets and in long-acting spansules of 5, 10, and 15 mg strength. As with Ritalin, the dose is established more by clinical observations than by the specific body weight. The Food and Drug Administration guidelines set the lower age limit at age three. The upper dose limit recommended is 40 mg per day; however, more can be used if clinically necessary.

Cylert is available in 18.75, 37.5, and 75 mg tablets and in 37.5 mg chewable tablets. It is administered as a single oral dose each morning; though, an evening dose may be used. The recommended starting dose is 37.5 mg per day. The dose can be gradually increased by 18.75 mg each time. The maximum recommended daily dose is 112.5 mg; although, older adolescents and adults may need a higher dose.

Since Ritalin is the most frequently used of the Group One medications, I will use it to discuss the clinical use of these Group One medications. Ritalin in the short-acting form begins to work in 30 to 45 minutes in most individuals. Recent studies show that it is not necessary to take the medication on an empty stomach. Food does not impair absorption of these medications; thus, it can be given with a meal or after a meal. Each dose lasts between three and five hours. It appears that the amount needed per dose is a reflection of the speed with which the medication is absorbed and metabolized. The functional blood level may be the same for the individual who needs 5, 10, 15, or 20 mg per dose.

Given these clinical factors, the three questions noted earlier have to be addressed by the clinician: (1) how much medication is needed per dose, (2) how often is the medication needed, and (3) during what time periods should the medication be used?

I strongly believe that parents must be informed. Thus, I will discuss in more detail each medication. You must know what I expect each physician to know.

The initial medical work-up should include measurements of height, weight, pulse, and blood pressure. The child or adolescent should be observed for tics and involuntary movements and a history of tic disorders in the family should be obtained. If Cylert is to be used, liver function tests should be performed. No such tests are required for Ritalin and Dexedrine. Medical follow-up at each visit should include observing for tics and involuntary movements and measurements of pulse, blood pressure, weight, and height. If Cylert is used, liver function tests should be done every four to six months.

Establishing the Dose

The dose-response relationships widely vary among individuals. The best way to establish the dose that is needed is not by obtaining frequent blood levels but by clinical monitoring of therapeutic effects and side effects.

The usual starting dose is 5 mg each time taken. For a younger child, 2.5 mg might be considered. The dose can be increased by 2.5 mg or 5 mg per dose every two to three days until the maximum benefit is noted. I usually start each individual on a three-times-a-day, seven-day-a-week program. Only in this way can the parents, the child or adolescent, the teachers, and I assess the benefits from the medication. Later, as will be discussed below, the specific times of coverage can be determined.

Clinical judgment is used to establish the best dose. I start at the lowest dose I believe best and increase the dose by 2.5 mg or 5 mg until all report maximum benefit. At times, I might increase the dosage in steps to build in a model for observation. That is, I might increase the morning dose but not the noon dose (e.g., 10 mg at 8:00 A.M. and 5 mg at noon and 4:00). I then ask the teacher to observe if the child or adolescent is better able to sit and attend in the morning as compared to the afternoon and evening.

Feedback from the teachers and parents is critical in assessing the improvement in the hyperactivity, distractibility, and/or impulsivity. One efficient way to do this is to ask you to talk to the teacher each day at the end of the school day and then relay this information to your physician. Thus, one call to the physician can provide feedback from the school and home.

When determining the best dose to reach maximum benefit, it is useful to increase the dose until this point is reached. As will be discussed later, there are two side effects that suggest that the dose is too high. If either occurs, the dose should be lowered. One side effect is emotional lability. For example, the child or adolescent becomes upset easier than would be normal for this individual, crying or having tantrums. The other side effect is that some children or adolescents appear to be "in a cloud" or "in a daze." They appear to be spaced out, possibly described as glassy-eyed.

I find it best to start with a short-acting form of the medication until the appropriate dose and time of dose is established. Then, a longer-acting form might be considered. If the child is started on Ritalin-SR 20 first, the clinician cannot judge if the individual might have needed less per dose. If 10 mg per dose is too high for this person, the use of the long-acting form might result in emotional lability or spacey behavior. Once the dose is established, the long-acting form can be considered if the amount needed for two consecutive doses equals the amount released in the long-acting form.

Establishing the Dose Interval

The average length of action for a short-acting tablet is four hours. However, for some individuals, the medication may last two-and-one-half to three hours and for others it might last up to five or more hours. Thus, the dose interval must be established for each individual. There is nothing special about using Ritalin every four hours.

The dose interval is determined clinically, using the feedback from the parents, the individual, and the teacher, as previously discussed. As an example, a child is placed on Ritalin, 5 mg, at 8:00 A.M., noon, and 4:00 P.M. daily. If the feedback throughout the day is good, the dose interval may be best. If the teacher says, "You know, John is great in the morning. But, about 11:00 or 11:30 A.M. he begins to wiggle in his seat and cannot stay on a task. He is perfect again after he gets his noon medication." Perhaps, the dose interval for John is three hours. He may need his medication at 8:00 A.M., 11:00 A.M., and 2:00 P.M. A 5:00 P.M. dose may be added.

If the teacher reports, "Alice is great in the morning. Only, between 12:30 and 1:00 P.M. she gets so upset. If I look at her the wrong way, she cries (or, she seems to be in a cloud and cannot be reached). By 1:00 or 1:30 P.M. she is fine again." Perhaps, for her, the dose interval is five hours. The noon dose starts to work at about 12:30 to 12:45 P.M., before the morning dose has been metabolized. For a period of time, she is getting too much medication. The interval dose for her might be every five hours. She might take medication at 8:00 A.M., 1:00 P.M., and 6:00 P.M.

Sometimes parents will report that their child or adolescent is significantly improved when on the medication. The morning dose is given just before he or she leaves for school at about 7:45 to 8:00 A.M. However, between the time the child gets up and the time the medication starts to work, he or she is impossible. The hyperactivity, distractibility, and/or impulsivity result in difficulty staying on a task, getting dressed on time, and cooperating with siblings, resulting in nagging, yelling, and fighting. In this situation, it would be ideal to provide the benefits of the medication during the early morning hours as well. The first dose may need to be given earlier and the following doses adjusted accordingly. For example, I might advise the parents to wake the child about 30 to 45 minutes before he or she has to get out of bed and give the first dose. By the time he or she gets up, the medication is working. The morning goes well for all. If this time is 6:30 A.M., the child may need to take the later doses at 10:30 A.M. and 2:30 P.M. A fourth dose may be needed at 6:30 P.M.

The same reasoning can be used for other problem situations. Suppose the child gets the first dose at 8:00 A.M. as he or she leaves for school. There are problems on the school bus. He or she will not sit in the seat or gets into trouble with the other children. By the time school starts he or she is fine. The morning dose may have to be given earlier so that it is working by the time he or she gets on the bus. Further illustrated, if the third dose is at 4:00 P.M. and wears off by about 8:00 P.M. and the parents report behavioral difficulties from 8:00 P.M. until bedtime at 9:30 or 10:00 P.M. (e.g., the child or adolescent has trouble getting ready for bed, following routines, and getting along with siblings), it might be appropriate to consider a fourth dose at 8:00 P.M. to help the child through these evening hours.

The theme is that the medication lasts about four hours. The clinician, the parents, and the child or adolescent need to learn just how long the medication lasts and then look at units of time to assess if the ADHD behaviors are interfering with functioning. If the behaviors are interfering, medication coverage for these hours may be indicated. The model of giving the medication at 8:00 A.M., noon, and 4:00 P.M. needs to be individualized for each child or adolescent.

Establishing the Periods of Time to be Covered

Since ADHD is a neurologically based disorder, the child or adolescent will be hyperactive, distractible, and/or impulsive throughout his or her awake hours. It is important to clinically assess each individual in his or her total environment to determine during which hours medication coverage is needed. There are no confirmed contraindications to the use of these medications on a continuous basis. Further, clinical research has shown that the amount of the medication in the blood at any one time is the same for individuals who take the medication on a chronic basis as it is for the individual who takes a single dose. Thus, medication can be programed around three-, four-, or five-hour units of time without concern that time is needed to accumulate the appropriate blood level or that such treatment will make the child or adolescent worse.

The key is to observe the effect of the ADHD behaviors. Hyperactivity, distractibility, and/or impulsivity can be a problem whenever such behaviors interfere with what is expected. Each behavior may interfere with functioning in the classroom. Each behavior can interfere as much with any school-like activity such as religious education, Sunday School, or homework. These behaviors might interfere with scout meetings or related activities.

Some children or adolescents (or their coaches) note that they can concentrate and play sports better on the medication.

The effect of some of these behaviors will depend on the age, grade, school demand, and family style. For example, a first or second grader might have little or no homework. Thus, if he or she is distractible, medication will be needed during school hours but may not be needed during the after-school hours. However, this same child, when older and in a higher grade, might have homework and might need medication during the after-school hours. A hyperactive child might need medication during school hours. However, if he or she is young and spends most of the after-school hours playing outside and if the family does not mind the fidgetiness, medication may not be needed at home. The same child might need medication for these hours when older and homework or family demands increase.

Weekends and holidays must be thought through in the same way. If the behaviors of ADHD interfere with expected activities or performance, medication will be needed. As an example, suppose the child is an eight-year-old boy who is hyperactive. The family plans a weekend trip. They will drive for four hours to get to the grandparents. Once there, he will run around and play with his cousins for most of the time. Finally, there will be the four hour ride home. He might need medication coverage during each four hour car ride. He might need coverage during the quiet family dinners. However, he might not need medication during the remainder of the weekend.

In determining which hours must be covered, I try to educate the parents and the individual on how the medication works. If they know that it starts to work in about 30 to 45 minutes and that it lasts between three and five hours and if they know that on the medication there is a decrease in whichever behaviors they know their son or daughter has, they can think through units of time with the clinician and decide when medication is needed. Often the child or adolescent will be the best clinician. One recently asked me if he could use the medication when he played soccer. He told me, "I can concentrate on the game so much better when I am on the medicine."

Using the Long-Acting Medications

Once the dose, time of dose, and time of coverage is determined, the clinician can consider using a long-acting form of the medication. For Ritalin, the long-acting form can be considered only if 10 mg is needed for each of two successive doses. Recent studies suggest that for some individuals the Ritalin-SR 20 appears to take longer to begin to show an effect and to only last four to five hours. Thus, it may not work as well as taking two individual 10 mg doses, four hours apart. If the Ritalin-SR 20 tablet is chewed instead of swallowed, the blood level is unpredictable and the child or adolescent might show evidence of too high a dose for part of the time and of too low a dose for other times. For Dexedrine (generic name: dextroamphetamine), the options for a long-acting form are greater since there are 5, 10, and 15 mg spansules available, each lasting about eight hours.

Cylert (generic name: pemoline) only comes in a long-acting form. The amount taken each morning must be determined. The time of dose is not an issue. Since the medication must be used each day to maintain the proper level, the time of coverage is not an issue.

Side Effects and Their Management

Again, Ritalin will be used to demonstrate the Group One medications. I will review the side effects most often seen and how they might be managed. Later, I will note the less frequent side effects listed in the pharmaceutical literature.

The two most frequently found side effects are loss of appetite and difficulty falling asleep at night. Of much less frequent occurrence, some individuals will complain of a stomachache or a headache. Of even less frequent occurrence, tics (these will be described later) may develop with some children or adolescents. As noted earlier, there are two side effects that suggest that the dose of the medication may be too high for the individual: emotional lability and a confused, cloudy cognitive state.

Loss of appetite

Ritalin may decrease an individual's appetite. This side effect may decrease over the first several weeks and cease to be a problem. If it persists, something must be done. The first step is to observe eating patterns. The medication may take the edge off of the appetite; thus, the child might not finish his or her meals but may eat candy, cake, and other sweets. If this is true, parents need to limit such sweets unless the meal is eaten. Some children are not hungry and do not eat their lunch at school. They return home at about 3:30 P.M. as the noon dose wears off and are hungry. They eat a huge snack and then cannot eat dinner. Parents need to offer smaller or lower calorie snacks after school.

For some, all of the above approaches do not work and the child continues to eat less than before starting the medication. He or she may lose weight or not gain weight. The next step is to try to create "windows of opportunity." I try to give the first dose after breakfast if at all possible. Since the child will have been off of medication overnight, he or she should have a normal appetite and eat well. I accept that lunch will not be great. Parents might try to make a meal he or she is more likely to want (e.g., a jelly sandwich rather than a tunafish sandwich). Teachers should be alerted that he or she may not eat lunch and that this is alright. For some children, this free time might mean the need for more supervision during lunch. Rather than give the third dose at 4:00 P.M., I try to hold off until dinner time or around 5:30 to 6:00 P.M. In this way, there might be a period of time off of medication when the appetite might return. The child might need more structure and supervision during the time off of medication. Homework might be delayed until later. If none of these approaches work, a Group Two medication might have to be considered.

Sleep difficulties

Some children and adolescents have difficulty going to sleep when they take Ritalin. This problem often lessens or goes away over the first two to three weeks. If it does not, an intervention is needed. For some, it is the medication that keeps them awake. For others, it is the lack of medication that keeps them awake. Each possibility must be explored. Each reason leads to a different management approach.

For some, the medication results in difficulty falling asleep. If the problem only occasionally occurs, your physician might recommend Benedryl. A dose of 25 to 50 mg at bedtime might assist the child or adolescent in falling asleep. It is important for the individual to know that the medication is not a sleeping pill. They cannot read or play until they get sleepy. However, if they lie quietly in the dark and try to sleep, the medication may help them fall asleep. This medication might help the child or adolescent return to a pattern of sleeping and then be phased out. For some, it might be occasionally needed. It is best not to use it every night on a regular basis. If the sleep problems persist, the 4:00 P.M. dose may have to be decreased or stopped. If this change creates behavioral problems in the afternoon and evening or when doing homework, a Group Two medication might have to be considered.

Lack of medication might cause sleep problems with some. If the individual takes the medication three times a day, he or she is functioning "normally" from about 8:00 A.M. to about 8:00 P.M. That is, he or she is no longer hyperactive, distractible, and/or impulsive. Then the medication wears off and the behaviors return, sometimes in greater intensity. He or she is not used to being this way and cannot lie still, block out stimuli, and fall asleep. For these individuals, a fourth dose of medication at about 8:00 P.M., allowing for the decrease or stopping of the ADHD behaviors may allow them to fall asleep with no difficulty.

I know of no way to distinguish which of the above reasons cause the sleep problem. I advise parents and the child or adolescent of the possibilities and ask them to help decide which is causing the problem. I ask that they pick an evening when staying up very late will not be a disaster, maybe a Friday or Saturday. I have the individual take a fourth dose of the medication at 8:00 P.M. If the medication is causing the sleep problem, he or she will have great difficulty going to sleep. I advise the family that if this happens, Benedryl can be used. If the added evening dose of the medication results in the individual going to sleep with no difficulty, I have learned that it is the lack of medication that is causing the problem. This fourth dose might be used every day.

Stomachache

The reason for a stomachache side effect is not known. It is my suspicion that the cause relates to the fact that the stimulant medications decrease gastrointestinal motility, resulting in food remaining in the stomach longer. I have tried a high fiber diet based on this possibility with no success. I know of no approach that corrects this side effect. If it persists, a Group Two medication may be needed.

Headache

The reason for a headache side effect is not known. If the headaches persist, it will be necessary to try a Group Two medication.

Tics

These tics might begin immediately or months after the medication is started. The most common tics are of the head or neck muscles. Some will involve the pharyngeal muscles (those in the back of your throat), resulting in sniffing, snorting, or coughing. Once the tics begin, I prefer to stop the medication and to change to a Group Two medication. Sometimes it takes up to six months for the tics to completely stop. If there is a family history of a muscle tic disorder or of Tourette's Disorder, there is an increased concern that the stimulant medication might initiate this disorder earlier than it might have been genetically set to start and that stopping the medication will not result in the tics going away. If such a tic disorder already exists, there is the concern that the stimulant medication might aggravate the disorder. Thus, it is important to explore if there is a family history of a tic disorder prior to starting a Group One medication and, if there is, to inform the physician. There are two views in medicine at this time: One group believes that if there is a history of a tic disorder, Ritalin should be used and if tics develop they should be treated. The other group believes that if there is a history of a motor tic disorder or Tourette's Disorder or if such a disorder has been diagnosed in the child or adolescent, the ADHD should not be treated with a stimulant medication. Each clinician must decide what to do. My preference is to use a Group Two medication or other medication if there is any concern about a tic disorder.

Emotional lability and cloudy cognitive ability

As noted earlier, these two behaviors suggest that the dose of the medication is too high for the individual. The reason for these behaviors is not known. The dose should be lowered. These side effects stop once the dose is at the appropriate level.

Height growth impairment

I discussed this problem earlier. Since many parents worry about it, I will mention it again. Research does not support the earlier fear that the stimulant medications inhibit growth. The few studies that suggest this to be true show that slowing of height gain rarely reaches clinical significance. It is important to understand that even these studies show that height loss, if it occurs, may be only 1 to 3 cm (about ⅓ to 1¼ inches).

My clinical understanding of the data leads me to use the medication without concern about height. I do not feel there is a need for vacations off medication nor for the need to stop the use of these medications before age 15.

Other side effects

The pharmaceutical literature describes other cardiovascular, central nervous system, gastrointestinal, allergic, and endocrine difficulties. These are extremely uncommon. The clinician should be familiar with these possibilities and will watch for them.

Unlike the other stimulant medications, Cylert can affect liver functioning. Thus, as noted earlier, periodic liver function tests should be done.

Other Clinical Issues

Preschool children

When stimulant medications are used with preschool children, there may be a higher frequency of side effects, especially emotional lability, manifested by sadness or irritability. It is possible that these side effects are secondary to the preschool child's sensitivity to the medication and to the need for lower doses.

Tolerance

No research data has shown the appearance of tolerance to stimulant medications throughout time. The exception is a suggestion of such when Ritalin-SR 20 is used.

Rebound

Some children and adolescents seem to experience a rebound effect when the Ritalin is metabolized and the blood level drops. They not only return to their previous level of hyperactivity, distractibility, and/or impulsivity, but may be excitable, talkative, impulsive, or have insomnia. This rebound behavior might last for an hour or more. Often, the problem lessens or stops after several weeks on the medication. If the rebound does not stop, the last dose of the day might need to be decreased. If this change creates a problem, one might try to add a fourth dose to see if the evening can be handled without the rebound and the child can go to sleep before the dose wears off. If nothing works, a change to a Group Two medication might be needed.

Effects of other medications

The pharmaceutical literature covers the effects of using other medication in great detail. Your physician will monitor for any possible problems. I will discuss the more common medications only. For some individuals, the additional use of a decongestant medication might increase the hyperactivity or make the individual feel agitated. The use of Theophylline (a medication often used for asthma) might do the same. In each case, if the new medication must be continued over a long period of time, a change to a Group Two medication might be considered. If the new medication is to be used for a short period of time, the amount of Ritalin might be increased for this period of time.

Some sedatives and antihistamines appear to decrease the effectiveness of the Ritalin. The individual appears to have "broken away" from the medication. The ADHD behaviors return. It may be necessary to increase the dose during the time that these other medications are used, returning to the appropriate dose after they are stopped. This problem might be seen when a child with ADHD and on Ritalin gets a cold and is placed on an antihistamine. He or she becomes more hyperactive, distractible, and/or impulsive. The physician concludes that the child is older and may need more medication. With an increase in dose, the behaviors improve. However, once the cold improves and the antihistamine is stopped, the child might become emotionally labile or appear to be in a cloud. Not knowing why this happened, the physician might stop all medication to "reassess" and the child begins to have problems at school and home.

Another situation might relate to surgery. Certain sedatives appear to cause the ADHD behaviors to become worse. This problem may be greater if your son or daughter is taken off of the Ritalin prior to surgery. The child or adolescent is given a preanesthetic, usually a short-acting sedative such as a barbiturate. Rather than calming down and getting sleepy, he or she becomes more active. More barbiturate may be given and the child gets even more active.

Fever

For reasons that are not yet understood, when a child with ADHD has a fever he or she often becomes calm and mellow. The ADHD behaviors seem to lessen or stop. Some parents report that they love it when their child has a fever because he or she will cuddle in their lap and be so calm. It is unclear at this time if a child on Ritalin should go off of the medication during the period of the fever. I usually do so and find that the behaviors remain under control.

Other Information

In earlier literature, some professionals raised the question of "state-dependent" learning. That is, if a child learns something while on a medication, will he or she retain this information when off of the medication? Studies show no such problem with any of the Group One medications.

Since the dose appears not to be related to weight, children and adolescents on a Group One medication usually do not need a higher dose as they grow in size or height. Many may need the same dose throughout many years.

At one time the use of a Group One medication with a child or adolescent with a seizure disorder was considered unwise. At this time this concern no longer appears to be an issue. Children and adolescents with a seizure disorder should be evaluated on an individual basis; however, the use of a Group One medication can be considered.

The question of addiction is noted in the pharmaceutical literature. Reference is made to the possibility of abuse. At the low doses used, addiction has not been reported to be an issue. Current studies suggest that Dexedrine probably carries a higher risk than Ritalin and that Cylert probably carries relatively less risk. For those children or adolescents with ADHD who also have a conduct disorder, special supervision may be needed to observe if the medications are being sold to peers. There is no evidence that substance abuse is increased by the use of stimulant medications. You should be advised of the concerns but assured that under proper management, addiction is not likely to occur.

Group Two Medications:
The Tricyclic Antidepressants

Group Two medications are used if the Group One medications do not work or if they produce side effects that cannot be clinically managed. Another indication might be an attempt to obtain a smoother, even effect from medication when a Group One medication does not last long or there is a rebound effect. Both Tofranil (generic name: imipramine) and Norpramine (generic name: desipramine) are long acting; thus, the time for each dose and the time period covered by the medication are not issues.

Tofranil Imipramine

Tofranil is available in 10, 25, and 50 mg tablets. The Food and Drug Administration guidelines suggest its use by individuals from age six and older. There is no apparent relationship between plasma level and clinical improvement. A starting dose for children might be 10 mg in the morning and 10 mg at bedtime. Unlike the Group One medications, Tofranil might take three to five days before its benefits can be assessed. The dose can be increased every three to five days until the maximum benefit is reached. Usually, the additional dose can be added in the evening or morning. If the feedback suggests that the child or adolescent is not doing as well during the middle of the day, the total dose can be divided into three parts and taken in the morning, early afternoon (thus, avoiding the need to give at school), and evening.

Tofranil works best in decreasing the hyperactivity and distractibility. My clinical experience shows it to have less of an effect on the impulsivity. If the impulsivity persists, a small amount of a Group One medication might be added. Often, since the Group One and Group Two medications each produce a relative increase in the suspected neurotransmitters at the nerve interface, less is needed of each when used together. If a Group One medication was stopped because of side effects, the lower dose needed in conjunction with a Group Two medication may not result in the side effect.

Side effects

Tofranil may produce electroencephalographic (EEG) changes at doses higher than the recommended level. It should not be used if the child or adolescent has a seizure disorder, since it might lower the threshold for seizures. It cannot be used if the individual is on a particular antidepressant called a mono-amine-oxidase inhibitor. Adolescents must be warned that Tofranil may enhance the nervous system depressant effects of alcohol.

The primary clinical side effect is sedation, thus, sleepiness.

If the child or adolescent complains of being tired or is observed to fall asleep in class, the dose may have to be lowered, given in divided doses throughout the day, or given primarily at bedtime. Other clinical side effects might be a dry mouth or constipation. Although very uncommon, Tofranil can have an effect on blood cell production, primarily causing a decrease in a particular blood cell called a neutrophil. Also uncommon, Tofranil can have an effect on liver function. Thus, a differential blood count and a liver function battery should be done initially and every four to six months thereafter while the medication is being used. If changes are noted, the medication should be discontinued.

Tricyclic antidepressants can cause heart blockage or irregular heart rhythms. There might be specific EKG changes. These effects appear to be dose-related and uncommon in children and adolescents. Most deaths associated with these drugs have been with adults and have occurred after deliberate or accidental overdosage or in patients with preexisting abnormalities in cardiac conduction. To detect a preexisting cardiac conduction defect, a baseline EKG is recommended. Follow-up EKGs should be part of follow-up care.

Norpramine (Desipramine)

Norpramine (generic name: desipramine) is a metabolite of Tofranil. It is available in 10, 25, 50, 75, 100, and 150 mg tablets. At this time the pharmaceutical literature does not recommend its use for children. It is not listed as a treatment for ADHD. However, studies show that it can be effective for ADHD.

The contraindications and the side effects are the same as for Tofranil. Three cases have been reported of a child having a sudden death while being treated with Norpramine. With one eight year old, there was no known cardiac abnormalities. He had been on the medication for two years as a treatment for ADHD. Plasma levels of Norpramine obtained from all three of these children were in the therapeutic or subtherapeutic range. Although there was no clear link, the studies suggested possible cardiac toxicity. Perhaps you have read about these children.

The currently available information about these sudden deaths is limited but suggests that the children were not receiving unusually high doses of Norpramine nor were their blood levels reported to be above the therapeutic range at the time they were obtained. In each case, the cardiac status of these children before the event is not known. Thus, there is no way to show that Norpramine caused a direct toxic effect that led to a sudden death in healthy children.

It could also be possible that the deaths occurred in children with preexisting but undetected cardiac conduction defects or structural anomalies and that the deaths were completely unrelated to exposure to Norpramine. Another suggestion is that Norpramine exacerbated a preexisting, undetected cardiac conduction defect or structural anomaly. Or, Norpramine had unusual effects on an immature cardiac conduction system. There is no data to support any of these possibilities.

The current literature suggests increased caution in the use of Norpramine and, possibly, other tricyclic drugs in the treatment of prepubertal children. Although the limited information available does not provide an adequate basis for developing an informed recommendation, it is suggested that an EKG be obtained at baseline and during medication "loading" and steady state. It may be contraindicated to administer tricyclic antidepressants to children who have suggestions of conduction problems. A more comprehensive evaluation may be needed for children with a positive family history of cardiac conduction defects or sudden death.

My preference at this time is not to use Norpramine with children and adolescents.

Catapres (Clonidine)

If the use of a Group One medication results in minimal improvement or in side effects that cannot be controlled, the use of Catapres (generic name: clonidine) might be considered.

Catapres appears to be more helpful in treating hyperactivity or aggressiveness. There may not be as significant an improvement in distractibility. This medication appears to improve frustration tolerance and compliance with children and adolescents who also have an Oppositional Defiant or Conduct Disorder.

Catapres comes in 0.1, 0.2, and 0.3 mg tablets and in a transdermal therapeutic system (TTS patch). The patch comes in different strengths programmed to deliver either 0.1, 0.2, or 0.3 mg of Catapres per day for one week.

The usual dose is 0.15 to 0.3 mg per day. The medication is given in divided doses three to four times a day with meals and at bedtime. The usual starting dose is one-fourth to one-half of the 0.1 mg tablet (i.e., 0.025–0.05 mg) given in the evening. The dose can be increased by adding a similar dose in the morning. If needed, a third similar dose might be added in the morning. Catapres is a short-acting medication; thus, such frequent doses may be necessary. Once the best dose is established with oral medications, the use of the patch might be considered. It might take several months to observe benefits from the medication.

The patch provides slow absorption through the skin and avoids the marked changes in blood levels when using the tablets. It is suggested that one-fourth to one-half of a Catapres-TTS patch be used.

Side effects

The most frequent side effect with Catapres is sedation, usually seen during the day. This sleepiness is most likely to occur during the first two to four weeks and then often decreases. Catapres, as an antihypertensive agent, may produce hypotension (a drop in blood pressure). In children, a 10 percent decrease in systolic pressure may be detected; but, this change generally produces no clinical symptoms or discomfort. The patch might produce an allergic skin reaction and have to be discontinued.

The initial medical work up should include a recording of blood pressure and pulse. Blood pressure and pulse should be obtained weekly during the first month of Catapres treatment. Once the dose is stabilized, these measurements can be obtained every two months. Information on sedation should be obtained on a regular basis.

If Catapres appears to work but some behaviors remain, and the clinician is hesitant to increase the dose, Ritalin or Dexedrine might be added. The two in combination might produce better results.

Wellbutrin (Bupropion)

As noted earlier, Wellbutrin (generic name: bupropion) has been suggested for use when all other Group One and Group Two medications are not effective. The research on the use of this medication is new and much of it has not yet been published. The clinician must refer to the pharmaceutical literature for suggested dose and possible side effects.

Group Three Medications

Each of the medications in Group Three is very different and must be discussed separately. Often the amount of medication needed is less than would be used for the primary clinical disorders usually treated by these medications. Because each is different, it is necessary for the clinician to review the pharmaceutical literature in detail with the parents.

Mellaril (Thioridazine)

Mellaril (generic name: Thioridazine) comes in 10, 15, 25, 50, 100, 150, and 200 mg tablets as well as in a concentrate form of 30 or 100 mg strength and in a 25 and 100 mg suspension. The Food and Drug Administration guidelines approves the use of this medication starting at age two. It is approved for ADHD. The starting dose can be as low as 10 mg in the morning and 10 mg at bedtime. The effect of the medication might not be noticed for three to five days. The dose can be increased by 10 mg each three to five days until maximum benefit is noted. If the child or adolescent does not do as well during midday, the dosage can be given in three divided amounts throughout the day.

The main side effect noted is sedation. If present, the dose may have to be decreased, given in divided doses, or given primarily at bedtime. At the low doses used for ADHD, a specific muscle problem called *tardive dyskinesia* is not common; however, they must be looked for. With this condition, the child appears not to be able to move the muscles of the face and cannot make facial expressions. Other side effects include sensitivity to sunlight with the need for more sunscreen, dryness of mouth, or nasal stuffiness.

A rare few may show motor restlessness. This is sometimes difficult to distinguish from certain forms of hyperactivity in children and can be confused with a worsening of symptoms or agitation. This clinical condition is characterized by pacing, restless feelings in the legs, a central state of agitation, dysphoria or irritability, and an inability to sit still. It is uncommon with children.

There are no specific laboratory tests needed prior to the use of this medication. During follow-up visits no specific studies are needed. Careful observations for the presence of abnormal movements should be done.

Tegretol (Carbamazepine)

Tegretol (generic name: carbamazepine) is available in 100 and 200 mg tablets. A starting dose of 100 mg at bedtime is recommended. For children under age 12, the dose can be increased by 100 mg given in the morning and at bedtime for a recommended maximum dose of 1000 mg. For individuals over 12, a maximum dose of 1200 mg can be considered. The dose needed for ADHD is usually less than that needed for control of a seizure disorder.

It is important to monitor the blood level to maintain a therapeutic and to avoid a toxic level. The more common side effects are dizziness, drowsiness, nausea, and vomiting. Because of possible side effects affecting the blood or cardiovascular system or on liver function, careful monitoring is needed. More details on side effects should be provided by the physician.

Lithium

Lithium carbonate comes in 300 mg capsules and 300 mg tablets as well as in 450 mg controlled release tablets. The amount needed will vary with each individual. The goal is to reach a therapeutic range in the blood.

Side effects might include hand tremor, frequent urination, and mild thirst. Transient and mild nausea and general discomfort may be seen. These side effects may decrease throughout time. More details on side effects should be provided by the physician.

Other Nonmedication Treatments for ADHD

The use of special diets, the role of allergies, and the effect of sugars will be discussed in Chapter 16.

In Summary

Medication to treat ADHD must be seen as part of a multimodal approach that includes education, counseling, behavioral management, along with the medication. If any of the associated disorders are present, they must be treated as well.

If your son or daughter has ADHD and medication is needed, work with your physician. The information provided in this chapter is meant to help you be informed so that you know what is being done and why. If you find that you now know more than your family doctor, find a way of lending him or her a copy of the chapter. If he or she does not believe in medication or refuses to work with you on establishing dose (e.g., "Give him these pills and come back in a month"), or handling side effects, consider another physician.

15

Treatment for Emotional, Social, and Family Problems

AS I HAVE SAID REPEATEDLY, the crucial question is whether the emotional, social, or family problems are causing the academic difficulties or whether these problems are a consequence of the frustrations and failures brought on by the academic difficulties. If the problems are a consequence of learning disabilities, the initial focus should be on developing appropriate educational programs and educating the family. If Attention-Deficit Hyperactivity Disorder (ADHD) is present, the addition of the appropriate medication must be initiated. After these initiatives are in place, the emotional, social, and family problems often lessen or disappear. If they do not, you and your family may need to look for clinical help.

In Chapter 11 on evaluation, I described the types of assessments that are available. Now, I would like to look at the different types of mental health professionals and the types of psychological therapies that are commonly available, including social skill training. Specific behavioral approaches that you can use at home to make your family life smoother whether or not your son or daughter is in treatment are also addressed in this chapter.

The Mental Health Professionals

There are four basic groups of mental health professionals: psychiatrists, psychologists, social workers, and psychiatric nurses. In addition, many school systems use school or mental health counselors. Each has a core of common knowledge and skills in diagnosis and treatment as well as unique areas of expertise. Being an intelligent consumer requires that you learn all you can about the qualifications of any clinician who is going to work with your child or your family. Don't be any less concerned about seeking the best qualified person in this field than you would be about selecting a brain surgeon.

Any of these professionals might practice one of several forms of therapy. The type of therapy offered will depend on the individual's interest and areas of training.

The *psychiatrist* is, first of all, a medical doctor, a physician. A general psychiatrist has taken four to five years of additional specialized training after graduating from medical school. Part of this training includes experiences in psychiatric work with children and adolescents. A *child and adolescent psychiatrist* has completed the medical education and training required to become a general psychiatrist and then has taken two additional years of training in child and adolescent psychiatry. Because of her or his medical training, the general or child and adolescent psychiatrist may be best able to differentiate the biological, psychological, and social—the "bio-psychosocial"—aspects of a problem in the process of establishing a diagnosis. Only psychiatrists of the mental health profession can prescribe medication or admit patients to a hospital. All psychiatrists are trained to do individual psychotherapy; most are also trained to do group, behavioral, and family therapy. The child and adolescent psychiatrist, because of his or her additional training, is most qualified to do bio-psychosocial diagnosis and treatment of children and adolescents.

The *psychologist* may have a doctorate or a master's degree. Most states require a doctorate degree to be licensed. Their doctorate is usually in clinical, counseling, school, or developmental psychology, although there are other possible areas. The doctorate-level psychologist has completed at least four to six years of graduate training beyond college, including a year of special clinical training called an internship. Because one can be trained in so many areas and because there are so many different types of internships available, any specific psychologist may have differing skills with different age groups or types of therapy. The depth and variety of training with children or adolescents also greatly varies. The master's level psychologist has completed a two-year graduate program beyond college. Because training and experience vary so widely, you may want to discuss the background of your psychologist before starting any therapy. Psychologists do have the unique skill of being able to administer psychological and often educational tests.

The *social worker* has completed college plus two years in a graduate school of social work. Following graduation, he or she must work under supervision for several years before being eligible to take their clinical certifying examination. If they pass they become a licensed clinical social worker (LCSW). The level of diagnostic and treatment skills in working with children and adolescents depends on the social worker's additional experiences following graduation or on other postgraduate training they have sought out. The kinds of therapies offered will also be based on this required experience or other experiences. Thus, being a social worker does not necessarily mean that the individual is experienced in working with children and adolescents. You need to learn what training and experiences they have had since graduation from their school of social work.

The *psychiatric nurse* may have completed a two-, three-, or four-year training program leading to a certificate as a registered nurse (RN) or a bachelor's degree in nursing. Some have taken a two year master's degree program in psychiatric nursing and some have obtained the experiences by working in the field. To be certified as a clinical specialist in psychiatric nursing, he or she must have a master's or doctor's degree in psychiatric or mental health nursing or an acceptable equivalent and must pass a national examination. The psychiatric nurse with graduate school training has core knowledge and skills comparable to those of the other mental health professionals with a similar master's level of training. Many focus on family therapy, but many are also skilled in individual, behavioral, or group therapy. As with the social worker, you will want to know if he or she has had special training experiences with children and adolescents.

The *counselor* is a mixed bag today. Many have a master's degree and are highly qualified. Some have less training and may be less qualified. If the counselor is part of the school team, he or she can be a valuable part of the intervention program. If he or she is in private practice, ask questions about qualifications and experiences.

You can see that there are several professionals within the mental health field, and within each profession, practitioners have widely different levels of training and experiences. Not all are equally well trained to work with children or adolescents. I am surprised at times when I see friends search the country to find the "best" surgeon for a specific procedure or the best physician to treat their specific disorder. They learn of the person's training and qualifications and how many years of experience they have had. Yet, this same friend will take a family member to a local mental health practitioner without asking for training, qualifications, and experiences. Is the mind any less important?

Be an intelligent, informed consumer. It is not inappropriate to discuss a person's training, experiences, and specialty. After all, you are entrusting your child and possibly your family to her or him. Be assertive. It is not rude to reject a therapist and look for another if you don't like the person or feel that he or she does not relate well to you or your child.

The Psychological Therapies

The various behaviors of children and adolescents reflect many kinds of emotional problems. Any evaluation must look at all aspects of behavior, and depending on the findings, specific types of therapy are recommended that best address the problems that are identified. Often, several problem areas are noted, calling for a combination of treatments. Be concerned about a mental health professional evaluating your child or adolescent or family who always recommends the same form of therapy following the evaluation. All cannot have the same problem areas every time. Let me briefly review the different types of evaluations and therapy that are offered.

The *dynamic or psychoanalytic evaluation* or "intrapsychic assessment" is done by talking with the child or adolescent. For younger children, play materials may be used as a vehicle for communicating. The evaluator looks at the interactions between internal thinking processes (basic wishes and needs, conscience, or value systems), the ability to mediate what to do, and the ability to assess the realities of the outside world. He or she explores questions that are related to the relative strengths of each process, the coping skills available, the types of problems or conflicts the child or adolescent is struggling with, and whether all of these factors are age-appropriate or not. If conflicts are found, *individual psychoanalytically oriented psychotherapy* might be recommended.

In a *behavioral evaluation*, the clinician observes and records behaviors in an attempt to observe how the behaviors were learned and why they persist. If they are not successful or are dysfunctional, how might they be changed? What reinforces the behavior? In addition, he or she might assess the individual's ability to handle anxiety or certain thoughts, feelings, or experiences that are causing stress and difficulty with functioning. *Behavioral therapy* might include a behavioral management program, techniques for better handling anxiety (e.g., relaxation therapy), or techniques for better handling feelings and thoughts (called *cognitive behavioral therapy*).

The *interpersonal evaluation* often involves directly observing the child or adolescent in several settings or obtaining information from people who observe him or her in these settings. How does the child interact with peers and adults? What roles does he or she play? Are there patterns of behavior that explain difficulties relating or communicating? If problems appear in these areas, *group therapy* might be recommended. If the difficulties relate to social skills, *social skill training* might be considered.

The *family evaluation* or systems evaluation looks at the most important system, the family. The family is seen together. What roles does the child or adolescent play? What effect does this role have on other family members? What effect do the other family members have on the child? Difficulties in these areas might lead to *family therapy*.

By the time some children are evaluated, their problems have become so complex that a multiple approach is needed. The full family may be seen initially both to educate and to help parents regain control and confidence. At this time a behavioral modification system might be introduced to assist in setting some limits on the child's or adolescent's unacceptable behaviors. Once the behavior is under control, the child or adolescent might be seen individually and the parents seen as a couple. The family continues to be seen together on occasion as well.

You can help your child or adolescent and your family in many ways. The first thing to do is to select a competent clinician, one who is well trained, experienced, and skilled, and one whom you like and feel you can talk to easily. Preferably, the clinician should be comfortable with more than one model of therapy and be flexible in using whichever approach is most helpful at any given time. The clinician must be knowledgeable about learning disabilities, ADHD, and the special problems of the child or adolescent with these problems and their family.

Behavioral Management Programs

I would like to teach you a model for assessing behaviors within your family and for setting up your own behavioral program to change unacceptable behaviors. It should work. If it does not, you may need to seek help from a professional. Let me describe the types of problems, the models for clarifying what needs to be changed, the basic model for demanding change, and additional models that might be used along with the basic model.

In an initial evaluation session with parents, a clinician might hear a child described as a tyrant who must have his or her way or all hell breaks loose with screaming, throwing things, hitting sister or brother, messing up his or her room, or "something." Later, he or she meets this "tyrant"—a 4-foot, 70 pound little boy who could be picked up and carried under one arm. Where is the monster?

Then the clinician begins to work with the family and soon finds out. This child's behavior does dominate the family. The parents avoid too many confrontations because they do not want to face the consequences. They "look the other way" until pushed so far that they have to react. By that time, feeling helpless, the only possible reaction often is anger. They yell, hit the child, or give out a punishment like "no television for one week" then have to back down because they have no way to enforce it or because enforcing it leads to more confrontations and fights.

As the evaluation progresses, the clinician may gain clues or clarify the dynamics within the child or within the family that explain the behaviors. What is more likely to occur is that the clinician cannot clarify the underlying issues but can see that something has to be done and quickly. One has to "put out the fire" before an in-depth assessment can be considered. What is clear is that the child is in control and the parents are not in control or are out of control. What may also be clear is that parents disagree and, rather than supporting each other, they are split and fighting with each other. This situation in the family is anxiety producing for the child and not compatible with healthy psychosocial development. This situation is dysfunctional for the parents and other members of the family as well.

Perhaps the clinician can see patterns. Without meaning to do so, the parents are reinforcing the very behaviors they do not want. The child acts badly and gets a lot of attention—negative attention. The parents get upset and this proves to the child that she or he can control one part of the world—the family. This, along with getting what the child wants, is the reward for bad behavior. The other children see the parents forced to give in. They become angry. Soon, they may learn that the only way to get attention or to get what one wants is to be bad.

Whatever the dynamics or initial cause, the family dysfunction must be corrected. The parents must regain control. The child or adolescent must feel that he or she can be controlled. These changes are essential for the parents, the child or adolescent, and the family. Such negative control of parents is unhealthy and unproductive for the child. He or she must learn different behavioral patterns before they generalize out to the school, to peers, or to the community.

Once the behaviors are in control, the child or adolescent can begin to learn new and better techniques to function within the family and to cope with stress. Parents and children or adolescents can rework styles of interacting and roles within the family. First comes the behavioral changes, then comes awareness and insight.

It is not uncommon to find that the same child or adolescent who is out of control at home is functioning very well in school, at friend's houses, or when playing with friends away from the house. Sunday School teachers, activity leaders, sports coaches might think the child is great and a perfect lady or gentleman. In this case, one might assume that the behavioral difficulties are not neurologically driven or they would occur in every setting. If the behaviors are only expressed at home, it is possible that they reflect family dynamics or conflict. It is also possible that the child or adolescent holds in all of his or her frustration and anger all day so as not to get into trouble and then lets it all out at home where it is safe to do so. Another possibility is that the child has ADHD and is on the appropriate medication and doing well during the hours that the medication is working; however, he or she is not taking the medication during other than school hours. The addition of the medication for evenings and weekends might lead to a significant improvement in home behaviors. If the behaviors are only seen at home, a behavioral management program might be needed just for the family.

The clinician might observe that the negative or aggressive behaviors are seen in school, with peers, during activities, and at home. Often this picture is associated with ADHD. In this situation, the possibility that the neurologically driven behaviors of hyperactivity, distractibility, and/or impulsivity might be seen as causing or contributing to the difficulties. Once medication is established, the behaviors might decrease or stop. If not, the behavioral management program will have to include school and outside of the house activities as well as home time.

Behavioral Management Concepts

Any behavioral plan must be based on several important concepts of the learning theory. First, one is more likely to succeed in changing behavior by rewarding what is desired than by punishing what is undesired. Second, for a plan to work, the responses to acceptable and unacceptable behaviors must be consistent and must occur each time. Inconsistent responses or inconsistent response patterns may reinforce the negative behavior.

As parents you must learn that there is no right or wrong way to raise children. You must collaborate in developing a plan with which you both can be comfortable and can agree. Once decided, the plan must be practiced in a consistent and persistent way.

Initially, you must be omnipotent. No more reasoning, bargaining, bribing, threatening, or trying to provoke guilt. Parents make the rules; parents enforce the rules; parents' decisions are final. As parents you must learn that if you "step into the arena" and agree to debate or argue with your child, you will lose. If a parent says it is time to go to sleep and a child says, "but can I stay up 15 minutes more," the answer must be, "I did not ask

you what time you wanted to go to sleep. I said it is bedtime."
Argue about the 15 minutes and it becomes 20 minutes, then 30
minutes. Soon, the parent's frustration and anger will result in
fighting. Later in the plan there can be flexibility, but not initially.

Developing the Initial Intervention Strategy

Initially, parents are usually overwhelmed. They have exhausted
their choices of actions. They may feel helpless and failures as
parents. If there are two parents, there may be stress between
the two, disagreeing on how to handle the behaviors or blaming
the other for the problems. Try to follow this plan. If you are too
worn out or overwhelmed, seek professional help.

The first step is to collect data on your observations of the
behaviors. Each parent should collect data separately. The differences between the two will be very useful. Don't be embarrassed by what you do. Record what really happens without
worrying what someone will think. We already know that things
are not working well. Just record what you live so that you can
begin to change things.

You will need a structure to collect these data. The easiest
model to use is an "ABC" chart. You record three things: (A) the
antecedent to the behavior, (B) the behavior, and (C) the consequences of the behavior. The chart will look like this:

Date/time	Antecedent	Behavior	Consequence

A typical entry might read like this:

Date/time	Antecedent	Behavior	Consequence
Monday 4:30 P.M.	Don't know; not there	John hit sister; she hit him back	Told both to go to room

Date/time	Antecedent	Behavior	Consequence
6:00 P.M.	Talking to Mary	John teased her; she cried	Yelled at John
9:00 P.M.	Told John to get ready for bed	Refused to take bath, get in P.J.'s yelled at me when told	Took 30 minutes of reminding; finally hit him and he went to take a bath

Each parent may have different lists. In part, this reflects when each is home and with the child or adolescent. One may be the firm disciplinarian and the other the easy-going, "give them another chance" type. Each parent will see and list different things. Each has different experiences and expectations. Father may come home at 6:00 or 6:30 P.M. looking forward to being with the children and playing with them. Frustrated and short of temper, mother may have had it by then and wants the kids to be quiet and to get their homework and other chores done so that they can go to bed.

Neither parent is right or wrong. The important goal is that both parents agree on their expectations and be consistent in asking that they be met. Consistency is the key. Inconsistency reinforces the behavior; consistency stops the behavior.

Certain patterns should become clear for each column and for overall behaviors. Certain antecedents lead to certain behaviors. The consequences that follow the same behaviors are inconsistent. Or, one parent gets mad and yells at everything or other family members seem to get punished as much as the child who caused the problems. A common theme may be that when a child or adolescent does not get what he or she wants or is asked to do something he or she does not want to do, this child or adolescent misbehaves.

Once the data are collected, it is analyzed. Patterns are sought out. The first task is to clearly define the unacceptable behaviors that need to be changed. Often, parents start with a long list of behaviors. Once the data are studied, the behaviors can be clustered into two or three major areas. By doing this, you will not be as overwhelmed. You are not dealing with an impossible list of problems but can focus on a few major areas.

Frequently, the unacceptable behaviors fall into three basic groups:

Physical abuse: Such behaviors in this category could include:
- ~ Hitting sibling
- ~ Hitting parent
- ~ Hurting a pet
- ~ Damaging property

Verbal abuse: Such behaviors in this category could include:

~ Yelling at sibling
~ Yelling at parent
~ Teasing
~ Cursing or other unacceptable words
~ Threatening someone

Noncompliance: Such behaviors in this category could include:

~ Not listening to what is said
~ Not doing a requested chore
~ Defying a parent's request

Once the behaviors are identified, it is useful to study the relationship between the antecedents and the behaviors. Look for themes. The behaviors are more likely to occur if the child is tired, hungry, or about to be sick. The behaviors are more likely to occur during the first hour after coming home from school. The behaviors are more likely to occur when he or she is off of medication. The behaviors appear to relate to the child's or adolescent's learning disabilities or Sensory Integrative Disorder. These themes will be useful in helping the child or adolescent understand why he or she has difficulty and in helping you know when to be most alert to the possibility of problems.

Setting up the Initial Program

Once you have a clearer idea of the behaviors that need to be changed, a plan can be developed. Define the behaviors as clearly as possible and work out a consequence that can be consistently imposed. Work out the plan in great detail, then introduce it to the family. The plan should be for all siblings. Even if the other children or adolescents do not cause problems, it will not negatively affect them to be part of the program. It might benefit them by rewarding them for their good behavior. It might have been that the "bad" child took so much attention that the "good" child was ignored or not thanked for being good. This plan will help you remember to reward good behaviors. If a sibling is provoking or encouraging the negative behavior, it will become clear if he or she also is on the plan.

As parents, you need to understand that there are several basic principles to reverse the pattern of punishing bad behavior and usually ignoring or occasionally rewarding good or positive behavior. This plan will reward positive behaviors and withhold rewards for negative behaviors. Furthermore, you will have pre-planned responses that can be used every time. Your child or adolescent cannot catch you off guard, making you feel helpless and therefore angry. Each time a behavior occurs there will be the same response from either parent.

Let me illustrate this point about consistency. Suppose a boy hits his sister five times in a week. On one occasion the mother was in such a rush she yelled at him but did nothing about the hit. On another occasion she was tired and did not want to deal with him so she pretended she did not see what happened. On the other three times she did punish him. If this child gives up hitting his sister because mother tells him to, he has to give up hitting her 100 percent of the time. If he continues to hit her, he has a 40 percent chance of getting away with it. He would be a fool to give up the behavior. If a parent is consistent, the behavior will stop. If the parent is anything less than consistent, the behavior might persist or get worse.

Step one

Divide the day into parts. For example, on a typical school day there will be three parts: (1) from the time the child or adolescent gets up until he or she leaves for school, (2) from the time he or she returns from school until the end of the evening meal, and (3) from the end of this meal until bedtime. Weekend or summer days can be divided into four parts by using meals as the dividers: (1) from the time the child or adolescent wakes up until the end of breakfast, (2) from the end of breakfast to the end of lunch, (3) from the end of lunch to the end of dinner, and (4) from the end of dinner until bedtime.

Step two

Make a list of the child's or adolescent's unacceptable behaviors. This list should be brief and limited to the major problems. If the basic three noted earlier are used, a list might read:

1. No physical abuse (define in detail for the child; for example, no hitting sister, pulling cat's tail, kicking mother, breaking toys).

2. No verbal abuse (define in detail for the child; for example, no cursing, calling someone stupid, teasing).

3. No noncompliance (define in detail for the child; for exam-

ple, refusing to do what you are told to do). For younger children, the term "not listening" might be used. Make it clear that you will request several times. Then you will say, "If I have to ask you again, I will call it noncompliance." Any behavior continuing after this warning is called noncompliance. In this way the child or adolescent can never say, "But, you never told me I had to do this."

Step three

The purpose of the plan is to reward positive behaviors. Negative behaviors are not mentioned as such. The child or adolescent can earn one point for each behavior he *does not do* during a unit of time. Later we will talk about "time out." With time out, too, the focus is on the positive and not the negative; thus, the wording is important. The parent says, "What you did is so unacceptable in this family that you must go to your room and think about the need to change what you do." The parent does not say, "Go to your room" with the connotation that doing so is punishment.

The child can earn points by not doing the unacceptable behaviors. He or she can earn one point for each negative behavior not done. For example, suppose a boy gets up in the morning, does all of his chores, and gets to breakfast on time. He does not hit anyone but he does call his sister "stupid." As he leaves for school the parent would say, "I am pleased that you earned two points this morning. You followed all rules and you did not hit anyone. I wish I could have given you the third point but you did call your sister a name and that is verbal abuse." This parent might say to the sister, "I am happy that you earned all three of your points. Thank you for not calling your brother a name when he called you one." Remember, behavior is changed by rewarding what you want and not by punishing what you do not want.

A book or chart should be available and the points recorded. If the child is too young to understand points, a calendar or chart can be used and stars pasted on, or a jar can be filled with marbles to represent each point earned.

Each part of the day is handled in the same way. In the model designed above with three units of time during school days and four units of time on the weekend, the maximum number of points that can be earned on a school day is 9 and the maximum each weekend day is 12. The total for a week will be 69. These points can be used in three ways: a daily reward, a weekly reward, and a special reward. The points are counted daily, then continue to be counted weekly or accumulatively. The child or adolescent should participate in developing the rewards. Parents make the final decisions but keep in mind the request. If the child or adolescent says, "This is stupid. I won't participate," the parent replies, "The plan starts tomorrow. Either you suggest what you might like to work toward or I will make the decisions for you."

Each reward must be individualized for each member of the family and each must be compatible with the family's style and philosophy. Rewards that involve interpersonal experiences are preferred to material reward. The daily reward could be an additional half hour of TV watched with a parent, being able to stay up 30 minutes later, reading a book or playing a game with a parent, or 30 minutes of special time with one parent.

The weekly reward might be going to a movie, or out to eat with the family, or having a friend sleep over, or any other special activity. Points are counted from Saturday morning to Friday night, thus you know if the child or adolescent has enough points before the weekend starts. In this way, a babysitter can be lined up before any family activity. In the past, your son or daughter might have been impossible all week, yet he or she would go out with the family on the weekend. Now, this child or adolescent stays home and your other children go out.

A special reward might be something important that must be worked toward. A new bicycle, or toy, or a special trip might be selected. It should take a month or more to accumulate enough points for this reward.

For the daily and weekly rewards, set a goal initially of 80 percent of the maximum number of points that can be earned. After a month of success (which might take several months to reach), the goal can be raised to 90 percent. It is best not to set the goal at 100 percent. No one can be perfect all of the time. Any negative behavior early in the day or week could destroy all hope of a reward and the child or adolescent might give up.

For the plan described earlier, the child or adolescent would need seven points each weekday evening to get the reward (80 percent of nine points). He or she would need 55 points by Friday night for the weekend reward (80 percent of 69 points).

Time out

Before starting the plan, define which behaviors will be considered so unacceptable to the family that they will result in the child not earning a point plus being removed from the family for a limited time so that he or she can think about the need to change this behavior. I always use this consequence in response to physical abuse. Other behaviors might be included. For the young child, 15 minutes is appropriate; for the older child or adolescent, 30 minutes is best.

This time is to be spent quietly thinking about what happened and why he or she needs to change. The child's or adolescent's room can be used if it is not filled with TV, stereo, games, and other pleasurable distractions. If his or her room cannot be used, a guest room or laundry room might be best. The door is to be closed and the child is to be quiet. Each time he or she opens the door or yells or throws something, the timer is reset to zero and the 15 or 30 minutes starts again. The child or adolescent soon learns that unless he or she is quiet and cooperative, a 15 minute time out can last for hours.

Time out can be used away from home as well. If in a restaurant and it is safe, take the child or adolescent to the car. If concerned, a parent might want to stand near the car and watch. If in a shopping center, try to find a safe place for the child to sit. Tell him or her that you will return in 15 (or 30 minutes). If concerned, the parent can stand away from the child or adolescent and watch during the time.

For the plan to work, it must be exact as to expectations, behaviors that are rewarded, and consequences. Once initiated, the child or adolescent will find loopholes. The parents must be smarter than their son or daughter and quickly close each loophole.

A common example is time out. The child or adolescent might be home with mother. He or she is told to go to their room and refuses. The child or adolescent might defy mother, run around the room, and dare her to chase him or her or run out of the house. If this happens, it is not good for mother to chase the child or to drag him or her to the room. The plan is developed and explained in advance. The child or adolescent knows that this plan will be implemented the minute he or she refuses to go to the assigned room for time out. This plan can have two parts:

1. The parent will announce a time that he or she is expected to be in the room (e.g., three minutes from the time that the parent informs the child to go to the room). After that time, he or she will need to spend two additional minutes in the room for every minute it takes to get to the room. This means that if the child or adolescent does not go to the room until father comes home two hours later, he or she will need to spend four additional hours in the room. This time cannot be counted after bedtime; thus, it is spent in the room the next day, perhaps after school. Sometimes, the child or adolescent spends all of a weekend day making up the time needed because he or she tested the parent earlier. Soon, he or she learns to listen.

2. The second part of the plan is for the child or adolescent to know that during the time he or she refuses to go to the assigned room a second thing will happen. The parent will say, "I will always love you dearly. However, when you abuse me as a parent, I do not choose to parent you." This means that the parent will not talk to the child or adolescent nor interact in any way. When mealtime comes, a place setting is set for everyone in the family but this person. If he or she wants to eat, he or she can make his or her own meal and sit somewhere else. If the parent was to carpool to a meeting or sports practice or game, it will not be done. The child will have to face the consequences of not attending. If the behavior persists till bedtime, the parent will not respond to the child or adolescent nor put him or her to bed. Once the son or daughter goes to the room to spend the quiet time, parenting starts again.

Some parents find that the, "I love you but if you abuse me as a parent I choose not to parent you" approach too painful to consider. I remind this parent that allowing the unacceptable behaviors is more painful and potentially harmful to the child than the model suggested.

There are other frequent loopholes. For physical abuse, the child or adolescent does not earn a point and goes to a quiet room to think; thus, the events are stopped. What about verbal abuse? For the first event, he or she will not earn a point. What does the parent do for the remainder of the time in this time period if this child or adolescent is verbally abusive again. I suggest that for the second occurrence, he or she must go to the quiet room for 15 to 30 minutes to think about the fact that such behavior is not acceptable in the family and he or she must change. What to do for noncompliance once he or she does not earn a point is harder to handle. What do parents do when the toys still need to be put away or a bath is still needed? Later in this chapter, several alternative plans are described.

This reward-point system along with a time out system will work. The key is to be consistent. You must be encouraged to develop and implement the plan. Your child or adolescent will test; but, if you stick to it, the behaviors will improve. To some parent's surprise, once the external controls work and the child or adolescent functions better, he or she is happier not more frustrated. Once they improve, the plan must be continued. If stopped too soon, the behaviors will return.

Setting up the Second Phase of the Plan

The goal of this second phase of intervention is to help the child or adolescent internalize the controls. The first phase provided external controls. Now, the effort shifts to helping build these controls into the behavioral patterns of this child or adolescent. The first phase continues; however, a more interactive rather than omnipotent approach is used by parents.

Once the unacceptable behaviors are under better control, *reflective talking* can be introduced. Initially, these discussions are held after the fact. The best time might be at night when sitting on the bed, talking. A child or adolescent has been in a fight or a yelling match. He or she has spent time in the quiet room. Later in the day a parent sits with the child or adolescent in private and discusses what happened. For example, "Fred, I am sorry you had so much trouble this afternoon. I love you and I do not like being angry with your behavior or having to ask you to remove yourself from the family. What do you think we can do to stop such things from happening?" Let him talk. At first he may only make angry accusations of unfairness or of others causing the trouble. The parent might respond, "I don't know if your brother was teasing you before you hit him or not. I was not there. But, let's suppose that he did. What else could you have done? By hitting him you got into trouble and he did not. There must be a better way. Maybe you could have told me what you thought he was doing." Such conversations may have to occur many times before the child or adolescent begins to think about his or her behavior and to consider alternative solutions to problems. It is important that you not only point out the behavior but offer alternative solutions.

Gradually, you will be able to point out themes. For example, "You know, Mary, I notice that you are most likely to get into trouble right after you come home from school. Do you suppose that you hold in all of your problems all day so that you will not get into trouble and then let it out the first time you are upset at home? If so, maybe we can do something to help. Maybe, as soon as you come home, you and I can sit in the kitchen, have a snack, and talk. Maybe if you tell me about your day and the problems you will feel better and will not have to act out your feelings."

Soon you will be able to do the reflective thinking before the fact. For example, "John, you and I both have learned that if you keep playing with your brother once the teasing starts, there will be a fight. Do you remember what we talked about? What else could you do?" Or, "Alice, you are forcing me to be a policeperson and to yell at you or punish you. I do not like doing that. I'd rather enjoy being with you than yelling at you or punishing you. Why do you think you force me to be a policeperson? Remember what we talked about the other night? Do you want to try some of the ideas we talked about?" Gradually, the child or adolescent will begin to try the new behaviors.

He or she can learn from hearing parents openly discuss feelings and thoughts. Let the child understand how you feel— angry, sad, afraid, worried. You can role model how to handle these feelings. For example, "I am so angry with what you did that I cannot talk to you. I am going into the other room to calm down. Later, we can talk." Not only will you feel more in control, but you have demonstrated a way to handle angry feelings.

It is important for parents to begin to explain or role model acceptable ways for their son or daughter to handle feelings. Many families are quick to tell their children how they may not show anger, sadness, or disappointment, but they do not teach them acceptable ways of showing these feelings. Anger is a normal feeling and children and adolescents must learn how to handle these feelings in an acceptable way in the family. Can they yell as long as they do not curse? Can they stamp their feet or slam the door shut as long as they do not break anything? Watch out for confusing messages. One parent in the family yells or throws things when angry. The other parent pouts or goes to a room alone when angry; but, when the child gets angry and starts to yell he or she is told, "You may not do that." If he or she walks off pouting, the parent says, "You come back here. I am talking to you." It is acceptable for families to have different rules for the adults and the children. However, parents must then teach their children or adolescents what are acceptable ways for them to express feelings in the family.

Additional Models

In addition to the basic plan, other concepts can be added to address specific problems. These plans may work best around issues of noncompliance. What do you do after the child or adolescent has not earned a point, yet the requested behavior is still required? The basic concepts are the same: the parents are in control, the rules and consequences are consistent and persistent.

Handling chores

To avoid any confusion about chores or other duties expected by the family, you must make a detailed list of expectations. For example, individual chores might include putting dirty clothes in the hamper, making one's bed, and picking things up off of the floor. Family chores might include setting the table, loading or emptying the dishwasher, and vacuuming. Place the list in an obvious place. Clarify if these chores are to be rewarded by money or if they are expected as part of family responsibility. If the family chores are to be shared on different days, make a clear list of what each child is to do each day. For example, Alice clears the table on even number days and Charlie clears the table on odd number days.

If the chores are expected and are not done, what will be the consistent consequence? What can you do if the child "forgets" or does not do an expected chore? Should you continue to nag, then shout? Several models are suggested below. Each gives the parents the controls. If a task is not done, there is a clear consequence. The choice is for the child or adolescent. If he or she does the chore there is the expected reward. If he or she does not do the chore there is the expected consequence.

The maid service Establish that all parent services are not supplied free of charge. If chores are not done by a set time, a parent will do them, but not for free. Make a list of the chores. Set a reasonable fee for each chore. Be realistic for the age and financial resources of the child or adolescent. For example, 25 cents to make the bed; 50 cents for picking up things from the floor of their room; 50 cents for putting a bike in the garage. Then, stop arguing, reminding, or nagging the child or adolescent. If the chore is done by the preset time, fine. If it is not done, do the chore without comment. At the end of each day or week, submit a bill for the service. If he or she gets an allowance, you might present a bill at the end of the week; for example:

Allowance:	$5.00
Maid service:	3.75
Balance due:	1.25

He or she might get upset and ask how lunch drinks or snacks are to be bought. You reply, "Think about that next week when you decide not to do a chore." If the child or adolescent does not get an allowance, use birthday or savings money. If there is no such money or if the child or adolescent owes the parent more than the allowance, he or she is given specific work details to earn the money owed. "I will pay you $2.00 per hour to clean the garage. You owe me $3.00; so, I expect you to work one and one-half hours this weekend."

No more getting angry. No more reminding. No more fights. They have two choices. Do their chores and get the rewards or not do the chores and pay someone else to do the chores.

The Sunday box Set up a "box" in a secure place. A closet or room that can be locked will do or the trunk of a car. Make it clear that any items left where they should not be after a predetermined time of the day (e.g., toys, bike, books, coat, shoes) will be placed in this "box." It will not be emptied until Sunday morning. This means that if a favorite game or bike or piece of sports equipment is left out or not put away, it is lost until Sunday. If the objects are clothes or shoes and cannot be done without, the child or adolescent must pay a fee to retrieve them early.

This plan has worked so well in some families that the mother placed the father on the plan as well. His clothes, work papers, or other objects that had been left lying around disappeared into the Sunday Box.

Handling property damage

The initial response from the parents regarding property damage will be based on the plan in place. If this behavior is called physical abuse, he or she will not earn a point and must spend time in a quiet room thinking. More might be needed. The child or adolescent could be made to pay to repair or replace the item. Money could come out of an allowance. If the amount is large, the money might come out in installments until paid off. If this model for payment is not possible because the child or adolescent does not have a savings account, he or she is given a way to earn the money. Assign other than expected tasks and pay by the hour—cutting the grass, washing clothes, washing the kitchen floor, or cleaning the garage. The first time a child or adolescent gets angry and kicks over a lamp, breaking it, then learns that it will cost $50.00 to replace and that he or she will have to work for 25 hours at $2.00 an hour to pay for the damage, may be the first time that he or she starts to think before acting. This is the goal, getting the child or adolescent to stop before acting and to think about the consequences of the behavior.

Handling dawdling

Many parents reinforce dawdling by reminding, nagging, yelling, screaming, and then, in anger, doing the task with or for the child. All this behavior does is teach the child that he or she can get away with their behavior, force the parents to help, or succeed in getting a parent upset. Instead, define the limits for a behavior then establish clear consequences.

A child may not get dressed on time. He or she is not openly oppositional, but is so busy playing or looking out of the window that tasks just never get done. As the time for the school bus gets closer he or she has not yet dressed or eaten because he or she is dawdling and playing. You probably go into the bedroom, yell at the child, and quickly dress him or her so that there will be time to eat and catch the bus. Your child has succeeded in getting you upset and angry and in getting you to help. It is important in this situation to think through if the difficulty getting dressed might relate to a learning disability (e.g., sequence, organization, motor), a Sensory Integrative Disorder, or ADHD behaviors present because the child is not on medication during these hours.

For this type of behavior, you might first establish the rules.

For example, the kitchen is open until 7:30 A.M. You must be dressed to enter. If you come in before 7:15, mother or father will make you a hot breakfast. If you come in after 7:15, you may . have cold cereal. No food after 7:30. You will have to go to school hungry. The child is expected to be ready to leave for the bus by 7:40. A.M.

What do you do if it is 7:40 A.M. and he or she is still not dressed? If it is an older child or an adolescent, he or she is told that if they miss the bus or car pool, you will not take him or her to school. Thus, unless this child or adolescent can walk or take public transportation, he or she will not be able to go to school. Furthermore, you will not write a note if he or she is late or absent, thus the school might issue a detention. The parent could say, for example, "Sorry, the problem is yours. Maybe tomorrow you will get dressed." If they remain home, they stay in their room during normal school hours. No television, and no interactions with parents. Obviously, if both parents work an alternative plan is needed.

If the child is young and the school cooperative, another plan can be developed with the help of the bus driver, the classroom teacher, and the principal. The child is told the plan in advance. When it is time to leave for the bus, quietly take all of the clothes that have not yet been put on and place them in a bag. Wrap the child in a robe or coat and walk him or her to the bus, pajamas and all. The bus driver, having been briefed, smiles and says hello. The child gets on the bus with the bag of clothes. The parent then calls the principal to have the teacher alerted. If the child dresses on the bus, fine. If he or she arrives at school in pajamas, the teacher quietly says, "Would you like to go to the bathroom and get dressed?" The child will not starve without breakfast on this day. He or she will have learned that dawdling no longer works. Only he or she is affected by the behavior.

This approach might work in other situations. At bedtime, whether in pajamas or still in street clothes, put the child in bed and turn out the lights. When the family is ready to leave for a movie, a visit, or a shopping trip and the child is not ready by the requested time, you should leave with the rest of the family. If the child cannot be left alone, have a sitter on call for the early phase of this approach so that you can follow through with the plan. Once the sitter is called, it is too late to change plans. Even if he or she quickly dresses, he or she still stays home. After a time or two when the child or adolescent loses rather than the parents or the rest of the family, this individual will get the message: "Finish your tasks on time or accept the consequences. You lose, not the rest of us."

Summary

When a consistent behavioral plan is used in a family, unacceptable behaviors begin to change to more acceptable behaviors. Both parents regain control and confidence in their ability to parent. Children and adolescents learn that they can be controlled and that they will not be overwhelmed by not being in control. They are usually happier. Now, all of the positive experiences with the family reinforce the behaviors as well.

If the plan does not work or does not work as well as desired because of learning disabilities, a Sensory Integrative Disorder, or other associated disorders or because the ADHD behaviors are not being managed by medication during all critical hours, these clinical issues must be addressed. The behavioral program should clarify these problems and help focus on the needs.

If the plan does not work either because the parents or one parent does not follow the plan or defeats the plan or because the child or adolescent has such emotional problems that he or she cannot give up being in control or the need to be punished, more intensive individual, couples, or family therapy might be needed.

Social Skill Training

Social skills needed for social competence include physical factors such as eye contact and posture, social responsivity such as sharing, and interactional skills such as initiating and maintaining conversation. If your son or daughter does not pick up social cues or has poor social skills, he or she might benefit from a form of group therapy called *social skill training*. Sometimes this is done as part of the special education program by the school psychologist or counselor. If not, check with other parents and find who does such work privately. Some parent groups have set up and run such programs on their own.

There are many types of social skill training programs. In general, they focus on a series of steps. The first step involves helping the child or adolescent to develop an awareness of and sensitivity to his or her social problems. This step is critical. Some have only limited awareness of their socialization difficulties and may deny their problems or blame others for their difficulties.

The second step involves having the child or adolescent generate alternative solutions for the identified problems. Here, the group leader and other group members can be of help. The third step involves helping the child or adolescent step-by-step through the process of learning the newly identified solution to the problems. Role-playing and practice are important ways of learning these new solutions. The final step is to help the child or adolescent link the new knowledge to past events and difficulties as well as to future happenings. He or she is encouraged to try out the new social skills in new settings and to report back to the group on successes and failures.

In Summary

The child or adolescent with learning disabilities and/or ADHD often develops secondary emotional, social, and family problems. Sometimes a parent or both parents will become as stressed or dysfunctional as the child or adolescent.

I have reviewed which professionals can be available to help and what types of help are available. Don't be hesitant to admit that your son or daughter, your family, yourself, or your marriage needs help. Seek competent professionals to help you assess the problems and to provide the needed interventions.

16

Controversial Therapies

OUR KNOWLEDGE OF learning disabilities and Attention-Deficit Hyperactivity Disorder (ADHD) is not complete. We do have approaches to treatment that are accepted practices and generally not controversial. These treatments have been discussed in this book. In this chapter, I would like to discuss the less acceptable or more controversial approaches to treatment. The controversy might be based on the theory behind the treatment, or on the way the treatment is done, or on the lack of research data to support the findings reported by the people using the treatment approach.

The acceptable treatments for learning disabilities take a long time and a lot of work. Training children—and parents—to compensate for problems while retraining them in better learning and coping skills is a slow, laborious, and often expensive process. I can understand that you would want to try almost any approach that might work better and faster. The same is true with ADHD. No parent wants to place their son or daughter on medication. Often they know that the medication may have to be used for years. And, even with the medication, all is not always well.

I can understand why parents would want to try almost any approach that might work better and faster. Especially, I can understand a parent wanting a cure rather than an intervention. But, you must be an informed and intelligent consumer. Before committing yourself and especially your daughter or son to any new or different approach, ask questions. Remember this general rule-of-thumb that I find helpful. If the treatment approach you are about to try is so successful, why is not everyone in the country using it? No professional, regardless of discipline, would avoid using a treatment that works.

Often you turn to your family physician for guidance and he or she knows no more about the proposed treatment than you do. The problem is that there are many professionals and non-professionals proposing approaches for helping these children and adolescents. If research has been conducted to support a particular approach, the reports and data will be published in professional journals. When research data are not available, the information may be in a popular book, the newspapers, lay magazines, or may be discussed on a television show. Thus, the professionals only know what they hear through the parents or through these sources.

I will discuss controversial approaches to treatment that have been proposed and are still being used. I will not review controversial research that focuses on cause but that has not resulted in treatment approaches. When research data supports reporting to you that a particular treatment approach does not work, I will let you know. When all of the facts are not yet in, I will review the information known and let you decide for yourself. At the end of the chapter I will give you two references to review articles that will provide the specific references for each treatment approach discussed in case you want to do more reading or want to show the specific references to a professional.

I find it helpful to group these controversial therapies by disorder; that is, by either learning disabilities or ADHD. I also find it helpful to group these controversial therapies when possible by their basic concepts—neurophysiological retraining and orthomolecular medicine. One broad area of treatment does not fit comfortably in either of these two groups, allergies. Another is the use of colored or tinted lenses for learning disabilities. These topics also will be discussed.

Neurophysiological retraining refers to a group of approaches that are based on the concept that by stimulating specific sensory inputs or exercising specific motor patterns one can retrain, recircuit, or in some way improve the functioning of a part of the nervous system. Four such approaches to treatment for learning disabilities are popular today: patterning, optometric visual training, vestibular dysfunction, and applied kinesiology.

Orthomolecular medicine is a term introduced by Linus Pauling, referring to the treatment of mental disorders by the provision of the optimum concentrations of substances normally present in the human body. The use of megavitamins or trace elements as well as the removal of specific food additives and refined sugar from the diet are examples of treatments proposed for learning disabilities and ADHD.

To summarize the controversial therapies by disorder:

Learning Disabilities

Neurophysiological Retraining
~ Patterning
~ Optometric Visual Training
~ Vestibular Dysfunction
~ Applied Kinesiology

Orthomolecular Medicine
~ Megavitamins
~ Trace Elements

Allergies
Colored Lenses

Attention-Deficit Hyperactivity Disorder

Orthomolecular Medicine
~ Food Additives
~ Refined Sugars
Allergies

Patterning

This theory and technique was initially developed by Dr. Glenn Doman and Dr. Carl Delacato. The underlying concept follows the principle that failures to pass properly through a certain sequence of developmental stages in mobility, language, and competence in the manual, visual, auditory, and tactile areas reflects poor "neurological organization" and may indicate "brain damage." The proposed treatments involve repetitive activities using specific muscle patterns in the order the child should have learned if development had been normal; for example, rolling over, then crawling, then standing, then walking, and so forth. The method is described in the literature as reaching ". . . all of the stimuli normally provided by his environment but with such intensity and frequency as to draw, ultimately, a response from the corresponding motor systems."

Reports from the American Academy of Pediatrics and other professional organizations, based on a review of all the literature, deny any evidence of success. The Report from the American Academy of Pediatrics concludes ". . . that the patterning treatment offers no special merit, that the claims of its advocates are unproven, and that the demands on families are so great that in some cases there may be harm in its use."

This approach is still popular and is often offered through Institutes for Human Potential. Be aware that patterning will not help improve your son's or daughter's learning disabilities.

Optometric Visual Training

Although this treatment approach is popular, the importance or value of developmental optometric visual training for children and adolescents with learning disabilities is controversial. The challenges and disagreements are often very public between the ophthalmologists (i.e., physicians specializing in eye diseases) who believe that this treatment approach does not work and should not be used and many optometrists who believe that it is effective. As parents, you are often caught in the middle between one professional telling you to use this approach and another saying not to use this approach.

When your son or daughter is seen by either professional working with eye disorders, several possible problem areas are checked. Does he or she have a refractive error (e.g., near-sighted, farsighted, astigmatism)? If so, this is corrected for by the use of glasses. Does he or she have an imbalance in the use of the eye muscles (e.g., strabismus)? There is no proven relationship between reading ability and strabismus. Yet, this disorder must be treated. Without intervention the youngster might develop suppression of vision in one eye, called amblyopia.

If there is no refractive error or eye muscle problem and the child or adolescent has a learning disability, the ophthalmologist believes that the preferred treatment is special education. At this phase of the evaluation, some optometrist would assess for two other possible areas of difficulty. If either is found, visual training (also called vision therapy) is recommended. The first area is the eye muscles ability to do tracking and pursuit of visual stimuli. The second is visual perception.

Not all optometrists are trained in or practice visual training.

Those who do tend to look rather broadly at their role in learning disabilities. They believe that learning in general and reading in particular are primarily visual perception tasks. They note that visual perception processes are also related to sensory and motor coordination. These optometrists employ a wide diversity of educational and sensory-motor perceptual training techniques in an attempt to correct the educational problem.

Most research to date has not confirmed that reading problems are visual perception problems. Some aspects of visual decoding relate to visual perception, but decoding and comprehension are central brain functions. The research studies on the effectiveness of visual training is split. The research in the optometric literature supports its effectiveness and the research in the medical literature does not.

Despite the questioning of eye function as a causal factor in reading disabilities and the reported absence of supporting data for the treatment approach in most studies, visual training continues to be widely used in many parts of the United States.

I try to share this literature with parents who need to decide what to do. I especially focus on the research showing that reading is not a visual perception function but a central brain function and on the lack of consensus that visual training works. If they still want to try optometric training I do not try to talk them out of it. I do, however, share two other concerns that do not relate as much to the theory as to the practice of this approach. First, some optometrists inform parents that if their child is not learning they can do an evaluation to find out why. Their evaluation assesses primarily visual perception and some visual motor areas. This is not a comprehensive evaluation. No auditory or language areas will be assessed, nor will many other areas of potential learning disabilities. A full team evaluation is needed. Second, much of the techniques used in visual training are similar to what a special education professional would do for visual perception and visual motor disabilities. Often, the services by this person are far less expensive and more likely to be integrated into the full educational program.

The American Association for Pediatric Ophthalmology and Strabismus and the American Academy of Ophthalmology stress that the treatment for dyslexia or a related learning disability is remediation with educational procedures. They report that "deficient visual perception of letters or words accounts for inability to read in only a small minority of children; the majority suffer from a variety of linguistic defects." They stress the need for a multidisciplinary approach to diagnosis and treatment and refute optometric visual training as a treatment.

Vestibular Dysfunction

Several investigators have suggested that the vestibular system is important in learning. The vestibular system consists of a sensory organ in each inner ear that monitors head position and the impact of gravity and relays this information to the brain, primarily to the cerebellum. These investigators claim that there is a clear relationship between vestibular disorders and poor academic performance involving children with learning disabilities.

The first to stress this view in the United States was Dr. Harold Levinson. In several books published since 1980 he proposes the causative role of the vestibular system and the vestibular-cerebellar systems with dyslexia. He proposes the treatment of dyslexia with anti-motion sickness medication to correct the vestibular dysfunction. If one reads Dr. Levinson's books, one will not find research to support his theory or the effectiveness of his treatment. His books refer to his clinical observations and case examples. In his most recent book, he proposes multiple other interventions along with the anti-motion sickness medication, including many other medications and special education.

Much research has been done on the vestibular system. The consistent finding is that there is no significant differences either in the intensity of vestibular responsivity or in the prevalence of vestibular dysfunction between children who are normal and those with learning disabilities. Furthermore, these researchers point out that the technique used by Dr. Levinson to diagnose vestibular dysfunction (i.e., a rotating cylinder with a picture on it, with the child reporting when the picture is no longer clear) is a measurement of "blurring speed" and, thus, a measurement of visual stimulation and not vestibular stimulation.

Dr. Levinson continues to write his own books. He has not published in professional journals. Much of the publicity for his approach is through appearances on television talk shows. Despite the evidence against his theory and treatment approach, he remains very busy with a long waiting list.

Applied Kinesiology

Some chiropractors and chiropractic clinics in the United States have actively advertised that they can cure dyslexia and learning disabilities. The literature that is distributed refers to the use of "applied kinesiology" and to the work of Dr. Carl A. Ferreri. The claim is that this treatment can result in an astounding reversal of all dyslexic and learning disability conditions. Often it is stated that, "This technique produces measurable results immediately, that is, after just one treatment."

The basis for the theory and treatment is a book written by Dr. Ferreri and Dr. Richard Wainwright, entitled *Breakthrough for Dyslexia and Learning Disabilities*. Produced by an obscure publisher and distributed by Dr. Ferreri's own Center, the book offers no research data. There is one reference cited over and over to a paper done by Dr. Ferreri. When I tracked down this article, I found it in an unknown and unedited journal. It was a page long and simply described Dr. Ferreri's theory.

In their book, Drs. Ferreri and Wainwright theorize that learning disabilities are caused by damage to two specific bones of the skull and by an imbalance within the "reflex centers" of the pelvis, the inner ear, and the head and neck. The treatment consists of manipulations of the bones of the skull, especially those around the eyes, as well as other bones and muscles of the body. I have seen videotapes of the treatment. It is painful to the child.

The proponents of this approach report that once specific bones of the skull are back in place, the learning disabilities are no longer present. They report that special education tutoring will be needed to correct for the problems that existed before the cure and that the bones might slip out of place again, requiring further treatment in the future. (They can never be the cause if the treatment does not work.)

You need to know that this proposed chiropractic treatment is not based on any known research; that some of it is based on anatomical concepts that are not held by the majority of anatomists; that there is no research that supports the proposed cures; and, that there are no follow-up research studies to document the claimed results. Furthermore, the national professional organization of chiropractors is also critical of Dr. Ferreri and his proposed treatment.

Megavitamins

Using massive doses of vitamins to treat emotional or cognitive disorders was first proposed for the treatment of schizophrenia, arguing that this disorder was the result of a biochemical problem that could be avoided by the use of massive amounts of vitamins, especially the B vitamins. No research supported the theory or the treatment and a rare few professionals still use megavitamins to treat this disorder. Dr. Allan Cott, in 1971, proposed that learning disabilities could be successfully treated with megavitamins. As with many professionals noted in this chapter, he presented his arguments without established research data in his own books. The American Academy of Pediatrics issued a report specifically focusing on megavitamin therapy and learning disabilities. The conclusion: "There is no validity to the concept or treatment."

Trace Elements

Trace elements are chemicals found in the body in minute amounts that are essential to normal functioning. They include copper, zinc, magnesium, manganese, and chromium along with the more common chemicals calcium, sodium, and iron.

No one to date has published data supporting the theory that deficiencies in one or more of these elements is a cause of learning disabilities; however, in some parts of this country children are tested for such deficiencies and treated with replacement therapy.

Colored Lenses

Helen Irlen proposes the treatment of certain types of dyslexia with colored or tinted lenses or templates. She specifically focuses on a group of problems she refers to as "scotopic sensitivity syndrome." Individuals with this syndrome show difficulty in six areas: (1) photophobia or sensitivity to light, (2) eye strain, (3) poor visual resolution, (4) a reduced span of focus, (5) impaired depth perception, and (6) poor sustained focus. She points out that the treatment is not used as a substitute for corrective refractive lenses.

Initially, informal and unpublished studies were cited to prove the effectiveness of this treatment. Recently, more formal studies have been published that suggest that some individuals with dyslexia (one specific form of a learning disability) might benefit from the use of these tinted lenses. Other studies do not support the findings.

The problem is that before the evidence is in, the treatment has become popular. Dr. Irlen's diagnostic test for scotopic sensitivity syndrome and the sale of tinted lenses is now in use throughout this country through a franchised chain. Dr. Irlen's unpublished paper suggest that the colored lenses are useful for the small percent of individuals with dyslexia who also have the scotopic sensitivity syndrome. Some concern has been expressed whether the facilities around the country are distinguishing this small subgroup of a subgroup of individuals with learning disabilities and only suggesting the lenses for these individuals.

The facts are not in. Parents must be aware of the difference between the claim and what is known.

Food Additives

In *Why Your Child is Hyperactive*, Dr. Benjamin Feingold proposed in 1975 that synthetic flavors and colors in the diet were related to hyperactivity. He reported that the elimination of all foods containing artificial colors and flavors as well as salicylates and certain other additives stopped the hyperactivity. Neither in this book nor in any of his other publications did Dr. Feingold present research data to support this theory. All findings were based on his clinical experience. He and his book received wide publicity. Parent groups advocating for the Feingold Diet formed all over the country. It was left to others to document whether he was correct or incorrect.

Because of a hope that he might be correct and a need to either counter his claims or to prove he was correct, the Federal government sponsored several major research projects to study the theory and the treatment. In 1982 the National Institutes of Health held what is called a "Consensus Conference" on this issue. A panel of experts is brought together. They read all available literature, hold hearings to allow anyone who wishes to present to do so, and question the experts. The panel members then spend time synthesizing what is known and finally write a current consensus on the topic.

The conclusions included:

1. There does appear to be a subset of children with behavioral disturbances who respond to some aspects of Feingold's diet. However, this group is small, possibly one percent of the children studied.

2. With notable exceptions, the specific elimination of synthetic food colors from the diet does not appear to be a major factor in the reported responses of a majority of these children.

3. The defined diets should not be used universally in the treatment of childhood hyperactivity.

Two more recent studies reached the same conclusion. The Feingold diet is not effective in treating hyperactivity in most children. There may be a small percentage (one percent) who appear to respond positively to the diet for reasons that are not yet clear.

There is no way for the physician to identify in advance which patients might be part of this small group. Sometimes a parent will report that if their child eats foods with specific food colors (e.g., Kool Aid, Hawaiian Punch, certain cereals) or medications with specific food colors (e.g., penicillin with red or yellow food coloring), he or she will become more hyperactive. Perhaps this is the only clue that this might be the child with ADHD who might respond to the Feingold Diet. In these cases, the full diet may not be needed. Elimination of these specific food colors might be adequate.

Refined Sugars

Clinical observations and parent reports suggest that refined sugar promotes adverse behavioral reactions in children. Hyperactive behavior is most commonly reported.

Several formal studies have been done to clarify and/or verify these parent claims. Each used what is called a "challenge study." Children who were reported by parents to become more hyperactive when they ate refined sugar were challenged with either refined sugar (glucose), natural sugar (fructose), or a placebo. The results failed to support the parent observations.

A recent study explored whether the reported increase in activity level with children who ate a high sugar snack or meal might be related to the amount of refined sugar eaten and not to the exposure to the sugar. In this study, each child was given a breakfast. This breakfast was either high in fat, carbohydrates, or protein. They were then given the challenge with either refined sugar, natural sugar, or a placebo. The researchers found that some children appeared to be more active after a high carbohydrate breakfast and exposure to refined sugars. Possibly, then, some children with ADHD will become more hyperactive if they eat high refined sugar foods and snacks throughout a period of time.

Allergies

Pediatricians and pediatric allergists have reported for many years that they see a higher percent of children and adolescents in their practice with allergies who also have learning disabilities and/or ADHD. Most studies have been done on the possible relationships between allergies and learning disabilities. As just discussed, Dr. Feingold, a pediatric allergist, focused on ADHD. No studies to date have shown how allergies and these disorders relate. No treatment approaches have been confirmed to be successful.

Two clinicians have written about specific issues relating allergies to learning disabilities and/or ADHD. Each has proposed their treatment plan. As with many such approaches, the books are written by the clinician and little or no research data are presented. Since you might hear of these clinicians or of their approach, let me review briefly what they propose.

Dr. Doris Rapp believes that there is a relationship between food or other sensitivities and hyperactivity. She proposes a diet that eliminates the identified foods or the avoidance of other suspected allergens as a treatment for hyperactivity. She believes that the traditional allergy skin testing for foods does not always detect the foods that cause problems. Her critics say that her challenge test, done under the tongue, is not a valid measure of allergies.

Dr. Rapp identifies certain foods or food groups that children might be allergic to: milk, chocolate, eggs, wheat, corn, peanuts, pork, and sugar. She suggests that the parents try a specific elimination diet described in her books. This diet consists of eliminating all of the possible allergy-producing foods then adding one back each week to see if there is a change in behaviors. She uses a food extract solution placed under the tongue in her tests. If the child is found to be sensitive to certain foods or chemicals in the environment (e.g., paste, glue, paint, mold, chemicals found in new carpets), these items are eliminated or avoided. She reports an improvement in the behaviors of the child. Most specifically, she reports less aggressive or oppositional behavior and less hyperactivity. Other professionals have not been able to duplicate her findings or claimed successes.

Dr. William Crook has written extensively on the relationship between allergies and general health, learning disabilities, and ADHD. He writes of the "allergic-tension-fatigue syndrome." He also reports that specific allergies can result in hyperactivity and distractibility. Much of his more recent publications and presentations focus on a possible allergic reaction to specific yeast and the development of specific behaviors following a yeast infection. He reports that treatment of the yeast infection improves or corrects the problem. No clinical or research studies have confirmed his theories or proposed treatment program.

Future Controversial Therapies

I find it hard to keep up with the many proposed treatments for learning disabilities and ADHD. There is a consistent pattern with these controversial therapies: one person or place claims that he or she has a "cure" for . . . ; all references relate to that person and are found in their papers or publications but not in scientific references; and, they accuse any professional who questions their results as being "blind" and refusing to believe anything that might be different from traditional treatments. In addition, it is not uncommon that these treatments are costly, payments must be made before treatment starts, and parents are made to feel guilty if they deprive their child of this "cure."

At the time I was preparing this second edition there were programs claiming to cure learning disabilities and/or ADHD by biofeedback techniques to "correct the brain waves," by "vibrating beds" that corrected the total bodies magnetism, by "electronic ears" that stimulate the brain to attend better, and by acupuncture. All I can say is that as parents, you must be cautious and learn as much as you can about these proposed treatments from as many sources as you can before you spend your money or place your son or daughter in the treatment program.

In Summary

There is a relationship between brain function and nutrition as well as between brain function and allergic reactions. These relationships appear to be true for learning disabilities, ADHD, and other neurological disorders. However, at this time we do not understand the relationship and there are no known treatments based on these relationships that are clinically successful.

When you learn of a new treatment or technique, you have good reason for showing interest. We all want a better and faster way to help these children and adolescents. Please take the time to become an informed parent. Ask yourself why this amazing approach is not used by everyone. If the person proposing the treatment tells you that "most professionals are biased and do not believe the findings because they are different from the usual treatments," ask to see the data supporting the concept and the treatment. Don't accept popular books published by the person proposing the theory or treatment. Discuss the approach with your family physician, with the school professionals, and with other parents. Don't put your son or daughter through something unproven and unlikely to help.

Further References

If you would like to have the specific references for the studies mentioned for each of the controversial therapies, please consult one of the following:

1. Silver, Larry B. "The Magic Cure: A Review of the Current Controversial Approaches for Treating Learning Disabilities. *Journal of Learning Disabilities,* 20, No. 8 (1987), 498–504.

2. Schaywitz, Salley E., and Schaywitz, Bennett E. "Hyperactivity/Attention Deficits." In *Learning Disabilities* : *Proceedings of the National Conference,* edited by James F. Kavanagh and Tom J. Truss, Jr., 488–492. Parkton, MD: York Press, 1988.

PART FIVE

Special Topics

17

The Gifted Student with Learning Disabilities

UNTIL RECENTLY, THE POSSIBILITY that a child or adolescent could be gifted and learning disabled at the same time was either ignored or disbelieved. Some educators believed that learning disabled and gifted were contradictory terms. Today, many school systems accept that students with learning disabilities can also be gifted (and talented) and programs are available for identifying and educating them.

Part of the difficulty relates to the way being gifted is measured. One approach has been to evaluate for high levels of academic performance in the classroom. Another has been to use scores from standardized tests. For example, to be eligible one must have a full scale IQ of 120 or higher. It is clear that many very bright and capable children and adolescents with learning disabilities would not meet one or the other criteria.

The State of Maryland, in a report to the U.S. Congress, offered a definition of gifted that is very compatible with the Federal definition of giftedness and that opens up the door to gifted students with learning disabilities:

> Gifted and talented children are those identified by professionally qualified persons (and) who by virtue of outstanding abilities are capable of high performance. These are children who require differentiated educational programs and services beyond those normally provided by the regular school program in order to realize their contribution to self and society.

Children capable of high performance include those with demonstrated achievement and/or potential ability in any of the following areas: general intellectual ability, specific academic aptitude, creative or productive thinking, leadership ability, and visual and performing arts.

How Have Gifted Students Been Selected

Although the legal definitions of giftedness do not automatically eliminate the student with learning disabilities, in practice the operational definitions used by many school systems do exclude many if not most of them. The experts in this area believe that the reason for this is that most professionals recommend the use of individual measures of intelligence such as the Wechsler Intelligence Scales. Schools then tend to screen for gifted students on the basis of group measures of intelligence or achievement tests, often in conjunction with teacher nominations or recommendations. In some programs self, peer, or parent nominations are also considered. Using this approach, many students who are gifted and learning disabled are overlooked because their performance on standardized group tests of achievement are not two or three years above their grade placement.

The Problem with the Concept of "Gifted"

Priscilla Vail makes a point of the problems with the concept of giftedness. The word *gifted* can create several problems. It implies its own opposite. If you are not gifted, what are you? Worthless, a "retard," "dumb." In addition, the label may be of such importance to parents that the pressure to qualify might place pressure on the child. She feels that it can create competition that sets learners against each other instead of joining them in the common goal of learning.

Some families have moved to school districts where their child could qualify for the gifted program. As one mother explained, "In my township you have to be 125 to be gifted and my child is 123. Two towns away you only have to be 120."

Children and adolescents with learning disabilities have difficulty because they can see that they do not do some academic work as well as their classmates. Yet, they often sense that they are as smart as their classmates. If some children are selected for the gifted program and this student is not, even though he or she might be as capable, it becomes but one more blow to self-esteem.

How Should Students with Learning Disabilities Be Evaluated

Professionals in the field of giftedness are moving toward a more sensible approach to identifying gifted students. They propose a wide variety of psychological tests that measure specific abilities (called psychometric testing) and nonpsychometric measures to initially screen as many children as possible for consideration for the available programs. Evidence of academic ability or potential can be assessed by nonverbal measures of deductive reasoning and some measurement of creativity might be evaluated in a way that allows the child with problems in areas of reading, spelling, or handwriting to compete for recognition in other areas.

Clearly any approach to identify the student with learning disabilities should assess the strengths of the child as well as the weaknesses. The key is for the classroom teacher, the specialist in the area of giftedness, and parents to be aware of the existence of students who are both gifted and learning disabled. With this awareness and a sensitivity to the need to modify the screening models, more such students will be found.

How Should Gifted Students with Learning Disabilities Be Educated

The answer to this question can be the problem for some students. In some school systems it is not clear who should be responsible for their education. Should these children be considered a subset of children with learning disabilities and identified and taught under the direction of programs for persons with learning disabilities or should they become the primary responsibility of educators and programs within the area of gifted and talented education? This concern is not a minor one. Basic to the answer is where the money will come from for the program. Some school systems would rather not hear about the existence of our students if it means that they must provide more testing and more special classes. If the programs are within the gifted and talented programs, there might be a concern that adding special programs for the gifted student with learning disabilities might have to come out of their existing budget and take away from the other programs. It seems clear that the best programs would involve cooperation between these two administrative groups. Yet, such may not happen.

Another problem in answering this question is that teachers of the gifted are not typically trained in the special educational methods needed for children with learning disabilities. And, teachers for children with learning disabilities have not been trained in gifted education.

There is no accepted model or program for educating students who are identified as intellectually or academically gifted. Most schools offer only one type of program. Some of these programs emphasize *enrichment* of the student's education by providing curricular content above and beyond the basic school program. Some programs allow students to progress rapidly through existing curricular content in an *acceleration* model. A few programs integrate acceleration and enrichment components, but most school systems focus on enrichment activities rather than acceleration.

Acceleration models for the gifted are usually not very realistic for gifted students who have learning disabilities. Most such programs require the student to learn a fair amount of material on his or her own in one way or another but probably primarily through reading textbooks. If a student is permitted to skip a grade, he or she must be able to learn the content of the skipped courses by some method, again, probably by reading a textbook on his or her own. Some who are permitted to skip courses must learn the courses on their own to pass such tests as the Advanced Placement Program.

Students with reading disabilities will have difficulty keeping up with the pace of the class. In mathematics, where acceleration is often recommended, students may be required to read the textbook on their own to learn theorems or problem-solving paradigms. Students with learning disabilities in accelerated programs have to be taught differently. What is needed are creative models for teaching materials that build on the student's strengths rather than demand a higher level of performance in the areas of weakness.

Gifted students with learning disabilities usually do best in programs that provide for acceleration using learning models that allow the individual student to succeed. These programs should provide enriching experiences above and beyond the basic school curriculum. To deny these experiences to the bright but disabled in order that they may spend more hours trying to master other skills is not right. As one professional put it, "After all, the skills of accessing and communicating information are often the means to the end, not the end in and of themselves for many bright people. It is wrong to neglect or overlook the talents and strengths of children in our diligent but perhaps misguided efforts to teach the cornerstones of education: reading, writing, spelling, and arithmetic."

Today, many bright students with reading or writing problems are excluded from enrichment programs for the gifted. Yet, their lack of these skills are, at best, minimally related to the purpose of the course or the content being taught. For example, this student might do extremely well in a creative writing class if he or she could dictate the story or speak into a tape recorder for someone else to type. Another student might do very well in an advanced chemistry course if he or she had a note-taker in class or the text on tape. An excellent math student might have no difficulty with complex mathematical concepts or theorems yet do poorly because of problems with simple computations and arithmetic. The ability to use a calculator in class might make all the difference.

Programs for the gifted student with learning disabilities must provide these accommodations for those with special needs. For some students, no matter how bright, no amount of special education remedial help will allow them to totally overcome a spelling, reading, or handwriting problem. Yet, these students should be given access to the advanced courses in high school that they need to prepare for college. They should be allowed to use appropriate "survival tools" to compensate for their disabilities. They must be permitted to use our modern technologies. They should be able to use word processors, maybe lap computers in class. They should be able to use tape recorders in class or calculators. If needed, they should be able to use books-on-tape. Adults who do not spell can now use word processors with editing programs and spell checking programs or they can hire secretaries who spell well. Why can't these students use such technical aids or let a parent help with editing (not thinking).

What Should You Do as a Parent

You may be so concerned with your son or daughter because of their learning disabilities that you have never focused on their possible giftedness. Ideally, programs for persons with learning disabilities should provide guidance to parents for those children who are of superior ability.

You should understand the characteristics of gifted children and the characteristics of children with learning disabilities and how these two might merge. You should know what programs exist in your school system and the criteria used for selection. If your school does not have special programs for the gifted student with learning disabilities (rather than expect all gifted students with learning disabilities to fit into the regular gifted programs), get together with other parents and try to get such programs started.

18

The Adult with Learning Disabilities and/or ADHD

THE CHILD WITH LEARNING disabilities becomes the adolescent with learning disabilities who becomes the adult with learning disabilities. Learning disabilities are lifetime disabilities. Since, in about 40 percent of cases, learning disabilities appear to be inherited and to run in families, it is not uncommon for me to discuss a child's or adolescent's learning disabilities with parents and have one say that he or she has the same problems. For some, the problems stopped being an issue in their life after they finished school. For most, the disabilities greatly affected their education and their educational accomplishments and continue to cause difficulties in their career and family life. If they continue to have Attention-Deficit Hyperactivity Disorder (ADHD), there are added problems.

When I hear this, I listen to the parent's story and explore what can be done now. A full psychoeducational evaluation might clarify where the difficulties are at this time in their life and might help in deciding what interventions would be most helpful. Often, if interventions are started, they are focused on specific difficulties in their work or home experiences.

This adult's life history often includes struggles through college and even through graduate or professional school. Somehow they made it. I frequently hear that they do well at the entry level jobs within their career or profession because they have the job and interpersonal skills to do well and knew how to compensate. The difficulties start when they get promoted to the middle management levels. Suddenly, the need to read, write, follow budgets or mathematical trends, or organize and operate a program or manage a group of people creates difficulties. Their learning disabilities prevent them from being as successful as they are capable of being. For those who make it to the upper management levels, the problems often become less. Now, they can go back to using their knowledge, intelligence, and reasoning abilities along with their interpersonal skills. For many, they never reach these higher levels because of their difficulties.

In the best of all possible worlds, this adult received the appropriate special education help in grade school and high school. For those who went into a trade or into the job market, they might have had vocational guidance and training designed for individuals with learning disabilities. For those who went to college, they might have had the necessary special programs to succeed. Some may have gotten assistance in graduate or professional schools. For most, I learn that they were never diagnosed or helped or that they got help in the earliest grades only. They made it by sheer drive and hard work—or, they did not make it.

For those who knew that they had learning disabilities, some feared disclosing their problem to their employer for fear that it would be misunderstood and result in not being hired, a lack of opportunities, or no promotions. For these adults, there can be no efforts toward accommodations. For those who only learn of their disabilities as adults, there is the need to rethink who they are and why they have had so much difficulty throughout their life.

Several factors have contributed to the increased number of adults identified as having learning disabilities as well as to the increased services available to these adults. The key was Section 504 of the Rehabilitation Act of 1973 (described in detail in Chapter 19 on legal issues). The public law that requires all public schools to provide services to the handicapped is an extension of this law. The significant increase in students with learning disabilities applying to and being accepted into a wide variety of colleges and universities has been because this law required these institutions to establish different acceptance criteria and to provide the necessary services.

Another major factor in the increase in the number of adults identified as having learning disabilities was the policy change of the Rehabilitation Services Administration, a component of the U.S. Department of Education. This federal agency is responsible for state and federal programs of vocational rehabilitation. This policy change resulted in the removal of a key barrier to the consideration of the eligibility of a person with learning disabilities for vocational rehabilitation services. Prior to 1980, adults with learning disabilities were not eligible for vocational rehabilitation services unless they also had a physical or mental disability.

I would like to discuss the definition of learning disabilities with adults and how evaluations are done. I will discuss the services available for you, for your adult family member, or for a friend or relative. Why do I suggest relatives? Sometimes at the interpretive session, a parent will say that he or she did not have problems but that a brother (or sister) was always a poor student and has never done well as an adult. The parent wonders if this person might be learning disabled. Since it "runs in families," the concern is valid.

How Do You Define Learning Disabilities in an Adult

The initial definitions as well as most revisions refer to children. In recent years several organizations have developed position papers that stress the need to consider adults under any definition of learning disabilities. The Learning Disabilities Association of America (a large, national, parent-based organization with chapters in each state and county and most cities) emphasized in their 1984 position paper that "Specific Learning Disabilities is a chronic condition . . ." This paper added: "Throughout life, the condition can affect self-esteem, education, vocation, socialization, and/or daily living activities."

The Rehabilitation Services Administration developed its own definition of learning disabilities for use in the vocational rehabilitation programs. Since the purpose of vocational rehabilitation programs is to facilitate the employment of individuals whose disability interferes with employability, the definition goes beyond verbal and academic problems and includes such issues as social competence and emotional maturity. This definition reads:

Individuals who have a disorder in one or more of the central nervous system processes involving perceiving, understanding, and/or using concepts through verbal (spoken or written language) or nonverbal means. This disorder manifests itself with difficulties in one or more of the following areas: attention, reasoning, memory, communicating, reading, spelling, calculation, coordination, social competence, and emotional maturity.

The difficulty with this definition is that it does not take into account the effect of the learning disability on employment.

There is no standard or accepted definition of learning disabilities for colleges. Each may use its own criteria for offering special admission standards or services. One state, California, established guidelines for its community colleges. This was done because of the significant increase in the number of students applying to and attending the community colleges and the inconsistency within this system. A student could be diagnosed as learning disabled and eligible for services in one college and not in another. In 1982 the following definition was established:

Learning disability in California Community College adults is a persistent condition of presumed neurological dysfunction which may also exist with other disabling conditions. This dysfunction continues despite instruction in standard classroom situations. Learning disabled adults, a heterogeneous group, have these common attributes:

1. Average to above-average intellectual ability
2. Severe processing deficit
3. Severe aptitude-achievement discrepancy or discrepancies
4. Measured achievement in an instructional or employment setting
5. Measured appropriate adaptive behavior in an instructional or employment setting

The reason for the last two factors is that many of these community colleges offer vocational training programs.

If your son or daughter is going to college, you will need guidance on how to select the best school and how to get the services needed. If your son or daughter (or yourself) needs vocational guidance and possibly vocational rehabilitation, you will need guidance on how to utilize the services of your state and county vocational rehabilitation services. I will try to give you the basic information in this chapter.

How Do You Diagnose an Adult as Learning Disabled

There will be many reasons for an adult to be referred or to refer oneself for a diagnostic evaluation. The underlying reason is to establish or verify a prior diagnosis of learning disability and to develop a plan of action that will help the individual achieve his or her goals. That is, perhaps of more importance than establishing the diagnosis is learning what can be done with the information gained to do career planning and/or to design the necessary interventions.

Depending on the need, the assessment might focus on the traditional areas relating to learning disabilities; that is, educational/academic functioning. A fuller vocational assessment would require evaluating social/interpersonal abilities and employment and life skills. Let me first discuss the assessment for the college bound and then the assessment for vocational rehabilitation. (I am very appreciative of Dr. Susan Vogel for helping me understand these important areas when working with adults who have learning disabilities.)

Assessment for the College Bound

This assessment should include the essential features of the previously discussed psychoeducational evaluation. Of importance is to clarify what residual problems may affect success in college. Often included are measures of receptive and expressive oral and written language, reading skills, mathematics reasoning and computation, and verbal and nonverbal concept formation. Also assessed are auditory and visual perception, memory, sequencing, analysis, and synthesis. Of equal importance will be the assessment of study habits and attitudes and study skills and strategies.

There are several needs for this evaluation. Parents and the adolescent or young adult must be realistic about college, and, if he or she is to attend college, what type of college and what services will be needed. The assessment will clarify which academic demands of college are most likely to cause difficulty and what interventions would be needed to remediate, compensate for, or accommodate for these areas of difficulty. The results will give clues as to which study skills and strategies are in place and which new or expanded ones might be needed. The assessment might clarify which required courses might need to be wavered since the student would have tremendous difficulty mastering the course. The purpose of the assessment is to select the right college and college services. The goal is to maximize the opportunities for success.

Assessment for Vocational Rehabilitation

The vocational rehabilitation assessment must first establish that there is a learning disability, using the criteria listed earlier in this chapter. Then, to determine eligibility for services and to develop a suitable vocational plan, the examiner must also ascertain the individuals strengths and functional limitations. The question is what, if any, areas would limit employment success. For example, would an adult with a reading disability have difficulty reading the classified ads, a job application form, or certain manuals necessary for job success? Or, in the math area, the questions might relate to the ability to do measurements, handle money, or keep track of time.

In the areas of underlying processing deficits, auditory perception problems may result in misperception of what is heard or difficulty in comprehending oral instructions.

The assessment of social skills and the ability to relate to coworkers and supervisors is essential. The adult might have all of the abilities and strengths to perform the job, yet not be able to keep the job because of personal interactions.

The Needs of Adults
with Learning Disabilities

The adult may have known he or she was learning disabled since childhood. However, once out of school, his or her way of thinking suggested that they no longer existed. Or, the adult might be aware that the learning disabilities were still there but think that nothing can be done. For this adult, it might be very helpful to do an updated assessment and to clarify what weaknesses and strengths remain. Specific targeted interventions might be tremendously valuable in the work situation as well as at home.

I have known adults who still cannot calculate money in their head. They have major problems with purchases. For example, how much do I give the salesperson, or how much should I get back? One man in his forties told me that he tried to carry large bills like $10s or $20s. In this way he did not have to worry about giving the proper amount. He just trusted that he got the correct change back. For this adult, targeted remedial tutoring focused on this area of difficulty and relieved him of a major worry.

I remember having dinner with a very successful lawyer who had learning disabilities. We often compared notes on survival. He shared with me that he still had tremendous trouble with reading. He joked about a problem he has had all of his life with restaurants and menus. "What is worse is if you are in a restaurant with atmosphere. I hate it. The lights are so low that I can't even see the menu. And then there are the fancy restaurants that write in French, Italian, or Spanish to impress you. They are my downfall." He shared with me how he survived. His first strategy was to fall back to a safe selection. If he went to an Italian restaurant, he could always order his favorite veal dish. In a French restaurant he had one favorite that every French restaurant served. And so it went. His other "trick" was to get into a conversation with the waiter. "Tell me about the chef. What is his or her specialty? What do you like? What do you recommend?" Here is a very successful and very competent professional still living under the fear that he will not be able to do something and that people will see that he is "stupid."

This lawyer illustrates a key concept for adults. It is important to learn how to improve on weaknesses as well as how to use strengths and minimize the need for the weaknesses. But, as an adult, of equal importance to survival is to learn how to compensate when you cannot avoid the areas of weakness. The people I discussed compensated by carrying $20 bills or by getting the waiter to discuss the menu. You must find your own survival skills.

When an adult first learns of his or her learning disabilities as an adult, there is more to do than diagnose and find the proper interventions. He or she may need to rethink their self-image and their past. For the first time, this adult might understand why he or she did so poorly in school or in college or on the job. Memories of childhood, adolescence, and adulthood might have to be explored and rethought. Deep feelings of being a failure or of disappointing parents have to be understood.

For some, going to or completing college was not realistic. They might have had a lifetime of underachieving. They are working in a job they feel is below their ability or they have never advanced despite their sense of competence. Some share with me that they will never see themselves as "smart" unless they finish college. They have had a lifetime of disappointments in their work and their personal world.

For others, the unrecognized learning disabilities have led to other life problems. Their spouse constantly complains of their disorganization or inability to complete what they start. Or they are told that they just never seem to listen or pay attention. This adult hears me describe his or her son or daughter and sadly says, "That's me . . . I do the same things." The spouse is only too quick to agree.

The Special Issues
for the Adult with ADHD

Since 25 percent or more of children with ADHD will continue to have this disorder as an adult, it is surprising how few adults are recognized and diagnosed. The literature on ADHD has only reported on the problems of adults in recent years. Few physicians who work with adults on health-related issues are aware of ADHD. Similarly, few psychiatrists or other mental health professionals who work with adults think of the possibility of this disorder. Thus, it is often missed.

As with learning disabilities, the first time the ADHD is recognized is when the adult's son or daughter is evaluated and diagnosed as ADHD. At the interpretive session one parent says "That's me," or the other parent says, "That's him (or her)." The other frequent way that adults recognize that they might have ADHD is when they read an article in a newspaper or magazine on ADHD and suddenly realize what their problem might be.

Fortunately, more and more of the professionals who work in college health and mental health services have become aware of the possibility of ADHD. Unfortunately, most professionals who see adults for health or mental health problems are not aware and the diagnosis is missed. Or, the adult goes to this professional because he or she reads about ADHD and the professional says,

"That is not possible. Kids outgrow ADHD at puberty." You may have to find another physician or talk to the professional who works with children and adolescents with ADHD.

The diagnosis of ADHD with adults is established in the same way as with children and adolescents. The history is most important. We look for a chronic and pervasive history of hyperactivity, distractibility, and/or impulsivity.

With adults, the hyperactivity might be less or more camouflaged. The distractibility might be the primary area of difficulty. Often, adults report that their thoughts are disorganized because it is so hard to stay on one thought or task. Impulsivity might be less but still present.

Fran was diagnosed as having learning disabilities in third grade. She had been in special classes through high school. During high school she had increasing difficulty doing her schoolwork. Teachers and parents complained that she would not stay on a task or complete her work. She was in psychotherapy during her senior year of high school and placed on an antidepressant, which she reported as being of little benefit.

She went to a college that offered resource help and accommodations for her learning disabilities; however, she found the work difficult. She could not concentrate when she studied in the dormitory and she became worried that she might not make it. Fran went to the college mental health service at the advice of her former psychotherapist. Both thought she was depressed. The psychologist who saw her at the college suspected ADHD and referred her to me.

Fran gave a classic history of hyperactivity and distractibility throughout her life. She was fidgety and had been so "forever." Her friends, even her new ones in college, teased her about her constant need to move some part of her body. She described being distracted by any sound. She could recall examples from elementary school of listening to what was going on in the hall rather than in class. Fran cried as she described her impulsivity. She constantly hurts friends' feelings by saying something before she thinks. Teachers always yelled at her for answering out of turn.

With Fran's permission, her mother was invited to a session. We asked her to bring all of Fran's old report cards and psychoeducational evaluations. The hyperactivity, distractibility, and impulsivity were described year after year, starting in kindergarten. The school and the parents assumed that these problems were part of her learning disabilities or her need to be sociable.

Fran was started on Ritalin. At a dose of 10 mg, three times a day, she showed significant improvement. "It's a miracle. I feel so relaxed. I can concentrate so much better, even in the dorm. I am getting my work done so much quicker and better. My friends have commented that I seem different. I pay attention when they are talking to me and I don't interrupt them when they are talking." Later she asked, "Why was I not given this medication when I was a child?"

The treatment of ADHD as an adult is the same as the treatment for children. The same educational and counseling efforts are important. The same medications are helpful.

Mr. S., a thirty-five-year-old attorney, came to see me after reading an article in the paper. He told me that he had been on a medication from age nine to sixteen because of overactivity and trouble concentrating. He remembered that two of his sisters took the same medicine. At my request, he contacted his parents who contacted their family doctor. He had been on dextroamphetamine.

During college and law school he occasionally was able to get this medication from friends. When he took it he studied better and more efficiently. He was now working for a law firm and having great difficulty staying on a task and getting his work done. He reported his frustration with his performance. He knew he could do the work. He had great difficulty staying organized and keeping track of his "billable hours."

I restarted him on dextroamphetamine. At a dose of 5 mg every four hours he reported a dramatic improvement. He was able to concentrate and stay on a task. His thoughts were more organized. He became effective and efficient at work. His supervisors noted the change and wondered what he had done. His wife was so excited about her husband's ability to relax and stay with a conversation that she called me to thank me.

In Summary

Learning disabilities continue into adulthood. ADHD might continue into adulthood. Since many professionals are not yet aware of these disabilities, you might have to be the person who recognizes the need for assessment and help. This effort might be for you, for your adult son or daughter, for your spouse, or for a brother or sister or cousin who does not realize yet what his or her problems might be.

If college or graduate studies is the issue, seek out counselors who specialize in helping individuals with learning disabilities find the right programs. Several reference books are listed in the Appendix of this book.

If vocational planning or vocational training is the issue, contact your county office of Vocational Rehabilitation. The people at this office are required to do assessments and interventions.

Whichever direction you or someone else needs to go, be aware of the impact that these problems have had throughout life. If you think it would be useful, find a professional to help you think this through.

19

Legal Issues of Importance to Parents

FORTUNATELY FOR YOUR son or daughter and for you, today laws require school systems to provide services for children and adolescents with learning disabilities. This was not always the case. Before 1975, about half of the children with disabilities in this country could not get an appropriate education. About one million were excluded entirely from the public school system. For the child with learning disabilities the situation was worse—about 90 percent were not even identified.

These laws, however, do not automatically assure that your child or adolescent will receive the educational programs he or she needs. This reality is even more true now because of the decrease in federal and state funding for education. As I have repeatedly noted, you must be an *informed consumer* and an *assertive advocate*. You must know the laws and know your rights, and then you must work actively with the school while insisting on these rights. The school personnel care about the education of *all* students. You care especially about the education of *your* student.

What are these laws? What do they mean for your son or daughter? What must you know and do to assure the best help you can possibly get? What can you do if you are not pleased with your school's effort? Let me try to answer these questions.

Parent Power

The major force behind today's legislation was a consumer movement led by organizations of parents of children with disabilities. Later, the people with disabilities themselves joined in this effort. They focused on the lack of an appropriate public education and on the exclusion of children and adolescents from programs provided by the public education system.

In the 1960s various groups of parents whose children had different disabilities, used publicity, mass mailings, public meetings, and other well-organized, opinion-molding techniques to put pressure on state legislatures. They wanted laws making educational opportunities for persons with disabilities not simply available but mandatory. Most states responded with legislation, some more than others. A few states did nothing. Most of the more progressive state governments passed the laws but provided no enabling funds for facilities or trained professionals to carry out their intent. The focus of these pressure groups then shifted toward enactment of a federal law that could have an impact on all states.

In 1971, the Pennsylvania Association for Retarded Citizens filed a suit in that state that directly involved the federal government in these issues for the first time. Citing constitutional guarantees of due process and equal protection under the law, they argued that the access of children with mental retardation to public education should be equal to that afforded other children. The court agreed. A year later the Federal Court in the District of Columbia made a similar ruling involving not only persons with mental retardation, but those with a wide range of disabilities. This 1972 decision established two major precedents critical to future progress: (1) Children with disabilities have the right to a "suitable publicly supported education, regardless of the degree of the child's mental, physical, or emotional disability or impairment"; and (2) concerning financing, "if sufficient funds are not available to finance all of the services and programs that are needed and desirable . . . the available funds must be expended equitably in such a manner that no child is entirely excluded from a publicly supported education." More than 40 such cases were won throughout the United States following these two landmark decisions.

These court actions also had a profound influence on federal legislation. The Rehabilitation Act of 1973, referred to as "The Civil Rights Act for the Handicapped," prohibits discrimination on the basis of physical or mental handicaps in every federally assisted program in the country. Public education, of course, accepts federal assistance. Section 504 of this law focuses on the rights of the individual people in these programs, and it has been the keystone of parents' demands and of numerous successful court actions. The most critical issues in this section are:

1. As disabled job applicants or employees, handicapped people have the same rights and must be guaranteed the same benefits as nonhandicapped applicants and employees.

2. They are entitled to all of the medical services and medically related instruction that is available to the general public.

3. They are entitled to participate in vocational rehabilitation, day care, or any other social service program receiving federal assistance on an equal basis with the nonhandicapped.

4. They have the equal rights to go to college or to enroll in a job-training or adult post-high school basic education programs. Selection must be based on academic or other school records, and the disability cannot be a factor. (If a person has learning disabilities, the standard entrance testing procedures, the Scholastic Aptitude Test, for example, can be modified, and admission standards can be based on potential as well as on past performance.)

5. State and local school districts must provide an appropriate elementary and secondary education for all handicapped students.

In 1990 this law was expanded to all programs and not just to federally funded programs. The required services and opportunities for persons with disabilities must be phased in throughout a several year time frame.

This last part of Section 504 became the basis for Public Law 94–142, the "Education for All Handicapped Children Act," which was passed overwhelmingly by the House and Senate and enacted in November of 1976. This landmark legislation capped a heroic effort begun by a few parents who joined with others to form organizations, these organizations then working together to successfully lobby for the needs of their children. The law is unique in several ways. There is no expiration date. It is regarded as permanent. It does more than just express a concern with children with disabilities, it requires a specific commitment. The law sets forth as national policy the proposition that education must be extended to persons with disabilities *as a fundamental right.*

Thanks to these parents, the right of the person with learning disabilities to a good education is now guaranteed by law. The challenge of today's parents is to insist on the transformation of this promise into reality.

Your need as parents to educate yourself and to be appropriately assertive is more crucial now than ever. With federal, state, and county budget cuts, services to persons with disabilities have been significantly cut. Because of budget cuts and loss of personnel, some school systems lead parents to believe that their child is not entitled to services or that the minimal services offered are adequate. This crisis in services is compounded by another problem. The initial law, Public Law 94–142, provided services for parent education. There was an understood need to inform parents of their rights under the law. This knowledge helped parents enter the system and function within the system. These parents have sons and daughters who have graduated from high school. None of the parents of the current public school students benefited from this initial educational process. As I lecture around the country I am distressed by the frequency with which I meet parents who do not know of their rights or how to fight for the services their son or daughter needs.

Public Law 94–142: Education for All Handicapped Children Act

Because Public Law 94–142 is so important to you, let me review first what the original law included and then explain the amendments enacted since. I will suggest how you can work within this law to be an advocate for your child or adolescent.

The initial law listed 11 categories of children with disabilities: mentally retarded, hard-of-hearing, deaf, deaf-blind, speech-impaired, visually handicapped, seriously emotionally disturbed, orthopedically impaired, other health-impaired, *specific learning disabilities*, and multihandicapped. In a 1986 addition (to be discussed later), two new groups were added: autism and traumatic brain injury.

The phrase "children with specific learning disabilities" is defined as applying to those children "who have a disorder in one or more of the basic psychological processes involved in understanding or in using language, spoken or written, which disorder may manifest itself in imperfect ability to listen, think, speak, read, write, spell, or do mathematical calculations. Such disorders include such conditions as perceptual handicaps, brain injury, minimal brain dysfunction, dyslexia, and developmental aphasia. Such term does not include children who have learning problems, which are primarily the result of visual, hearing, or motor handicaps, or mental retardation, of emotional disturbance, or of environmental, cultural, or economic disadvantage."

In 1990–91 a parent-based initiative attempted to have Congress add a 14th category, Attention-Deficit Hyperactivity Disorder (ADHD). This effort did not succeed. At this time a child or adolescent with ADHD who also has learning disabilities can be eligible for services under the category, learning disabled. If he or she has emotional problems, the category seriously emotionally disturbed, can be used. If neither exist or are of major concern, this individual can be eligible for services as "other health impaired."

Let me review what this law entitles children and adolescents with a handicapping condition.

1. A *free public education* is guaranteed to all between the ages of 3 and 21.

2. Each handicapped person is guaranteed an "individualized education program" or IEP. This IEP must be in the form of a written statement, jointly developed by the school officials, the child's teacher, the parent or guardian, and if possible by the child her- or himself. It must include an analysis of the child's present achievement level, a list of both short-range and annual goals, an identification of the specific services that will be provided toward meeting these goals, and an indication of the extent to which the child will be able to participate in regular school programs. The IEP must also be clear about when these services will be provided and how long they will last, and it provides a schedule for checking on the progress achieved under the plan and for making any revisions in it that may be needed.

3. Handicapped and nonhandicapped children must be *educated together* to the fullest extent that is appropriate. The child can be placed in special classes or separate schools only when the nature and severity of his or her handicap prevents satisfactory achievement in a regular education program.

4. Tests and other *evaluation materials* used in placing handicapped children must be prepared and administered in such a way as not to be racially or culturally discriminatory. They must also be presented in the child's native tongue.

5. An intensive and ongoing effort must be made to *locate* and *identify* children with handicaps, to evaluate their educational needs, and to determine whether these needs are being met.

6. In all efforts, *priority* must be given to those who are not receiving an education and to those severely handicapped people who are receiving an inadequate education.

7. In all decisions, a *prior consultation with the child's parents or guardians* must be held. No policies, programs, or procedures affecting the education of handicapped children may be adopted without a public notice.

8. These rights and guarantees apply to handicapped children *in private as well as public schools.* Any special education provided to any child shall be provided at no cost to the parents *if* state or local education agency officials placed the child in such schools or referred the child to them.

9. States and localities must develop comprehensive *personnel development programs*, including in-service training for regular as well as special education teachers and support personnel.

10. In implementing the law, special effort shall be made to employ qualified handicapped persons.

11. All architectural barriers must be removed.

12. The state education agency has jurisdiction over all educational programs for handicapped children offered within a given state, including those administered by noneducational agencies.

13. An *advisory panel* must exist to advise the state's education agency of unmet needs. Membership must include handicapped people and parents or guardians of those people.

This law guarantees *procedural safeguards.* Parents or guardians have an opportunity to examine any records that bear on the identification of a child as being disabled, on the defined nature and severity of his or her disability, and on the kind of educational setting in which he or she is placed. Schools must provide written notice prior to changing a child's placement. If a parent or guardian objects to a school's decision, there must be a process in place through which complaints can be registered. This process must include an opportunity for an impartial hearing that offers parents rights similar to those involved in a court case—the right to be advised by counsel (and by special education experts if they wish), to present evidence, to cross-examine witnesses, to compel the presence of any witnesses who do not voluntarily appear, to be provided a verbatim report of the proceedings, and to receive the decision and findings in written form.

The rights and safeguards of Public Law 94–142 are critical. Take the time to reread the above paragraph. Each school system is required to provide you a written guideline explaining your rights of appeal. If they have not, ask for it.

Revisions to Public Law 94–142: Public Law 99–457

In September, 1986, Congress passed Public Law 99–457. This law, entitled the "Education of the Handicapped Act Amendments of 1986," includes provisions for children with disabilities of all ages. The upper age was kept at 21. The original age of three, however, was lowered to include "handicapped and 'at risk' children between the ages of birth and age six and their families." There are two major components to this law.

A new mandate for state education agencies to serve all three, four, and five year old children with disabilities by 1990–1991 was created. All of the rights to an education in the original law for ages 6 to 21 are now required down to age three. As with the initial law, services for these children in the three to six age group are not encouraged but mandated. If a state does not comply, it can lose many areas of federal funds.

The second landmark in this early intervention program established by Public Law 99–457 is the "Handicapped Infants and Toddlers Program." This section of the law creates a brand new federal program for children with disabilities and who are at risk, from birth to age three years and their families. While the infant and toddler program is voluntary for states, that is, they may elect to not participate, if a state does choose to participate or to apply for funding under this law, it must meet the requirements of the law and assure that services are available for all eligible children.

Public Law 99–457 stresses the importance of a coordinated and multiagency approach to the planning and dialogue that is necessary to implement the new early childhood initiatives. A wide variety of local providers, public and private, must work together to provide the services.

One last update. The 101st Congress approved a change in the name of Public Law 94–142 from Education for All Handicapped Children to Individuals with Disabilities Education Act (IDEA). The other change was in the term "handicapped children," which is now preferably "children with disabilities."

Your Child or Adolescent and Public Law 94–142

Each state has developed its own laws, rules, and regulations for carrying out the intentions of this federal law. You will have to speak to your school officials, other parents, or other knowledgeable people to learn about the specifics as they apply in your state and community.

It is useful to look at the several steps in the process used to help your son or daughter. In Chapter 11 on the evaluation procedures, I briefly outlined the process required by this law. Let me be more specific.

1. *Search* Each school system should have a system for seeking out students who might have a disability.

2. *Find* Once a student with a potential problem is identified, there should be a system for collecting information and designing an evaluation process.

3. *Evaluation* A comprehensive, multidisciplinary evaluation should be done.

4. *Conference* Parents or guardians should meet with the school personnel and evaluation professionals to review the evaluation conclusions, any labels or diagnoses established, and any proposed placement and IEP. The details should be presented in writing.

5. *Parent's Decision Process* Parents or guardians, with consultation from educational or other professionals and lawyers when needed, decide to accept, request clarifica-

tion, request changes, or reject the proposed placement and IEP.

6. *Appeals Process* If parents reject the label, placement recommendation, or IEP, there should be an appeals process that starts with the local school system and can go to the county or state level.

7. *Follow-up Progress reports* should be provided to the family. As the end of the school year approaches, a reassessment is done (with many school systems, a full, formal reevaluation is only done every three years). There should be a *conference* to plan the next year. Steps 5 and 6 are repeated before implementing the next year's plans.

Throughout this book I have urged you as parents to be informed and assertive. I have suggested what you need for your son or daughter and how to get the services from your school system. Please note that what I have encouraged you to fight for is not based only on what I believe children and adolescents with learning disabilities need, but it is based on a federal law. This federal law requires every state and every school system within the state to meet the requirements of the law. School systems can only get away with not meeting the requirements of the law if you do not know your rights. Since this is so important, let me go into more detail.

Search

If someone from your school system suggests that your son or daughter has a problem and wants to do some tests, be positive and agree to the testing. If the tests reveal a problem, you can get help. If the tests find nothing wrong, that should relieve both you and the school. If you are concerned about your child's academic progress and suspect a problem but the school has said nothing about it, speak to the classroom teacher. Share your observations and concerns.

If the teacher agrees with you, he or she can initiate the process through the principal. If you cannot get the classroom teacher to start this process, meet with the principal. (It is better not to go directly to the principal first because this may antagonize the teacher.) When there are two parents, it is always better for both to be present at such meetings. Explain your concerns again, and ask the principal to start the evaluation process. If the principal does not agree and/or refuses to request such an evaluation, contact the head of the special education (or special services) team assigned to your school and request the evaluation. You have the right to go above the principal's head once you have met with the principal. In many school systems, if a parent requests an evaluation in writing to the principal, the principal *must* forward the request to the evaluation team within 30 working days.

When you reach the person at the special education office, get his or her name. Explain your concerns and make it clear that you have already spoken to the teacher and the principal. Ask if this person or someone else could observe your child and then meet with the teacher and you.

These efforts should result in an evaluation or a very substantial reason why one is not required. If you are still not successful, several other strategies may work. You can send a letter to your superintendent of schools, explaining why you are concerned, what you have done, and what you believe you are entitled to under Public Law 94–142 (quote from the material in this book). Always send a copy to the person in the special education office, the principal, and the teacher. Request a meeting. At best, you will have the meeting. At the least, pressure will be building on the evaluation team to do something. Hopefully, you will get the evaluation. You also can have the evaluation privately conducted. If significant results are found, they can be presented to the principal and the special education staff.

The school may find it hard to identify certain types of children who are having difficulty. One is the quiet, shy, withdrawn student who is not causing trouble. Unfortunately, the school professionals may wait until this child is so frustrated and unhappy that he or she refuses to go to school, cries in class, or gets into trouble before they become concerned. With the parents' permission, of course, I have occasionally taught such children how to get into trouble—how to slam or throw books, yell at other kids or the teacher, refuse to do certain work, run out of class—just to get the kind of attention they need at school.

Another such type is the very bright child who manages to do at least average work in spite of his or her problems. This child may have a superior intelligence, but because of learning disabilities, he or she performs at a C or D level. The school personnel see the child or adolescent as "just average," yet actually they are looking at a case of gross underachievement.

As I stated before, parents might be doing two or more hours of homework with the child each night, essentially teaching the child or doing the work for him or her. In addition, parents might be providing a private tutor to help this child. Thus, the child appears to be doing well in school. Must this parent remove all help and supports and let the child fail before he or she is seen as in need of an evaluation?

Find

Once the school agrees to the need for an evaluation, make yourself as informed as possible about what the evaluation is and what is being assessed. Find out what is planned, make sure that the plans cover the areas discussed in Chapter 10 on the evaluation process. Be sure that someone prepares your son or daughter for each step.

Conference

School personnel and special educators will meet with you. If your family has two parents or guardians, be sure both of you are present. You may also bring your own professional consultant to review the results and recommendations and to advise you. If necessary, you could bring your lawyer.

Angry, defensive, or demanding behavior won't get you anyplace. Assume that everyone there has the best interest of your son or daughter at heart. In reality, this is true for more than most school conferences. Listen, ask questions, reflect. Even if you completely agree with everything that is advised, ask for time to think and to read the recommendations in detail. On the one hand, anger or defensiveness polarizes the sides. On the other, too quick an agreement may prevent you from asking questions that occur to you after you read the reports and reflect on them.

Do your homework prior to the conference. Reread Chapters 10 and 11 on evaluation. Talk with other parents who have been in the same situation and, if possible, learn something about what programs are likely to be suggested.

During the conference, ask questions. If someone says that your child has learning disabilities, ask for specifics. You know what learning disabilities are. Impress them with your awareness and their need to be precise. Don't let the evaluator(s) over-whelm you with professional words. Ask for definitions and clar-ification in a calm, concerned way. Let them know that although what they say is important, this is *your* child or adolescent about whom you care very much.

Remember, for the school professionals, the question is not whether your son or daughter has a learning disability—the question is whether he or she is eligible for services. Each school system has a definition of eligibility based on a discrepancy for-mula. That is, how far behind does the child or adolescent have to be in what areas to qualify for services. It has been my expe-rience that when the budget is adequate the amount of discrep-ancy between ability and performance required to be eligible for services is small and that when the budget is tight the formula is changed to require a greater discrepancy.

If you do not agree with the findings, don't challenge them just now. Tell the evaluation team that you would like a copy of the test results to show to another professional for a second opin-ion. You wouldn't consent to your child having open heart surgery or even to being sent to the hospital without a second opinion. Committing your child to at least one year of a special education program or to another year in a regular program without the ap-propriate help has just as great an impact on his or her life.

You will have to agree to the diagnosis, or label; that is, to the name your school gives to the problems they say your son or daughter has. You also will have to agree to the placement rec-ommendations and to the Individualized Education Program (IEP) that is proposed. Ask for clarifications and definitions. Carefully read the documents and be sure you understand.

Keep in mind the difference between an emotional problem that *causes* academic difficulties and an emotional problem that *results* in an academic difficulty. If your son's or daughter's be-havior problems are due to the frustrations and failures experi-enced because of learning disabilities, don't agree to having him or her labeled "emotionally disturbed." If the school personnel insist that your son or daughter has learning disabilities and an emotional disorder, they are probably correct. In making your decision, consider this possibility. If he or she is coded as learn-ing disabled first and emotionally disturbed as the secondary di-agnosis, the placement will be in a program for students with learning disabilities with supportive psychological help. If he or she is coded as emotionally disturbed first and learning disabled as the secondary diagnosis, the placement will be in a program for students with emotional disorders with supportive special education help for the learning disabilities. Which do you believe would be best for your child or adolescent? The primary label is critical. Fight for the correct one.

Your school system is responsible for placing your child in an appropriate program within their system. Only if this is not possible will they consider an out-of-system or private placement. You may prefer that your child go into a particular private program that you know about. The school does not have to concur, however, if an appropriate placement is available within their own system. You might argue that the private placement is better, and this might be true. But even if it were, the law states only that each child must receive an *appropriate* education, not necessarily the *best* education possible.

There are several program levels. You want to find the *least restrictive program* that still provides the *most effective educational support* for your child. Remember that this does not always mean being in a program that resembles a regular class program. The least restrictive environment for some children might be the most restrictive environment available. A child may need the security and support of a small, separate, self-contained classroom in order to feel safe enough to relax and become available for learning.

Ask for the details on any placement. Where is it? Will your child have to be transported out of the neighborhood? Ask about the qualifications of the teacher, the size of the class, and the age distribution of the students. Ask for the mix—diagnosis, level of intellectual functioning. Ask if you can visit the program. Even if it is spring and you will see a different group of students, you will get a feel for the teacher and program. Try to speak to several parents of the children who are currently in the program. If the teacher has not been selected yet or the class makeup established, ask for a written statement of the qualifications that this teacher must have and the probable makeup of the class.

What about the IEP? This is the written plan identifying the instruction designed especially for your son or daughter and listing reasonable expectations for the child's achievement. There should be a specific system for monitoring progress.

At a minimum, each IEP must cover the following points:

1. A statement of your child's or adolescent's levels of educational performance.
2. A statement of yearly goals or achievements expected for each area of identified weakness by the end of the school year.
3. Short-term objectives stated in instructional terms that are the steps leading to the mastery of these yearly goals.
4. A statement of the specific special education and support services to be provided to the child.
5. A statement of the extent to which a child will be able to participate in regular education programs and justification for any special placement recommended.
6. Projected dates for initiation of services and the anticipated duration of the services.
7. A statement of the criteria and evaluation procedures to be used in determining, on at least an annual basis, whether short-term objectives are being achieved.

In addition to an appropriate placement and IEP, your child or adolescent may need other services. These are called *related services*. They are to be provided at no expense to the family. The formal definition of related services is: "transportation and such developmental, corrective, and other supportive services (including speech pathology and audiology, psychological services, physical and occupational therapy, recreation, and medical counseling services, except that such medical services shall be for diagnostic and evaluation purposes only) as may be required to assist a handicapped child to benefit from special education, and includes the early identification and assessment of handicapping conditions in children." These services are usually provided by the school system and built into the school program.

Related services are expensive. Your school personnel might make many suggestions about getting the child or adolescent into psychotherapy but never formally recommend it verbally or in writing. They know that if they recommend a service, thus identifying it as a related service, the school system must pay for the service.

The Parents' Decision Process

After the conference, you are entitled to a full transcript of the meeting. You can also get copies of all tests that were done. The placement and the IEP recommendations must also be provided in writing.

Read all of the documents. If necessary, ask for clarification or more details. If you see something in writing that was not mentioned at the meeting, ask for an explanation. If you need help, seek consultation and advice from other parents or from professionals.

If you are comfortable with the school's plan for your child or adolescent, you may agree to it and sign the necessary documents. If you do not agree and cannot get the school personnel to modify their proposals, inform them that you wish to appeal. Ask that they review with you their appeal process. Remember that you are entitled by law to due process of appeal.

The Appeals Process

The appeals process differs with each state and local school system. Your school system is supposed to have the step-by-step process in writing for you. If you feel that you need legal guidance, try to find a lawyer who works in the area of special education law. Other parents may be of help in finding the right person. The final step in this appeals process is usually a meeting between you and your school system before a "hearing officer" who is not part of the school system. His or her decision is binding. It is usually best to have legal help if you get to this level.

The appeals process may go quickly or may take months. Meanwhile your son or daughter must attend school. You might decide to accept a placement and IEP under protest, allowing an educational program to begin while the appeals process proceeds.

Implementation

The best designed plans of April and May may fall apart in September. Be observant when school opens. Be sure the placement, the teacher, the related services, the makeup of the class, and the implementation steps for the IEP are correct and in operation. Be concerned, ask questions, but try not to be a nuisance. If you believe that some departure from the plan agreed upon has been made, ask about it.

Be sure that the regular classroom teachers with whom your child has contact are aware of any special needs or programs. Be certain that they are familiar with the evaluation and the IEP and that they are in regular contact with the special education professionals.

Programs begun in September may get changed or diluted as the year progresses and the number of students in need of service increases. Ask your son or daughter to keep you informed or check this for yourself. Does each person see your son or daughter the amount of time noted in the IEP? Are more children being added to the program time your child or adolescent receives services? Know your child's IEP and insist that he or she gets what it promises. Remember that no changes can be made without a written notification and your concurrence.

Other Thoughts

Your son or daughter must be kept informed. How much you share, what you explain, and how you explain it will depend on the child's age. If you need help, ask the professionals involved to meet with you and your child or adolescent. If you think it would be helpful, make it a family session.

I touched earlier on how to handle any resistance by your son or daughter to accepting help. Let me mention one other problem—*stigma*. Other children can be cruel, sometimes on purpose, sometimes they just say all the wrong things. The special programs may be called "retard" or "mental" classes and the children in them may be called "retards" or "speds" (for *special education*). It all hurts. Speak to the teachers. Ask that they talk to the offending students. Perhaps the teachers could discuss the theme of being different with the whole class. Alert the teacher if his or her insensitivity contributes to the teasing. If necessary, speak to the parents of an offending child in as positive a way as you can. (Here, as elsewhere, hostility won't get you very far.) Support your child and empathize with his or her feelings. Don't be afraid to show your own emotions, and don't be afraid to have a good cry together. You would do anything in the world to spare the child these problems, but they exist. Make sure the child knows that you care too much to ignore what is going on and that you will do everything possible to support and help. Keep at it until the teasing is minimized or stopped.

Work closely with your school personnel. And make them work closely with you. As a team, both the school people and the family can do the best job of helping your son or daughter reach his or her maximum growth and potential.

PART SIX

Conclusion

20

In Conclusion

PERHAPS YOU REMEMBER VICTOR, the boy whose victorious story opened this book.

Let us for a moment look at another young man who had the same extent of learning disabilities. Bob struggled through elementary school, did poorly in junior high school, and finally quit school at age 16. Early on, his parents tried to get the school to provide help. Later, they gave up in frustration. Once he quit school, they lost control and lost track of him.

The next time they heard of him, he had been arrested for killing two policemen while trying to rob a bank.

The newspaper coverage was painfully revealing (*Washington Post*, August 8, 1976). The psychiatric report noted, "Every time he struggled hopelessly with a math problem, every time he stumbled over a sentence from his first reader, every time his brother beat him in a fight . . . (he) grew a little more hostile, a little more withdrawn, a little more convinced of his worthlessness. . . . He thought of himself as stupid and worthless and developed intense anger at himself and the world."

Bob's parents were professionals. His older brother was an honor student. Bob had been labeled "slow" in elementary school, but the first testing was not done until eighth grade. It revealed learning disabilities and an IQ in the bright range. No programs were offered. The high-school counselor never knew of these studies. After Bob quit school, he moved from job to job. He spent more and more time riding his motorcycle and getting into trouble with the police. The bank robbery and killings were an almost inevitable outcome of his lifestyle.

Bob is now in prison.

You have probably heard all of this before, but let me mention a few other people with learning disabilities before getting to my point. Leonardo da Vinci often wrote backward. His writing shows evidence of perceptual problems. Woodrow Wilson didn't learn the alphabet until he was eight years old. He didn't read until he was 11. At school, he excelled only in work that was related to speech. He was labeled as "dull and backward."

Auguste Rodin, the famous artist-sculptor, did poorly with math and spelling. He was described as "ineducable" and "an idiot." General George Patton was severely learning disabled and could not read or write at age 12. A special reader worked with him all through his time at West Point. Winston Churchill had learning disabilities. Albert Einstein did not talk until age four or read until age nine. He was considered backward and made progress only after his family moved him to a special school where he could learn using his own style.

Thomas Edison couldn't learn anything in public school. He entered at age eight and was removed three months later by his mother who decided to teach him herself. His autobiography is revealing. Edison wrote, "I remember I used never to be able to get along at school. I was always at the foot of the class. I used to feel that the teachers did not sympathize with me and that my father thought I was stupid." Later, he added, "It was impossible to observe and learn the processes of nature by description, or the English alphabet and arithmetic only by rote . . . it was always necessary to observe with my own eyes and to do things or to make things. . . ." To see for himself, to test things for himself, he said, was, "for one instance . . . better than to learn about something I had never seen for two hours." His mother noted that he never learned to spell. His grammar and syntax were appalling. He was hard to teach. Whatever he learned, he learned in his own way. In fact, she said, she only inspired him—no one ever taught him anything. He taught himself.

There are others. Perhaps you have met successful people who overcame or learned to compensate for their learning disabilities. Perhaps you are one. I know that I am. You should have seen the first draft of the first edition of this book—spelling errors, letter reversals, illegible handwriting. But, I had something then that I didn't have when I was in school. I had a secretary who learned to read my handwriting, who could spell, and who no longer laughed at my errors. That was compensation. By the time I started the second edition I had discovered a miracle—the computer and the word processor. I can now type almost as fast as I think. (How exhausting it is to have to slow my thinking down to the rate my hand can write.) I can use a spell checker. The product can be read by everyone. I think back at the pain of writing by hand at such a slow rate and with fatigue. Then, the secretary would type it and I would edit it. Finally, a first draft.

But I did not always have such help. My grades in elementary and junior high school were less than good. The principal recommended to my mother that I would be happier in a vocational high school. My mother refused and insisted that I go to the regular high school. She won—or, I should say, she gave me the chance to win. Somehow I got my act together in high school. I taught myself how to learn and how to pass exams. My grades improved in college. Medical school was a mixed blessing. My strengths plus study skills permitted me to do well and to graduate, for the first time in my life, near the top of my class. But, I still remember the Chief of Surgery calling me in during my senior year. I had just completed my required rotation on surgery. My visual motor and fine motor skills are at best poor. He said to me, "Larry, if you promise never to go into surgery I will pass you." I agreed, and I passed. It is no surprise to me that I chose a specialty of medicine that requires listening and talking skills.

My inability to sit still for more than a second has always been the center of humor in my family. If not my wife, then my kids will say, "Can't you sit down and relax?" I guess the answer is no. I still remember a fifth-grade teacher who tied me in my seat and a fourth-grade teacher who made me sit on my hands whenever she was teaching something to the class. I also remember the sadness and the embarrassment as my classmates looked at me.

All of this was the beginning. The ending never comes. I still face new frustrations and challenges. As the Acting Director of the National Institute of Mental Health, I attended a congressional hearing on our budget with the director of the agency. I needed to pass information to him so that he could answer a Senator's questions. When the hearing was over he handed back my note. On the top he wrote, "Thanks"—then he proceeded to correct two spelling errors and one reversal. Writing notes will never be a comfortable thing for me. There is always the fear that I will show someone that I cannot spell. And, of course, I know that if you can't spell you must be dumb.

What, then, determines the outcome for us? Why is it that some children and adolescents make it and some do not? It seems to me that the outcome depends on the interaction of several factors:

1. The types and the extent of the learning disabilities.
2. The level of intellectual potential.
3. The time when these disabilities are recognized and an appropriate program developed. If this is not done early, additional academic and emotional problems develop. The child grows farther and farther behind.
4. The kinds of help provided in school and in the family.
5. The child's or adolescent's personality. Does he or she take on the disabilities as a challenge, accept the need to work harder, develop styles of coping? Does he or she relate in a way that makes people want to reach out and help or in a way that pushes them away?
6. The parents' and the whole family's ability to be supportive and caring.

Current research efforts will someday give us the knowledge to minimize or to prevent learning disabilities and ADHD and to improve the existing problems through education, medication, and/or special nutritional approaches. For now there is little we can do to "cure" the learning disabilities or the ADHD that your son or daughter has. His or her intellectual potential is established. You can only work for programs that will maximize this potential.

Out best hope for achieving the best outcome is to work on the other factors that affect the child and adolescent—those factors that we *can* influence.

By being an *informed consumer* and an *assertive advocate* you can work to get the necessary evaluations and school interventions. Through your own understanding, you can help your child or adolescent understand and maximize strengths rather than magnify weaknesses. You can help with his or her self-image and personality development. You can help your family understand and support the child. You can support your other children. And, equally important, you can support yourself.

There is a saying that you never know how good a parent you have been until it is too late to do anything about it—until your child is an adult. Perhaps this saying is true for those delightfully "normal" children. But it cannot be the philosophy for our children with special problems or disabilities to overcome. We must stop and assess ourselves as they grow. If everything has been done to help him or her get through the challenges of their current stage of life, we must then look ahead for the challenges of their next stage of life.

I hope that this book has given you more understanding than you had when you began it. I hope that it has suggested a new way of thinking and some ideas that will help you help your son or daughter reach his or her full potential as a happy, healthy, productive adult. That will never be easy, but I wish you the best of success.

Appendix

Resources

Parent Organizations

Attention Deficit Disorder Association (A.D.D.A.)

Attention Deficit Disorder Association is a national alliance of Attention-Deficit Hyperactivity Disorder (ADHD) support groups that provides referrals and information to parents and parent support groups.

> 8091 South Ireland Way
> Aurora, Colorado 80016
> (800) 487–2282

Children with Attention Deficit Disorders (CH.A.D.D.)

Children with Attention Deficit Disorders is a national alliance of parent organizations that provides information and support to parents of children with ADHD.

> 1859 North Pine Island Road
> Suite 185
> Plantation, Florida 33322
> (305) 857–3700

Learning Disabilities Association of America, Inc.

The Learning Disabilities Association of America, Inc. was formerly called the Association for Children and Adults with Learning Disabilities (ACLD). It is a national parent association with state and local chapters. Membership is open to parents and professionals. The local groups provide educational programs, advice on local issues and programs, and support systems for parents, families, and the children and adolescents. To find your nearest chapter, contact the National Office:

> 4156 Library Road
> Pittsburgh, Pennsylvania 15234
> (412) 341–1515

The Orton Dyslexia Society

The Orton Dyslexia Society is for parents of children and adults with dyslexia as well as for professionals concerned with dyslexia.

> 8600 LaSalle Road
> Suite 382
> Baltimore, Maryland 21204
> (301) 296-0232

Other Useful Organizations

American Association of Children's Residential Centers

The American Association of Children's Residential Centers represents most of the residential treatment centers available for children and adolescents.

> 440 First Street, N.W.
> Suite 310
> Washington, DC 20001

American Association of Psychiatric Services for Children

The American Association of Psychiatric Services for Children represents many of the programs and organizations providing mental health services for children.

> 1200-C Scottsville Road
> Suite 225
> Rochester, New York 14624

Council for Exceptional Children

The Council for Exceptional Children is the branch of the National Education Association for educators in special education. The Division on Learning Disabilities is the specific group within the Council concerned with learning disabilities.

> 1920 Association Drive
> Reston, Virginia 22091

Epilepsy Foundation of America

The Epilepsy Foundation of America is an organization for parents of children and adults with seizure disorders.

4351 Garden City Drive
Landover, Maryland 20785

National Center for Learning Disabilities

Formerly called the Foundation for Children with Learning Disabilities, the National Center for Learning Disabilities does extensive fund raising. This money is used to support research relating to learning disabilities. In addition, the Center provides information for parents and professionals.

99 Park Avenue
New York, New York 10016

National Congress of Parents and Teachers

The National Congress of Parents and Teachers is the national organization representing parent-teacher groups throughout the country.

700 North Rush Street
Chicago, Illinois 60611

National Council of Community Mental Health Centers

The National Council of Community Mental Health Centers represents most of the Community Mental Health Centers in the country. Mental health services are available for children and adolescents at an adjustable rate.

12300 Twinbrook Parkway
Suite 320
Rockville, Maryland 20852

National Mental Health Association

The National Mental Health Association consists of volunteers who are concerned with the mental health needs of the country. It has state and local chapters.

1021 Prince Street
Third Floor
Alexandria, Virginia 22310

Parents without Partners

Parents without Partners is a national organization with local chapters for parents raising children alone.

8807 Colesville Road
Silver Spring, Maryland 20910

Professional Organizations

American Academy of Child and Adolescent Psychiatry
3615 Wisconsin Avenue, N.W.
Washington, DC 20016

American Academy of Ophthalmology
1101 Vermont Avenue, N.W.
Washington, DC 20036

American Academy of Optometry
5530 Wisconsin Avenue
Chevy Chase, Maryland 20815

American Academy of Pediatrics
P.O. Box 927
141 Northwest Point Road
Elk Grove Village, Illinois 60007

American Medical Association
535 N. Dearborn
Chicago, Illinois 60610

American Nurses' Association
2420 Pershing Road
Kansas City, Missouri 64108

American Occupational Therapy Association
1383 Piccard Drive
Rockville, Maryland 20852

American Psychiatric Association
1400 K Street, N.W.
Washington, DC 20005

American Psychological Association
1200 17th Street, N.W.
Washington, DC 20036

American Speech, Language, and Hearing Association
10801 Rockville Pike
Rockville, Maryland 20852

American Society for Adolescent Psychiatry
3843 Massachusetts Avenue, N.W.
Washington, DC 20016

National Association of School Psychologists
8455 Colesville Road
Silver Spring, Maryland 20910

National Association of Social Workers
7981 Eastern Avenue
Silver Spring, Maryland 20910

Sensory Integration International
1402 Cravens Avenue
Torrance, CA 90501

Legal Organizations

Many law schools have special units or programs offering reference materials or counsel on children with disabilities. If you or
your attorney needs such help, contact your nearest law school
and find out what they offer. The following national programs
may be of help or may provide a local resource.

Children's Defense Fund
122 C Street, N.W.
Fourth Floor
Washington, DC 20001

Mental Disability Legal Resource Center
American Bar Association
1800 M Street, N.W.
Washington, DC 20036

Colleges and Other
Post-High School Training

The number of programs and the kinds of programs available
change and increase all the time. Rather than list those programs
in existence when this book was being prepared, I will provide
resources you can contact to get a current list.

You might contact the Graduate School of Education at your
nearest university. Ask for the Department of Special Education.

The faculty of this department can advise you of resources or people at their school or others.

Peterson's Colleges with Programs for Learning Disabled Students

This list of colleges with detailed descriptions is published in current editions. It can be found in most libraries and book stores.

Peterson's Guides
Princeton, New Jersey 08540

Schoolsearch Guide to Colleges with Programs or Services for Students with Learning Disabilities,
by M. Lipkin

This guide can be found in most libraries or ordered from:

Schoolsearch
127 Marsh Street
Belmont, Massachusetts 02178

Unlocking Potential: College and Other Choices for Learning Disabled People: A Step-by-Step Guide,
by B. Scheiber and J. Talpers

Adler and Adler Publishers
4550 Montgomery Avenue
Bethesda, Maryland 20817

Special Note

To obtain the specific details on how your son or daughter can take the Scholastic Aptitude Test (SAT) untimed, with a preceptor, and/or with other special considerations, contact:

College Board
American Testing Program
Box 592
Princeton, New Jersey 08541

Index

About the Author

Dr. Silver, a Child and Adolescent Psychiatrist, is the Clinical Professor of Psychiatry and Director of Training in Child and Adolescent Psychiatry at Georgetown University School of Medicine in Washington, DC. Prior to this appointment, he was Acting Director and Deputy Director of the National Institute of Mental Health. Before going to the National Institute of Mental Health, he was Professor of Psychiatry, Professor of Pediatrics, and Director of Child Psychiatry at Rutgers Medical School (now the Robert Wood Johnson School of Medicine).